A Church That
Can and Cannot Change

ERASMUS INSTITUTE BOOKS

For over three-thousand years, in much of the world, slavery existed.
It was a way of life, accepted as beyond change. It was not condemned by any
major religion. Robinson Crusoe, a slaveowner and slavetrader, was a national hero.
Théodore Géricault's "African Slave Trade" exhibits a new sensibility.
Focused on the weakest point in the slave system, the making of slaves
by violence, Géricault addresses humanity.
Art courtesy of École nationale supérieure des beaux-arts.

A CHURCH THAT
Can AND *Cannot* CHANGE

The Development of Catholic Moral Teaching

JOHN T. NOONAN, JR.

A John W. Kluge Center Book
Library of Congress, Washington, D.C.

University of Notre Dame Press

Notre Dame, Indiana

Library of Congress Cataloging-in-Publication Data
Noonan, John Thomas, 1926–
    A church that can and cannot change : the development of Catholic moral
teaching / John T. Noonan, Jr.
        p.   cm. — (Erasmus Institute books)
    "A John W. Kluge Center book."
    Includes bibliographical references (p.   ) and index.
    ISBN 0-268-03603-9 (cloth : alk. paper)
    1. Catholic Church—History.   2. Slavery and the church—Catholic Church.
3. Usury—Religious aspects—Catholic Church.   4. Divorce—Religious
aspects—Catholic Church.   I. Title.   II. Series.
BX946.N66   2005
241'.042—dc22
                                                              2004026983

To Erasmians, Everywhere

And this I pray:

That your love abound more and more

In knowledge and in insight of every kind

So that you test what is vital.

(Paul to the Philippians 1:9–10.)

CONTENTS

Intrinsic Evil

Folly, Championed

Conjoined by God, Disjoined by God

The Test of the Teaching

P R E F A C E

In the fall of 1947, I began the study of Catholicism with a series of tutorials at the Catholic University of America. One of the first subjects I investigated was the Church's stand on religious freedom. Doing so, I encountered the unhappy story of Félicité de Lamennais, whose newspaper *L'Avenir* was the champion of religious freedom when the Church would not recognize it. I went on from Lamennais, whose mistake was being ahead of his ecclesiastical superiors, to Alfred Loisy, the quintessential Modernist, whose mistake was to reduce revelation to subjective satisfaction. Looking for a subject whose development in the Church was debatable, I turned to the history of the prohibition of usury and in 1951 completed a doctoral dissertation in philosophy upon it. It is a pleasure now, over half a century later, to bring together what I have learned about the development of moral doctrine and to think once more about Lamennais, the usury rule, and the relation of revelation to human needs.

My first effort to tie together the themes of this book occurred in the fall of 2002 when at Emory University I held the Alonso L. McDonald Chair of Jesus and Culture, addressing a topic that invited both biblical exploration and historical investigation.

Research for this study was largely conducted at the John Kluge Center for Scholars at the Library of Congress, where I held in turn the Maguire Chair of Ethics and the Kluge Chair of American Law and Government. I am grateful to James H. Billington, librarian of Congress, and to Prosser Gifford, director of Scholarly Programs, for these appointments; to Cary Maguire and John Kluge for funding them; and to Linda Harrington and Charlotte Allen, my research assistants at this center. Working at the Library of Congress, I returned occasionally to the great reading hall where I first encountered Lamennais.

I am also indebted to the librarians of the Graduate Theological Union, Berkeley; of the Theodore M. Hesburgh Library, Notre Dame; of the Robbins Collection at Boalt Hall, the law school of University of California, Berkeley; and of the United States Court of Appeals for the Ninth Circuit.

The encouragement and the insights of my wife, Mary Lee, have as always played an important part. Neither theological cant nor legal fustian can survive in her vicinity. I am grateful to the comments and suggestions of Charles Curran, David Brion Davis, Katherine Eldred, Nancy Eisenhauer, Dagfinn Føllesdal, Richard Helmholz, Ladislas Orsy, S.J., James J. Sheehan, and Robert Sullivan. I have been greatly benefitted by the secretarial skills of Evelyn Lew.

I appreciate the invitation of the Erasmus Institute to give the Erasmus Lectures. They form the core of this book. The institute and the lectures carry a name evoking the highest standard of scholarship and the most demanding Christian commitment.

John T. Noonan, Jr.

Notre Dame, Indiana
March 25, 2004

THREE UNAVOIDABLE ISSUES

Father Newman Startles

The inventor of the idea that Christian doctrine develops is John Henry Newman. Ignoring the boast of Bossuet that doctrine is unchanging, escaping the thin theorizing that would restrict development to a movement from the implicit to the explicit, Newman pointed to transformations of doctrine as tangible and as organic, as many-sided and complex and real, as the passage from childhood to adulthood. An Anglican arguing his way into the Catholic Church, Newman saw that the anomalies and novelties of his new spiritual home were the marks of vigor, of maturity, of being alive. What Newman noticed and defended were changes in the ways that piety was expressed, in the rules guiding the governance of the Church, in the understanding of the nature of Christ. What he spent no time in either enumerating or explaining were changes in the rules of moral conduct.

On October 26, 1863, Thomas William Allies, a lecturer on history at Oxford University and a convert to the Catholic Church, sent Newman the draft of a lecture in which he pronounced slavery to be intrinsically evil. He wanted his friend's opinion. Newman replied cautiously: "I do not materially differ from you, though I do still startle at some of the sentences of your Lecture." The source of his startle was St. Paul. Newman wrote:

That which is intrinsically and per se evil, we cannot give way to for an hour. That which is only accidentally evil, we can meet according to what is expedient, giving different rules, according to the particular case. St. Paul would have got rid of despotism if he could. He could not, he left the desirable object to the slow working of Christian principles. So he would have got rid of slavery, if he could. He did not, because he could not, but had it been intrinsically evil, had it been *in se* a sin, it must have been said to Philemon, liberate all your slaves at once.

Succinctly raising his central difficulty, Newman elaborated with examples of other institutions that he saw to be bad but not to be intrinsically evil. Any army and any government offered occasions of sin and provided temptations to sin and were instruments of sin. Neither an army nor a government was to be condemned as intrinsically evil. "Which did most harm to the soul the Jewish slavedom or the Jewish army?" Slavery, he surprisingly added, was not even as bad as polygamy.

Newman then appears to let his imagination wander from the slaveowner to the slave, declaring: "I had rather have been a slave in the Holy Land, than a courtier of Xerxes or a solider of Zingis Khan." This fantasy is not a digression. In putting himself in the place of a slave, Newman is following a classic pattern. He supposes his soul to be unaffected by the body's servile state. Imagined in this way, slavery does not destroy or even impair the essential self. Newman's vision of slavery is the antithesis of an account of slavery that sees it as an assault upon the person. The dualism implicit in this view is a prime reason why slavery was so long seen as acceptable.

Newman ends as he began: "left to myself, I might be disposed to speak as strongly as you do, but that the tone of the inspired writers held me back." The possibility that what was intrinsic was subject to development was not expressed. Imperatively, the intrinsic froze his moral judgment. Convinced that slavery was evil, he was constrained to affirm that it was not always and everywhere evil. Else, how could Paul have accepted it? That question, so fairly expressed by Newman, could not be exorcised but it could, for a long time, be ignored as the Catholic Church entered the modern world.

In 1993, Karol Wojtyla, Pope John Paul II, published a small treatise on the fundamentals of moral theology, the encyclical *Veritatis splendor*, "Truth's Splendor." In it the pope emphasized and elaborated the notion of the intrinsically evil, very much along the lines indicated by Newman in his refusal to find slavery to be intrinsically evil. As John Paul II expressed it:

Reason attests that there are objects of the human act which by their nature are "incapable of being ordered to God," because they radically contradict the good of the person created in His image. These are the acts which by the moral tradition of the Church have been termed intrinsically evil: they are such always and per se, apart from the person's reason for acting and apart from other circumstances.

A little later in the encyclical, the pope declared: "the norms which prohibit such acts oblige always and forever, that is, they oblige without any exception." Emphatically, he repeated: "the universality and immutability of the moral norms make manifest, and at the same time serve, the absolute personal dignity—that is, the inviolability—of the human being, on whose face shines the splendor of God." Universal, immutable, per se, everywhere and always, the intrinsic governed the empire of actions.

Formulating the same idea another way, the pope spoke of "the negative commandments"—the commandments "expressed in negative form in the Old and New Testaments," such as "You shall not commit adultery." These commandments he declared to be indistinguishable from "the negative commandments of the natural law." These commandments set the standard that was minimal. They ruled out any reason for actions that "never, under any conditions, can be held to be a response congruent with the dignity of the person."

The attraction of the intrinsic to a moralist is that, beyond its apparent self-evidence, the intrinsic removes contingency. The act that is intrinsically of a particular character is so regardless of circumstances and motive. Judgment of the act can be certain and unchanging. With this intellectual satisfaction the act of lending was once pronounced to be intrinsically gratuitous and marriage was described as intrinsically indissoluble, and John Paul II discovered slavery to be intrinsically evil.

John Paul II and John Henry Newman agreed that the intrinsically evil could never be done without sin. But Newman thought that to hold a human being in slavery was not intrinsically evil. For John Paul II, slavery was a prime example of what could never be lawfully committed, of what was indeed an instance of intrinsic evil. Their agreement on the nature of the intrinsically evil and their disagreement on slavery generates questions. Is it possible that what is intrinsically evil in one era is not so in another? How then can the intrinsically evil be universal, immutable, always and forever? Or, if the pope was right on slavery, was Newman wrong? Between Newman and John Paul II, there was a change in the theological judgment on slavery. How account for it?

Where the development of moral doctrine is concerned, the development on the subject of slavery is the prime case. At issue is not the mitigation of slavery for Hebrews that the Hebrew Bible called for, nor the fairness supposed to mark the Christian master's treatment of slaves, nor the doubts as to particular titles to slave ownership developed by Christian casuists, but the intrinsic character of a relationship in which one person bought, sold, mortgaged, and transferred another person without regard to that person's will or education or vocation, in which the one owned was a chattel of the owner. Slavery is, if you like, the elephant in the room, so large, so awkward, so threatening that everyone would prefer not to notice it or speak of it. But I will speak of it, for its own sake and for the light it sheds on what constitutes the intrinsically evil, a theme that cannot be avoided in considering the development of moral doctrine. The imperative to avoid the intrinsically evil must be confronted by the changes that have occurred in teachings on conduct, most notable of which is the teaching on slavery.

The focus of this book is on the teaching of morals within the Catholic Church. It is not, except incidentally, a sociological account of Catholic practice. In setting out the teaching on slavery, for example, I do not ask whether slavery was more or less pleasant under Christian masters or note that some slaves led more comfortable lives than others or emphasize that Christian owners sometimes gave freedom to those they owned. I focus on what appears to be true of slaveholding in every context: the right of the owner to determine the identity, education, and vocation of the slave and to possess the fruit of the slave's body. Acts exercising these kinds of domination were once accepted by the teaching Church as without sin. They are no longer.

Slavery is the first and largest subject of development that I address. Usury, religious freedom, divorce follow. Each development has had its own course—its own initiators, its own influencing events and formative forces, its own problems, compromises, and solutions. I have looked for the rules guiding development, and I have found only one, set out in the final chapter. I have discovered in the instances examined that neither the form in which a moral rule is cast, nor the analytic label attached to the acts regulated, nor the kind of human activity at issue can block development or make the teaching on it impervious to change.

The Church cannot change. In the Church's care is what is the deposit of faith—a core of revealed truth that no extrinsic force has power to enlarge or diminish. The deposit is secure in the Church's treasury. The Church proclaims what is necessary for salvation. God's requirements are stable. The revelation that was made in the person of Jesus Christ was complete and final. No subsequent revelation was needed nor has been made.

A Church without change and with change—is one a mirage, a distortion of the facts, a lie; or is reconciliation possible even if, like John Henry Newman, we may startle? To answer the question I do not start a priori. I determine and date the changes that have occurred, then see what reconciliation is possible.

Slavery, religious liberty, usury—on these topics, the teaching of the Catholic Church has changed definitively. On divorce a change is in progress. All change, the cynics say, is glacial. So it must seem to those struggling to foster it. Mutations are small, sometimes sudden. The major mutations that have occurred exhibit what the Church is capable of.

Change is not a thing to be ashamed of, to be whispered about, to be disguised or held from the light of day, as grave guardians sometimes think. Change, in continuity with roots, is the rule of human life. It has been the way of life of the Church. It is a way of teaching celebrated in the Gospel itself in the image of the scribe learned in the law of Moses who is "like a householder who produces from his treasury what is new and what is old" (Mt 13:52). The new and the old cannot in life be neatly distinguished as the old slowly comes to fruition in the new.

Concubines, Castrati,
Concordats—Is There Teaching There?

The magisterium of the Church is expressed in words—by definitions, conciliar pronouncements, catechisms. But is there not another kind of teaching by deeds? In the controversies prior to 1870 over the infallibility of the pope, the focus was on what was "defined" as doctrine by the pope. Evidently definition is done only by words. Analogously, when the teaching of the ordinary magisterium is referred to, what is meant is a doctrine that has been expressed verbally. But should teaching be so confined? Do not teachers teach by example? Do not the deeds of teachers convey doctrine too?

That teaching is, in fact, by example as well as by word is the experience of every teacher. That truth is embedded in the Rule of St. Benedict as it describes the key man in the monastery, the abbot:

> Therefore when anyone takes up the name of Abbot, he ought to govern his disciples by a teaching [*doctrina*] that is twofold; that is, to show all that is good and holy more by his deeds than by his words. To apt disciples let him propose the commandments of the Lord by words; but to the hard

of heart and the more simple, let him demonstrate the divine commandments by his deeds.

That truth is equally embedded in Catholic devotional tradition, as, for example, in *The Imitation of Christ,* whose very title proclaims that it is a person who is to be followed. As in the Gospel of John 14:6, Jesus declares that he is "the way," so *The Imitation of Christ* repeats the declaration adding, "Without the way there is no going." The disciple adds that "your excellent examples" are what sustain us. The examples furnished by the Lord are complemented as instruction by "the lively examples of the holy fathers."

The central place of conduct is at the heart of the exposition of moral theology by John Paul II in *Veritatis splendor:* "Therefore to follow Christ is the essential and proper foundation of Christian moral teaching." The pope focuses not on the words as much as on the reality of Jesus as an acting person: "It is not only a matter here of hearing the teaching and accepting it by obedience to the commandment, but, more deeply, of adhering to the very person of Christ." Quoting the words of Jesus after washing the feet of his disciples, "I have given you an example so that as I have done to you, you will do" (Jn 13:15), the pope continues: "His actions and his commandments are the moral rule of Christian life."

If Jesus's actions are part of his teaching, why should that not be true of the Church which is the body of Christ? If Jesus taught by example, has not the Church?

Let us, in true scholastic fashion, distinguish. Teachers do perform acts which they do not intend to be exemplary, which they themselves would characterize as bad. In this category, for instance, fall the acts of the members of the Roman curia, of whom St. Antoninus speaks in his *Summa theologiae moralis,* who kept concubines. As he observes, their practice did not prove that fornication is permissible. He takes it for granted that no one could conclude that the curialists considered their conduct to be legitimate.

Consider a second case: that of castrating willing boys, so that as *castrati* they might "sing the divine praises in churches more sweetly." This practice was in force in Rome until *castrati* were banned from the Sistine Chapel by Leo XIII. It was sharply criticized by some theologians, but was also cited by other theologians as an instance of acceptable self-mutilation. Until it was finally prohibited, an argument existed that what was "in practice today and tolerated by the Church" could not be wrong.

Another example: as early as 1307, Alessandro of Alessandria, a prominent Franciscan theologian, disputing at Genoa, noted, "The Church condemns and always prosecutes usurers but does not condemn and pursue exchange-bankers; rather it supports them, as is evident in the Roman Church." This practice made Alessandro inclined to distinguish the bankers from the usurers. He failed to develop a coherent theory. His position was repudiated by Antoninus of Florence with the counterexample of the curialists' concubines. In the end, theologians such as Cajetan vindicated the bankers. The move was from practice to approval.

A third kind of case is presented by a practice that challenges no explicit moral rule and that is uncriticized by theologians familiar with the facts—for instance, the practice of the Roman Curia to seek a privileged and even exclusive position for the Catholic Church in concordats between the popes and various secular states. Was not such a practice a form of teaching about the proper relationship of State to Church? Was it not altogether appropriate for Cardinal Ruffini at the Second Vatican Council to cite this practice as a doctrinal objection to the proposed Declaration on Religious Freedom?

In the great debate on religious liberty that culminated in *Dignitatis humanae personae,* the opponents of that declaration were able to cite, in addition to the concordats, a multitude of papal texts rejecting religious freedom. The majority who supported the declaration were hard-pressed to find precedents expressed in words. But they had a trump: the conduct of Christ and his apostles. Neither he nor his chosen followers sought to coerce any conscience. By their example, they proclaimed the freedom of the human person to accept or reject faith. Here was teaching by deed that was not ambiguous or neutral but entirely good. These examples were successfully invoked by the Second Vatican Council as precedent for its own proclamation of freedom.

If the practice of the curia could be cited as Ruffini cited it, if the example of the apostles could be cited as the council cited it, if the actions of Jesus form part of his teaching, is it not clear that teaching by the Church is sometimes done by what the Church does?

One or two examples are not enough. For instance, Pope Gregory II appears to have permitted divorce and remarriage in the case of a wife who was ill and incapable of intercourse but was possibly able to recover; she was not described as antecedently or permanently impotent, yet her marriage was not upheld. Pope Celestine III ruled that if a Catholic spouse fell into heresy, such contempt of the Creator was shown that the marriage was dissolved. These rulings were later overruled. A pattern, not an instance, is necessary for teaching to occur. *Ex facto ius oritur*—law is born from fact. The old maxim may be applied to show that teaching is done by deed, if the deed is repeated and not repudiated by authority.

If we may distinguish these four large categories—bad deeds, undefended; controversial deeds, sometimes criticized, sometimes vindicated; unchallenged practice, publicly engaged in by the popes; and conduct by spiritual persons that is unambiguously good—we may conclude that at least the third and fourth types of activity have a pedagogic function. They need to be taken account of in the development of moral doctrine.

Morals without Experience and Empathy Are like Sundaes without Ice Cream or Sauce

In his *Consilience: The Unity of Knowledge*, E. O. Wilson has a chapter entitled "Ethics and Religion," which begins with this declaration: "Either ethical precepts, such as justice and human rights, are independent of human experience or else they are human inventions." I hold that this simple dichotomy is false. It is false because the teaching of experience is not self-verifying. Raw experience is chaos. Billions of events could count as human experience. Which events count? Each event is good or bad and leads to further results, good or bad. Who decides the goodness or badness? Billions of persons have the billions of experiences. Whose experience is significant? None of these questions are answered by experience alone, nor can human invention by itself get beyond experience. The dynamisms of human nature, including the thirst for truth transcending material existence, provide the criteria by which everyone judges experience; and in the Church these norms are confirmed and deepened by the criteria provided by Christian revelation.

Vicarious experience, of course, counts. The more intensely another's plight or problem is appropriated the better. As far as moral judgment is concerned, that is the great function of great literature—to open us and to convey to us critical experience. Among those who have formed Christian moral thought, Dante and Shakespeare stand near the top. That persons who commit evil acts deform themselves is, I think, a fair reading of the *Inferno* and the *Purgatorio*. That forgiveness of a mortal injury is the measure of Christian love and that redemption is distinguishable from bribery are the insights of *Measure for Measure*.

In any community existing over time there is an additional factor:

> The past experience revived in the meaning
> Is not the experience of one life only
> But of many generations.

In the community that is the Church all its generations are included, and in assessing the experience prayer has a part, and the guidance of the Holy Spirit is assured. In this community it is ultimately the Church that judges what experience counts, whose experience is significant, what experience is good and what experience is bad. Certainly the experience of the Christian faithful counts—an experience that may not be captured in articulated rules but that underlies and influences development. Without experience for the Church to select, preserve, and judge, moral doctrine does not develop.

Experience, no doubt, does not come raw. It comes in the categories and vocabulary of a particular society. It is never pure data free of preexisting concepts. It is not difficult, however, to distinguish a person with experience of a particular situation from a person proceeding purely by concepts without such experience.

Empathy enlarges experience, enabling the individual to identify with some human beings in particular ways. St. Paul writing the Philippians prays that love "may abound in knowledge and insight of every kind" (Phil 1:9). Love, it may be objected, is not a form of knowledge. But love, as St. Thomas contends, seeks to serve the other as oneself. In that seeking, knowledge is acquired. Empathy is the name of this knowledge.

Why does the teaching not develop in the absence of experience? Because the expositors of the teaching have a consciousness formed by their own experience, actual and vicarious. They are not in a position to understand more. Open to experience, they learn; their consciousness grows; the teaching they deliver is developed. In theory, the experience of everyone is relevant. The experience of everyone—saints and sinners, pagans and the baptized, lay and clerical—counts, because, whether good or bad, it furnishes data for moral judgment. In practice, only a fraction of experience can be captured and brought into consideration by those making the judgment.

With these matters unavoidably in mind—the status of the intrinsic; the types of teaching; and the role of experience—I propose to proceed to "the unknown sin." By the unknown sin I do not mean a secret sin, as some might understand the title. I do not mean the sin against the Spirit, which in Luke 12:10 is said to be unforgivable but whose exact nature has never been established. I mean acts which were not known to be sins; acts for which no vocabulary existed to denominate them as sins; acts participated in by upright men and women, by popes and dedicated members of religious orders and canonized saints; acts now regarded with horror as the blackest kind of affront to the human person and among the most serious derelictions of duty to God, whose image is the person.

THE UNKNOWN SIN

God's Slaveowners

The Lord came down upon Mount Sinai and summoned Moses to the mountain top, and Moses went up . . . God spoke, and these were his words: . . . "You shall not covet your neighbor's house; you shall not covet your neighbor's wife, his slave, his slave girl, his ox, his ass, or anything that belongs to him." (Ex 20:17)

No suggestion here that there is anything wrong in owning slaves. In a language with gendered nouns, pains are taken to specify slaves of both genders. Slaves are not to be coveted because they are among what belongs to someone else.

The report of the Lord's words to Moses is almost the same in Deuteronomy 5:21 as that in Exodus, except that "land" is added to the list of what should not be coveted. In both accounts, the presence among the Hebrews of slaves and slave girls has already been remarked by the specification in the commandment to keep holy the Sabbath that they, like ox and ass, are not to work on that day (Ex 20:10; Dt 5:15). A slaveholding society is assured in two of the Ten Commandments promulgated on Mount Sinai that God is aware of its slaves and that God has protected the slaveholder by proscribing the desire to take what is the slaveholder's property. God issues his command protecting the slaveholder. The rest from labor prescribed for the slaves is no more than that prescribed for the domestic animals. Slaveholding as an institution is presented as divinely sanctioned. No Hebrew prophet, no Hebrew text condemns or criticizes the institution recognized and secured by the divine commandments.

Genesis put slavery almost at the start of biblical history. Noah, the first man "to plant a vineyard," becomes drunk. His son Ham enters his tent and sees "his father's nakedness" (Gen 9:20–26). When Noah wakes and learns "what his youngest son had done to him," he punishes him by cursing Ham's son, Canaan: "Cursed be Canaan, slave of slaves shall he be to his brothers," that is, to his cousins, the offspring of Noah's two good sons. The sin whose enormity earned this enormous punishment has never been clear. That slavery, however, was the punishment of the sin was clear. The story was probably told in order to pre-figure the enslavement of the Canaanites to the Hebrews as the latter took over the Promised Land. Some theologians, in later generations, would read it as showing slavery established by divine command. By a peculiar twisting of the text, Africans became identified as the children of Ham.

A second story in which God approves slavery in the family of a patriarch focuses on Isaac and Rebecca's twin sons, Esau and Jacob. As they clash in her womb, Rebecca asks the Lord why, and he answers that from her loins two people shall come, "the elder, the younger's slave" (Gen 25:21–23). This story pre-figures the enslavement of the Edomites, the descendants of Esau. Just as Noah's curse is carried out by God's power, so God's prediction for Esau is fulfilled.

In the book of Leviticus, the Lord as legislator on Mount Sinai declares:

> The slave and the slave girl shall come from the nations round about you; from them you may buy slaves. You may also buy the children of those who have settled and lodge with you and such of their family as are born in the land. They may become your property, and you may leave them to your sons after you; you may use them as slaves permanently. (Lev 25:44–46)

The notion, that, since God has given the land to the Hebrews the former inhabitants must be their slaves, is reaffirmed in the book of Joshua. The Gibeonites pretend to be from a far country but are discovered to be neighbors occupying land meant for Israel. Joshua tells them: "There is a curse upon you for this: for all time you shall provide us with slaves, to chop wood and draw water for the house of my God" (Jos 9:16–24). Inconsistently, the law in Deu-teronomy prescribes death for every creature in the patrimony. It is in distant lands that the conquering Hebrews "may take the women, the dependents, and the cattle for yourselves" (Dt 20:14).

The enslavement of enemies at the Lord's command is exemplified in Moses's victory over the Midianites. After every male child and every woman who has had intercourse with a man are slaughtered, the girls who have had no intercourse with a man are to be divided among the victors (Num 31:18). After deducting the Lord's share and the Levites' share, the booty is enumerated: "675,000 sheep; 72,000 oxen; 61,000 asses; and 32,000 girls who are still virgins" (Num 31:34–35). Uneasy about the quantities and perhaps about the actions recorded, a modern commentator suggests that the numbers are fantasy. Still, the reduction of the virgins of the vanquished to slavery is cause for the biblical author to celebrate, just as other peoples in the Near East celebrated. The basic pattern is taken for granted in Genesis in the story of the revenge of Jacob's boys on Sichem and his Hivite kin: the men are killed, the women and children enslaved (Gen 34:25–29). An Assyrian temple of Ashurnasirpal II (883–859) proclaimed his triumph after crossing the Euphrates: "I received the tribute of the king of Songura, the king of the Hittites: 20 talents of silver . . . all his own furniture . . . also 200 young females in linen garments with multi-colored trimmings. . . ." The conquerors rejoiced as they enlarged their properties with silver, animals, and human beings. Not unusually, in each of these three examples, slavery is not a way of sparing the life of defeated warriors; they are killed. Slavery is a form in which booty is acquired.

The enslavement of non-Israelites was recorded continuing in the tenth century; it was the fate of the survivors of the Amorites, Hittites, Perizzites, Hivites, and Jebusites (1 Kgs 9:21). Gangs of slaves were employed at Solomon's smelter at Ezion-geber on the north shore of the Red Sea. Slaves were dedicated to service in the Temple, so that, in the sixth century, Artaxerxes, king of Persia, is said to have sent Ezra, priest and doctor of the law of the Lord, back from Babylon to Jerusalem accompanied by templeslaves (1 Esd 8:5). Enslavement of the foreigner was the program prophetically proclaimed in the seventh century for Israel by Isaiah:

> Many nations shall escort Israel to her place, and she shall employ them as slaves and slave girls in the land of the Lord. She shall take her captors captive and rule over her task-masters. (Is 14:2)

As Second Isaiah, in the bitterness of the Babylonian exile, has visions of the vengenance of the Lord upon those who have oppressed Israel, he descends into detail on the life of the women spared to become slaves:

Down from your throne, sit on the ground, daughter of the Chaldeans;
never again shall men call you soft-skinned and delicate.
Take up the millstone, grind meal, uncover your tresses;
strip off your skirt, bare your thighs, wade through rivers
so that your nakedness may be plain to see
and your shame exposed.

(Is 47:1–3)

Slaves in the Mediterranean World

Slavery as an institutional arrangement ran throughout the world in which Christianity appeared. The Hebrew, Greek, and Roman acceptance of slavery formed the society in which Jesus lived, Paul's epistles were written, and Christian communities took shape.

The Apocalypse of John, for example, takes a saturnine satisfaction in the fall of "the great Babylon," where, enumerated among other vendibles such as "sheep and cattle, horses and chariots," are "slaves and the souls of men" (Apoc 18:13). The imperial household embraced a large number of slaves, as did other opulent houses where slaves were employed in domestic service. Gangs of slaves cultivated the land in Sicily and parts of the Italian peninsula. Other slave gangs were employed in mining or in intensive industrial work as they had been at Solomon's smelter. Slaves held high positions as managers for the rich and powerful. Slaves were craftsmen, weavers, and spinners. Slaves were gardeners, cooks, maids, cupbearers, doorkeepers. The *Digest* listed thirty-five specific jobs for slaves on a rural estate. Slaves were rented out as prostitutes or taken as concubines by their owners or merely used as occasional sexual outlets for the owner or his sons. Slaves could supply either heterosexual or homosexual tastes. Slaves were incapable of contracting a marriage recognized by law, and not many slaves lived within a slave family; such units as did exist were not taken into consideration when slaves were sold.

The total number of slaves in the Roman world is not documented. This number and the number supplied annually from different sources are matters of estimate and debate. The majority of rural domestic slaves were men; of domestic slaves, boys and women. A slaveowner might own only one slave or as many as one hundred, five hundred, or one thousand or more. In the time of Augustine, slaves are estimated to have been a substantial percent of the population; to have dominated agricultural production and large-scale production in the cities;

and to have been the chief source of income for the wealthy. In these three ways, Italy was a slave society, as, in lesser degrees, was the rest of the empire.

Why slaves? Four reasons: Economically, slaves were useful auxiliaries in the cities and close to indispensable on farms too large to be cultivated by a free family. Slaves were aliens, exploitable in ways that free citizens might resist. Slaves conferred status on their owners and at the same time gave all citizens a sense of superiority. Psychologically, slaves satisfied what St. Augustine acknowledged as a basic human desire, *libido dominandi,* the lust to dominate. And a fifth reason: it was the way life had always been organized.

Terrible moments of transition punctuated the institution—the reduction of free men or children to slavery to satisfy a debt; the reduction of noblewomen to slaves at the taking of a city, as in Euripides' *The Trojan Women;* the auction of naked captives; the taking of a slave child from the child's slave mother. Cruelty beyond these traumas was inherent in an institution in which one person's food, clothes, place of residence, sexual opportunities, education, and occupation depended on the will of another person, who could enforce his or her will by physical punishment and physical deprivations.

Slaves were sold in a Roman market under the same rules that animals were sold and were subject to the same sort of physical inspection. Their origin was supposed to be indicated by the seller, but their old identity disappeared. Their former names and any reference to relatives or ancestors were eliminated. Whatever name they subsequently bore was determined by the buyer. Obliteration of the old identity was often confirmed by transportation to regions unknown to the slave and to areas whose language was equally unknown by him or her. The expansion of the empire made this possibility more likely than it had been when the Hebrews warred on neighboring tribes.

War was a regular source of supply. Populations of entire cities captured in war might be enslaved, as were the thirty thousand inhabitants of Tiberias in Galilee in A.D. 67. Existing slaves bred fresh supplies. The home-born slaves (*vernae*) were conspicuous in the slave population. Children abandoned by their parents and then seized by persons who raised and sold them also formed part of the supply. Roman slavers traded for slaves in the Caucasus, in Gaul, in Germany, in Egypt and Armenia. Ephesus was a hub for slaves from the East. Outright kidnapping by pirates fed into the trade. The result was a large slave population "highly differentiated and complex" in its makeup.

The Romans did free a number of domestic slaves. The slaves paid for their freedom, so that humanity was complemented by self-interest. Emancipation was not the normal reward of those engaged in agriculture or in mining. Nor did the possibility of emancipation prevent slaves from becoming fugitives or soften the slaves' resentment. "So many slaves, so many enemies," ran a Roman proverb.

Apologists for the acceptance of slavery in the Bible have sometimes asserted that ancient slavery was different from the chattel slavery of the American South. This argument was used by nineteenth-century abolitionists, embarrassed by defenses of slavery based on the Bible. The argument appears to be without historical support. Chattel slavery is slavery in which persons count as things to be bought and sold. In this respect, the slavery of the non-Hebrew slaves of the Hebrews was no different from slavery more generally in the Roman world, although Roman law, as more developed, was more extensive in its regulation of the disposition of slaves as property. The *Digest*, for example, dealt with the equipment (*instrumentum*) of a farm, including slaves. The Romans divided the means by which farms were cultivated into the mute (vehicles); the inarticulate (cattle); and the articulate (slaves). In Varro's memorable phrase, a slave was an *instrumentum vocale* or talking tool.

The masters were aware that their instruments were human. Humane management was recommended. Perks for the slaves who acted as foremen would motivate them. *Verba* (words), not *verbera* (whips) should direct the farm slaves. But only if words got results. Force remained as the ultimate motivator.

The approach to slaves that had evolved at the time of the writing in the second century B.C. of "The Wisdom of Jesus Son of Sirach" for the Greek-speaking Jews of Egypt was marginally more complex than the Roman:

> Fodder, and stick, and burdens for the donkey;
> bread, and discipline, and work for the slave!
> Make your slave work, if you want rest for yourself;
> if you leave him idle, he will be looking for his liberty,
> The ox is tamed by yoke and harness,
> the bad slave by racks and tortures.
> Put him to work to keep him from being idle,
> for idleness is a great teacher of mischief.
> Set him to work, for that is what he is for,
> and if he disobeys you, load him with fetters.
>
> (Eccl 33:24–28)

The advice is immediately countered:

> If you have a slave, treat him with justice,
> because you bought him with your blood.

> If you have a slave, treat him like a brother;
> you will need him as much as you need yourself.
> If you ill-treat him, and he takes to his heels,
> where will you go to look for him?
>
> (Eccl 33:30–31)

An ox or a donkey are analogues for a slave; but a slave is to be cherished as a brother. The gnomic utterances invite a range of conduct by the master. No single rule governed all master-slave interactions. Nevertheless, the slave was stigmatized by more than poverty, disease, or physical disfigurement. Add the ancient disdain for women, and the female slave—or slave girl as she would normally be classed—was the lowest of the low.

Slaves in the Speech of Jesus

Slaves in the biblical world are partly hidden from us. What disguises their ubiquity is our translation. Hebrew for slave is *ĕbed*, male slave; *amăh*, female slave; *n 'r*, young slave. The Septuagint faithfully translated these words into Greek as *doulos*, male slave; *doule*, slave girl; and *pais*, slave boy. The Vulgate rendered the terms in Latin as *servus; serva* or *ancilla;* and *puer*. But when John Wyclif translated the Vulgate into English in 1382, he translated the Latin *servus* as "servant" and the Latin *ancilla* as "handmaiden." These conventions were followed in the sixteenth century by William Tyndal, by Myles Coverdale, and by the Geneva Bible. Wyclif and his early successors did not bowdlerize the Bible deliberately. Slavery, for them, was not a racist institution. Slavery as such was not current in England. "Servant" could carry the sense of "slave." By the time of the King James translators, "slave" was associated with blackness, as Shakespeare's treatment of Caliban in *The Tempest* demonstrates. A deliberate choice may have been made to avoid the new connotation by retaining "servant." *The New Oxford English Dictionary* lists as a special meaning of "servant" its use as the English translation of what means "slave" in biblical Hebrew and Greek. The editors also observe that in the American South, from colonial times through the eighteenth century, "servant" was a usual term for a slave. It may be supposed that Southern slaveholders adopted the usage from their English bibles.

Translators today do not always take note that modern English distinguishes servants from slaves. True, "slave" and "slave girl" have an unfamiliar ring in biblical passages where the ear is accustomed to bland reference to a servant. The ring is often not only unfamiliar but harsh, especially where the slave is presented as the ideal believer. That Jesus moves in a society in which slavery is an institution and that he draws on this institution for illustrations, metaphors, and sayings is not an impression one obtains from our English translations from which the vocabulary of slavery has been largely expunged. Today, it is a bowdlerization of the Bible not to use the rougher terms that accurately translate the Scriptures.

As a matter of course, Jesus uses the slave culture for illustrations, a rhetorical practice that treats slavery as normal. Slaves are dispatched to put sandals on the feet of the prodigal son (Lk 15:22). Slaves are sent to invite guests for dinner but are not themselves invited to dine (Lk 14: 16–24). In one of the most memorable sayings attributed to him, Jesus declares, "No slave can serve two masters" (Lk 16:13). "No slave" is far more pointed than "No servant," as Luke is often translated, or than "No man" as in Matthew 6:24. In the parable of the faithless superslave, who takes advantage of his position while his lord is away and beats the boy slaves and the girl slaves, the punishment inflicted when his lord returns is the unrestrained punishment a wrathful owner might inflict on property. The superslave, in Luke's account, is to be "dismembered" (Lk 12:42–46).

In a snatch of theological argument presented in John, Jesus tells his interlocutors, "The truth shall free you." They reply that they have never been slaves. He replies, "Everyone who commits sin is a slave. But the slave does not remain in the household forever. The son does remain forever. Accordingly, if the son frees you, you will be really free" (Jn 8:34–35). The actual difference between slaves and the son of the master is used to state a parallel relation between sinners and the Son of God. Paul sets up a similar parallel in writing the Galatians (Gal 4:21–5:1).

Slaves appear seven times in New Testament narrative. Three times they are named. They are Malchus and Onesimus, to be discussed below, and Rhoda, the doorkeeper who lets Peter in after his escape from prison (Acts 12:14). The slave exorcised by Paul (Acts 16:16–18), and the two slaves sent by Cornelius to find Peter (Acts 10:47–48) are not named. The slave girl who questions Peter suspects that Peter is a follower of Jesus when she sees him "in the light of the fire" by which he stands (Lk 22:56). Is the detail accidental, or does it emphasize the unnamed girl's acuteness?

Jesus explicitly praises the centurion of Capernaum, not on account of his owning an unnamed slave, but without notice of this fact as any sort of blemish. Matthew introduces the centurion's slave as a slaveboy (Mt 8:6); Luke describes him as "valuable" to his owner (Lk 7:2). The centurion needs help for his sick property. Jewish elders are sent by the centurion to urge Jesus to "save his slave's life"; for the centurion "loves our nation" and helped to build the synagogue. Jesus responds by approaching the centurion's house. The centurion sends friends to deter him, saying in the centurion's name:

> "Lord, do not take more trouble, for I am not worthy that you enter under my roof. On that account I did not think myself worthy to come to you. But say the word and my slave boy will be healed. For I am myself a man under authority, having soldiers under me, and I say to this one 'Go,' and he goes, and to another, 'Come,' and he comes, and to my slave, 'Do this,' and he does it." When Jesus heard this speech, he respected him and turned to the following crowd and said, "Amen, I say to you I have not found such great faith in Israel." When the messengers returned to the house, they found that the slave was healed. (Lk 7:2–10)

The text celebrates the faith of a soldier and opens the message of Jesus to gentiles. The subtext testifies to the virtue of a property owner concerned about preserving valuable and obedient property.

Jesus is never presented in conversation with a slave. Assuming that the evangelists present encounters with Jesus that will instruct those for whom they write, we may infer either that Jesus had no conversation with a slave or that the gospel-writers found it difficult, embarrassing, or pointless to recall such a meeting. Whichever inference is drawn, a distinct reserve is suggested as to slaves as potential followers. Jesus spoke to the Samaritan, the Roman centurion, the tax collector, the leper. Never, so far as is reported, did he speak to a slave. Only the slaveowning centurion is addressed and praised. As much as the slaveowners addressed and fortified by the Ten Commandments, this figure of the Gospels is confirmed in his human possession.

God's Slaves

Why should we be concerned with slavery in the Bible? It is not because anyone today would defend slavery because it was a biblical institution. It is because we need to understand the transformation of morals in which slavery has become intrinsically evil. What was always and everywhere the way life was organized has become what is always and everywhere evil. How did it happen? Ceremonial rules could be discarded. Commandments had to be kept. But what of an institution ingrained in the society as part of its way of life? The transformation begins haltingly, ambiguously, almost silently in the Bible itself. Hebrews who were slaves of fellow Hebrews were the subject of special legislation in ancient Israel.

Out of Egypt

The special status of Hebrew slaves was associated in Leviticus with God's deliverance of all the Hebrews from slavery in Egypt. Hebrew slaves "are my slaves whom I brought out of Egypt" (Lev 25:42). It is God who speaks. A transformation of Hebrew slavery is being attempted. It is because all Hebrews are God's slaves that the law seeks to make their treatment different from that accorded alien slaves. It is the law in Leviticus as well that "you shall love your neighbor as yourself" (Lev 19:18). It was not read as a prohibition of slavery. The general teaching that man was made in the image of God (Gen 1:26) was not understood as a prohibition against making slaves of men. An institution that was provided for by God's own precepts was not undermined while it was softened for those bound by blood and religion.

In Exodus, following the presentation of the Ten Commandments by Moses to the Israelites, Moses again consults the Lord, who tells him: "These are the laws you shall set before them" (Ex 21:1). The first of the laws regulates the treatment of a Hebrew slave bought by another Hebrew. He is to be free in the seventh year. A single man shall depart single; a married slave shall leave with the wife he brought with him. If his master gives him a wife, the woman and any children she bears belong to the master and, on being freed, "the man shall go alone." The slave also has the option of remaining a slave for the rest of his life, a commitment symbolized by the master "piercing his ear with an awl" (Ex 21:2–6). The sale of a Hebrew girl by her father is also covered. She has no right to freedom at the end of six years. The assumption is that she is sold for sexual purposes. "If the master has not had intercourse with her and she does not please him, he shall let her be ransomed" (Ex 21:7–8). "If he assigns her to a son, he shall allow her the rights of a daughter" (Ex 21:10). If the master "takes another woman," he shall not deny his slavewife "meat, clothes and conjugal rights." If he does, she shall go free (Ex 21:9–10). If the master strikes his slave or slave girl with a stick and he or she dies "on the spot," the master "must be punished," the punishment being unspecified; and there is no punishment "if the slave survives for one day or two" (Ex 21:20–21). If the master's blow knocks out an eye or a tooth of a slave or slave girl, the one struck goes free (Ex 21:26–27).

These restraints were ways of humanizing the institution, to give hope to the enslaved Hebrew male, to make enslavement the path to marriage for the Hebrew girl, to outlaw sudden death and violent blows as punishment. At the same time the Lord's legislation does not disapprove of Hebrews acquiring Hebrews, or of Hebrews subjecting Hebrews to corporal punishment. In the Lord's legislation in Leviticus, it is expressly stated that a Hebrew slave is "not to be driven with ruthless severity by his owner" (Lev 25:46). Every fifty years, counting from the entry of the Hebrews into the promised land, the ram's horn was to go round and sound a blast. It would be the year of jubilee. In that year, every Hebrew slave and his children were to be released from slavery, as the Israelites had been released from bondage in Eygpt (Lev 25:54–55). Enforcement of the mitigating rules, as in much of the legislation transmitted from the Lord to Moses, is not specified.

A remarkable break in ethics of a slave society is the preservation of the tribal tribute to Samson, the story of a Hebrew hero who is betrayed into captivity. The story does not identify him as enslaved but shows him mutilated and treated as a slave. In Milton's mighty line, he is

> Eyeless in Gaza at the Mill with slaves

Roman law wrote off warriors reduced to slavery by the enemy. Samson asserts himself again as a hero (Jud 16:21)—a dangerous recognition of humanity transcending enslavement, marginally less dangerous because the slave-hero is overcoming the enemy.

The conduct of a slave, instead of being beneath comment or contempt, can be a model. The psalmist prays:

> Deliver me, O Lord, I beseech you,
> for I am your slave . . .
> I am your slave, the son of your slave girl,
> you have undone the bonds that bound me.
>
> (Ps 116:4 and 16)

The devout Hebrew casts himself in this model:

> As the eyes of a slave are on the hand of his master,
> As the eyes of a slave girl are on the hands of her mistress,
> So our eyes are on the Lord our God
> Waiting for kindness from him.
>
> (Ps 123:2)

The time will come, God says through the prophet Joel, when

> I will pour out my spirit
> even upon slaves and slave girls.
>
> (Joel 2:29)

Two themes are detectable—on the one hand, an effort to enhance the status of actual slaves by relating them to God; on the other, the use of slavery as a metaphor for the service the good Hebrew owes to God. Neither approach effects an estrangement of the slave from society. The slave, Joel indicates, can receive the spirit. The slave, as presented by the psalmist, is exemplary. Both approaches lie behind a part of the New Testament treatment of slaves.

Christ's Purchases

Writing to the Corinthians, Paul adapts the teaching of the Hebrew Bible about the Israelites redeemed by God. "You are not your own," he tells the new Christians, "for you were bought at a great price" (1 Cor 6:20). Unlike the ancient Israelites, these purchased people were free in human terms, but slaves of sin. Called to union with Christ, the free man becomes "slave of Christ" (1 Cor 7:22). "Bought for a price," Paul reminds them, "do not become slaves of men" (1 Cor 7:23). The instruction that they are bought and enslaved to Christ is not an assault upon the dignity of the new Christians but a metaphor strenuously inculcating the fidelity and obedience their new Master demands. It is also a metaphor obliterating the difference—so far as a metaphor can—between Christians who are free and those who are actual slaves. "Paul, slave of Christ Jesus," Paul identifies himself to the Romans (Rom 1:1). In what Acts presents as the prayer of Peter and John, the two apostles beseech God to "give your slaves power" to preach with effect (Acts 4:29).

The metaphor is enthusiastically taken up in the Apocalypse or Revelation of John. A great multitude in heaven proclaims the judgment of God upon the great idolatress: "He has avenged upon her the blood of his slaves" (Apoc 19:2). An angel instructs the author not to worship him for "I am your co-slave" (Apoc 19:10; and again 22:9). The Lord has sent his angel "to show his slaves what must happen soon" (Apoc 22:6). These slaves are the followers of the Lamb. The throne of God and of the Lamb will be in the new city "and his slaves shall worship him" (Apoc 22:3). Like slaves branded by their owners, the slaves of the Lamb "shall bear his name on their foreheads" (Apoc 22:4).

Paul's letters, Peter and John in Acts, and the author of the Apocalypse chime with Jesus's parables and sayings. For example, the vigilant doorkeepers in Luke 12, ready to let in their lord at whatever hour he returns, are slaves who are stand-ins for Jesus's faithful followers. The superslave of Luke 12, about to be dismembered, is a sharp reminder of the accountability of leaders of the Christian community who abuse their position. If a slave has been ploughing or minding sheep and comes in from the field, his master will not invite him to sit down but will say, "Prepare my supper." The master is not grateful that his slave has obeyed him. So, too, the followers of Jesus, when they have carried out all their orders, should say, "We are slaves and worthless; we have only done our duty" (Lk 17:7–10). "Whoever wants to be great among you must be your servant (*diakonos*), and whoever wishes to be first among you must be everybody's slave" (Mk 10:45). In these sayings, the Hebrew concept of the slaves of God is applied to the followers of Jesus and especially to their leaders. No follower of Jesus is analogized to a slaveowner.

Jesus himself as the model for his followers is presented as a slave. Washing the feet of his disciples, he performs the office of a slave, reminding them after he has done so that he is their lord and master, and "a slave is not greater than his master," so they are to follow his example (Jn 13:3–16). Similarly, in the Gospel of Mark, after the saying about the leader's duty to be everybody's slave, Jesus adds in explanation, "because the Son of Man did not come to be served but to serve and to give his life to free many" (Mk 10:45). So Paul writes, or incorporates, a hymn that states that Christ Jesus was in the form of God but "emptied himself, taking the form of a slave" (Phil 2:6–7). In this extreme paradox one who is equal with God becomes God's slave.

If Jesus can be presented as a slave, as God's slave, there can be no indignity, no loss of honor, no social death implied in extension of the metaphor of slavery to Mary; and it is Mary who as a slave girl not only converses with Jesus but brings him into the world. As Luke presents her at the start of his Gospel, Mary responds to the angel's announcement of her forthcoming pregnancy: "See the slave girl of the Lord. Let it be according to your word" (Lk 1:38). A little later in the canticle responding to Elizabeth, Mary salutes God, who has "looked upon his slave girl in her humbleness" (Lk 1:48). Given the exploitation of slave girls by their masters, the imagery is bold. The relation of slave girl and master is used to accept and then to proclaim the most chaste form of procreation. The slave girl is the mother of the slave son, and both are God's slaves.

The obedience, the humility, the vigilance expected of all slaves, as well as the enterprise, loyalty, and responsibility demanded of managerial slaves, were expected of the followers of Jesus—so the parables and sayings made clear. To draw on slavery for a model of Christian life gave an implicit dignity to the slave. The slave had virtues now prized by the Christians.

That conclusion does not establish Friedrich Nietzsche's famous contention that Christianity was the revenge of the slaves on their masters. Nietzsche includes among "the slaves" those he calls "the little people," such as artisans, and he extends the term to include all the Jews, making Christianity their revenge on their Roman masters. Moreover, the virtues of those he calls "the weak" include willingness to forgive, a virtue an actual slave was not supposed to need; he could not ever assert that he was injured. Slavery in Nietzsche is a rhetorical trope not a historical explanation.

Orlando Patterson, a modern master of the sociology of slavery, has presented a strong case that, across cultures, the essential feature of slavery is the social extinction of the slave. Legally nothing, cut off from ancestors, deprived of any right to spouse or to children, the slave is a "dishonored being," radically reduced from humanness. Accurate as that case may be in capturing the slave condition, it cannot be simplistically applied in a world where "slave" functions as a metaphor, and there are God's slaves as well as man's.

As early as the story of Abigail and David, becoming a slave may be a path to greatness. The astute Abigail, when David sends his sons to ask her to be his wife, prostrates herself and says to them: "Behold let your servant be as a slave girl to wash the feet of the slaves of my lord" (1 Sam 25:41). In this way, Abigail moves from being the widow of Nabal (= Churl) to being the wife of the king-to-be. Being God's slave is a boast in Paul. God's slave is not alienated from the community, not reduced to powerlessness, not a nothing. A transvaluation of values has been effected. The metaphor's meaning is missed if it is read literally. Without strain or sense of incongruity, the centurion's plea for his sick slave boy was to enter the Mass as an appropriate prayer before receiving the Eucharist: "Say but the word and my soul will be healed."

To use slavery to model Christian life carried the risk of implied acceptance of the legal structure; in modern jargon, the slave parables "reinscribed" the structure. The risk lay in the effect on the literal-minded. In Hebrew scripture, Hosea's marriage to a prostitute symbolized God's faithful love to a faithless spouse, without showing an approval of prostitution (Hosea 1:1–2:17). The unjust judge is a figure for God responding to petitions, without unjust judging being recommended (Lk 18:2–8). The putting out of money at usury stands for productive faith without the prohibition of usury being called into question (Lk 19:12–27). That slavery should so often be taken as a structure symbolizing the believer's status before God arose from the absoluteness of God's claim. "The slave is not above the master," Jesus says in John 13:16. A little later and then surprisingly, the analogy of slavery is challenged. "You are my friends, if you do what I command you. I call you slaves no longer. A slave does not know what his lord is doing. But you I have called friends because whatever I have heard from my Father I have made known to you" (Jn 15:14–15). In this way, the Johannine Christ at the Last Supper deliberately departs from the metaphor of slavery to give the disciples a special status. This exception to the rule does not invalidate the evangelical use of the metaphor elsewhere, nor alter its effect of enhancing the status of those serving God as it increases what is demanded of them. Without reference to slavery, without acknowledgment of the abnegation of the slave, the imagery of the New Testament is impaired, the force of the demand made of the follower of Christ is diluted.

The message of Jesus as it relates to slavery is complex. Jesus in Luke declares near the beginning of his mission in Nazareth that he has come "to proclaim liberty to captives" (Lk 4:18). "Captives" could be understood to mean metaphorically those captive to sin. Jesus immediately speaks of giving sight to the blind, an undoubted metaphor. But "captives" is from Isaiah 61:1, where the prophet adds after "captives" the words "and release to those in prison." Isaiah does not appear to speak metaphorically. Jesus in Luke may be seen self-designated as a liberator. The captives are most naturally understood as the slaves. Whether slaves of the Romans or slaves of fellow Israelites, or both, is not spelled out. The reference to liberation is short, fragmentary, undeveloped. But would not any slave hearing the gospel have grasped a message? As Luke wrote not only the gospel bearing his name but also the Acts of the Apostles, it is not without significance that he attributes to Peter speaking at the Harvest Festival (= the Pentecost of Christians) Joel's lines on God pouring out his spirit on slaves and slave girls (Acts 2:18). The evangelist who gives kudos to the centurion-slaveowner is also the evangelist aware of slaves among those drawn to Jesus.

Jesus did not abolish slavery—that would have called for an uprising like Spartacus's. Jesus did not legitimate slavery, as some have claimed. It needed no legitimation. No one in the Mediterranean world of the first century wrote an abolitionist tract. Slavery was an institution as accepted as animals used for agriculture or as tables used to furnish a house.

The Gospels do present a story showing remarkable interest in a slave. The story is the last miracle of Jesus's pre-Resurrection life—the healing of the slave of the high priest whose ear Peter has sliced off. Jesus acts not at the slaveowner's request but spontaneously to help an injured human being. To effect the cure Jesus touches the slave (Lk 22:51). By the time of John's Gospel, the slave has a name—Malchus—although the miracle performed on him is not mentioned (Jn 18:10). The naming of the slave is one of the several indications in the New Testament that slaves were among the earliest Christians. Malchus, like Rhoda and Onesimus, must have been a member of a Christian community for his name to be preserved. The story can be read as testimony to Jesus's concern for the lowest of the low, to whom, nonetheless, he does not speak.

A subversive view of slavery lurks in the Apocalypse when it speaks of the great Babylon, where what is sold includes "slaves and the souls of men" (Apoc 18:13). It would have been enough to say "slaves." The author wants to indicate that souls are included in the sales. Later Greek Christians continued the usage, speaking of the sale of "souls" when slaves were merchandise.

That the gospel as preached by Paul opened Christian communities to slaves is incontestable. They who were stateless, ancestorless, personless were recognized as equal souls. There was opened for them a life that would transcend the life they lived. The promise to the Good Thief, "This day you shall be with me in paradise" (Lk 23:43), was, analogously, made to them as to their future. Instead of enlistment in a futile campaign for abolition, the Christian slave was given hope in place of hopelessness, purpose in place of mechanical obedience. Gifts of this kind should not be dismissed as cheaply given. They could make a world of difference. They do explain why slaves became active in the new faith.

Useful

That Paul has no doubt that slavery is an undesirable state is evident in his brilliant metaphorical use of slavery to describe the state of a spouse abandoned by his or her unbelieving mate but bound not to remarry. As discussed more fully below in chapter 24, Paul does not think such slavery a state that God intended Christians to be in.

Paul's letters, in general, preserve a delicate balance. In Christ Jesus, there is neither slave nor free, he repeats (Gal 3:27–28; 1 Col 3:11). But Paul is not an advocate of liberation. Slaves are told to "obey your human masters in everything." Masters are told to "treat your slaves justly and fairly, remembering that you have a Master in heaven" (Col 3:22). The only guidance given the owners is their idea of a just God. A little more specifically in Ephesians, Paul instructs masters to "stop bullying" and reminds them that with God there is no "noticing of faces," i.e., partiality (Eph 6:9). What is just, fair, not bullying in a slave-owning society is left to the imagination of the masters. But in two different contexts, Paul challenges the negative image of slavery. Writing the Corinthians, he declares that he is a free man, yet "I have enslaved myself to all" (1 Cor 9:19). Here, Paul challenges the hierarchy of status: the leader is to lead by lowering himself to serve. His action parallels that of Jesus becoming a slave. It is very far from becoming a nothing; it is the way of the Lord.

This kind of reference to slavery ennobles it while using the term metaphorically. In a second, nonmetaphorical context, in a remarkably dense letter, Paul embarks on a course which, if taken as exemplary, would have been revolutionary. Writing from imprisonment in Rome about the year 62, Paul addresses Philemon, his convert and the head of a house-church probably at Colossae: "the viscera of the saints have found peace through you, brother." He moves to the business of the letter. He is sending it with Onesimus (= Useful or, more colloquially, Handy):

> I appeal to you for my child to whom I gave birth in prison—Useful, who was once unserviceable to you and now is serviceable to you and to me. When I send him back to you, it's my own viscera. . . . Perhaps he left you for an hour that you might have him forever, no longer as slave but above slave, brother beloved very much by me and much more by you in the flesh and in the Lord. If you hold me your partner, receive him as me. If he has injured you in some way or owes you, impute it to me. I Paul have written in my own hand. I will repay. I do not say to you that you owe yourself to me. Come brother, I make use of you in the Lord. Rest my viscera in the Lord. If, therefore, you hold me your partner, receive him as me.
>
> (Philem 10–20)

This passage is sometimes read as acknowledging that Useful may have stolen something from Philemon. He clearly has stolen the service he owed his master; in legal terms as a runaway he is a thief. Whether he took something in addition is not clear. What is clear is that Paul takes on himself to pay whatever is owed. Sometimes his letter is seen as doing no more than that, excusing Useful's theft and promising to make it up. There is more. Paul states that he is free to command Philemon but prefers to appeal to him so that Philemon's "kindness might be voluntary." The emphasis on the voluntary is undercut by the mounting eloquence and urgency of the appeal. Paul does not exactly pun on Useful's name but first plays with it to indicate Useful's new status; then he asks Philemon himself to be useful. Three times he uses a term invoking the guts, the last time leaving "viscera" to be interpreted either as Paul's own guts or as Useful, who is identified with them. Born of Paul, his child, his guts, his very self, Useful is to be given rest, and Philemon himself is to become useful. Philemon would have to be a clod to miss what Paul is telling him. Lest he hesitate, Paul adds:

> I have written you, relying on your obedience,
> Knowing that you will do even more than I ask.
> (Philem 21–22)

It is impossible to read these lines and to think of Useful as a nothing, deprived of humanity. He is identified with his father in Christ. He is to be loved as Paul himself is loved.

Amazingly, this brief personal note of no more than twenty-five sentences survived. Tradition identifies Useful as "the faithful and loved brother" Paul refers to in Colossians 4:9, and the tradition goes on to say he became bishop of Ephesus. The tradition cannot be proved to be right. That the letter survived, however, is pretty good evidence that Philemon acted on it and emancipated Useful. Those who preserved it in the collection of Paul's letters could see what it meant for a Christian to treat a slave with love. Could enslavement in its essentials survive if Paul's letter presented the paradigm? Paul seeks freedom for one man only; he doesn't tell Philemon, "You must free all your slaves." Could slavery survive the commandment to love one's neighbor as oneself? The New Testament did not confront the institution with the commandment.

The Pope's Slaves

An old Northumbrian legend tells of the coming of Christianity to Anglo-
Saxon England; it had, of course, already come to Celtic Britain. As the story
is told by St. Bede, the first English historian, of Gregory I in Rome:

> On a certain day when merchants had recently arrived, many wares had
> been collected for the market and many men had congregated there to buy,
> and among others was Gregory himself; and he saw, among other things, boys
> put up for sale whose bodies were white and whose faces were beautiful and
> whose hair was remarkably shaped. When he saw them, he asked, as they say,
> from what region or land they had been brought. From the island of Britain,
> it was answered; such is the look of its inhabitants. He then asked whether
> these islanders were Christians or whether they were still bound by pagan
> errors. Pagans, it was replied. He drew from the depths of his heart some long
> sighs: "Alas, how sad," he said, "that men with such clear faces are possessed
> by the author of darkness and that such great gracefulness in appearance cov-
> ers minds empty of grace within." He asked, then, what was the name of their
> race. They are called Angles, it was replied. "Good," he said, "for they have
> angelic faces, and such should be co-heirs of the angels in heaven."

According to what Bede understands as a traditional tale, this epiphany in the slave market was what awakened Gregory's desire to teach the English. For Bede, St. Gregory was an ideal figure. Nothing unworthy of the future pope is intended to be conveyed by this description of him among those who have come to buy. Bede is telling the story as the prelude to the most wonderful event in his history—the making of the scattered tribes of England into a people and the making of the English into Christians. Bede does not think it discreditable that the English should first obtrude on the imagination of Rome as handsome boy slaves.

The slave sellers have recently arrived—so they are slave traders from somewhere else. Among "other things," among their "wares" (*venalia*), are the British boys. What captures the browsing buyer's attention first is the whiteness of the slaves' skin. His reaction is not to race but to pigmentation different from the Mediterranean. Gregory does not assume that Christians will not be sold; he has to ask their religious status. The story assumes that the slaves would not be spoken to directly even through a translator. Gregory addresses the sellers to know the source of their wares. Gregory's heartfelt emotion is not distress at their enslavement by the slave traders, but at their enslavement to the devil. His thought is not, "Let me end this horror and free these children." It is, "Let me go to Britain and evangelize their pagan relatives."

"In spite of the vast outpouring of works on slavery in recent decades, it is still remarkable how unaware the proverbial educated layman is of its extent and significance in human history." I quote that leading authority on the sociology of slavery, Orlando Patterson. In this regard, we are all proverbial educated laymen, a fortiori in regard to the significance of slavery in the development of Catholic moral doctrine. I cannot present in a single book all the evidence that has now been gathered as to the participation by Catholics in the perpetuation of slavery as an institution. I can only provide a set of illustrations of the pervasive practice engaged in without any sense of sinfulness.

A firm letter from Gregory in 591 to the subdeacon Peter, his deputy to rule the patrimony of the pope in Sicily, spells out what is to be done in the face of a number of complaints that slaves are escaping their masters by going to churches and becoming "slaves of ecclesiastical law." According to what the pope has heard, the fugitives will be defended by the rectors of churches as being under the law of the Church although no judgment has freed them. "This displeases me as much as it shrinks from judgment of the truth." Subdeacon Peter is instructed to restore the slaves to their masters without delay. If there is something within the competence of the Church, it is to be established by legal action against the possessors after the slaves have been returned to them. "Correct all these matters without hesitation, because then you will truly be a soldier of the blessed apostle

Peter." As for a slave desiring to become a monk without his master's consent, a canon of Chalcedon, a general council of the Church, forbade it.

Gregory as pope arranged his own purchase of some English boys, age seventeen or eighteen, writing to the priest Candidus, whom he was sending to France. The notes made by Gregory's secretary indicate that Candidus is to use Gallic money not usable in Italy to buy either clothes for the poor or "English boys," who are "to advance in servitude to Almighty God." As the boys are pagans, a priest is to accompany them when they are transported, so that they can be baptized immediately if they should fall mortally ill on the way. Gregory may have in mind their later instruction and conversion by his reference to "servitude to Almighty God" or he may have meant only that they would serve an ecclesiastical institution. It is unlikely that he thought those purchased for not much money in the market would become monks.

Nothing in the instruction to Candidus advises him to inquire into the title of those selling the slaves. What moralists at a much later time would consider a point worth considering is unmentioned. As in Bede's story of the Roman market, it is assumed in Gregory's correspondence that those who are sold are lawfully being sold.

Why these pagan adolescents are being purchased and transported is not evident from the letter, but the reason may be guessed from another letter of Gregory, this time in 599 to Vitalis, his representative in Sardinia. The pope notifies him that he is sending the notary Bonifacio "to buy Barbaricini slaves for the use of a parish." The pope wants to be sure that they are bought "at a good price" and that "those who are purchased" will be quickly brought to Rome. The Barbaricini were pagan inhabitants of Sardinia. Like the English boys bought with currency useless to him, the pope hopes to acquire them economically. In both cases, he probably has in mind menial work on behalf of the poor whom he is assisting.

Gregory shows no compunction about buying humans or about moving them around without their consent. Another letter casts light on his notion of "servitude to Almighty God." He writes Narses, a Greek monk, in this vein, sending him two shirts and one prayer book as gifts for others, adding: "Morever, a certain man at his death sent me a small boy. Thinking of his soul I have sent him on to Your Sweetness that in your land he may live in his servitude, through which he can come to the freedom of heaven." Pretty plainly, the small boy transmitted in this fashion is not free and is not expected to be freed by Narses. His servitude will be rewarded in heaven. In the same way Gregory graciously gave Felix, bishop of Porto, the ownership of the slave John, already in Felix's possession. The act of donation ran as follows:

Moved by the grace of Your Charity, and lest we seem unfruitful to you, especially because we know you have few slaves, therefore we give and grant by our plain right to Your Brotherhood the slave by ecclesiastical law John, of the Sabine nation, out of Flavian stock, of an age, more or less, of eighteen years, whom you have possessed for some time now, so that you may have him and possess him entirely and may protect and defend your right and property in him, and whatever you wish to do with him as his master you may do with free will, your rights made complete by means of this gift. Neither we nor our successors will contest the record of our gift. We have moreover registered this gift with our notary and signed it.

The legal precision of the instrument of gift reflects what must be a common form. The slave being transferred is identified by legal status, name, ethnicity, age; the unbounded rights of the new owner are affirmed. A pledge not to renege on the gift is made. A notary confirms the signature. John, the transferee, is not consulted.

The pope gave permission to the abbot of a monastery in Syracuse, who was moving to a bishopric, to take with him four or five monks from the monastery and "boys whom he has bought with his own money and codexes belonging to him and his father." Gregory lets the monks be moved almost as easily as the purchased boys; he puts the latter in the same category of property as the books.

Another case required lines to be drawn between types of property owners. Under the laws enacted by Christian emperors, the criminal law against adultery had no application to slaves. Parents could legally sell a newborn child as a slave. But one of the first laws enacted by Constantine to show his respect for Christianity was a prohibition against Jews buying and circumcising Christian slaves. Fortunatus, bishop of Naples, set out to remove those Christian slaves bought and brought from Gaul by Jews. One Basil and other Jews appealed to Gregory that they had "bought equally" among pagans and Christians. Gregory ruled that they should not sustain loss unjustly. Expanding on Constantine, Gregory directed Fortunatus to order the Christian slaves either to be returned to the seller or sold to Christian purchasers within forty days. Implicitly, the Jews were allowed to keep the pagan slaves. The Christians were to have their owners changed.

Acceptance of slavery as routine was accompanied by a belief that it was in the divine order of the world. "It is clear," Gregory wrote in his *Pastoral Rule,* "that nature bears all men equal, but fault puts one above another in the varying order of merits. That diversity, which arises from vice, is dispensed by divine justice." Because "not all men are able to stand equally, one man is ruled by another." That should not make the ruler proud. But rulers are necessary.

Gregory acknowledged the claim of nature in a grant of manumission to Montana and Thomas, two slaves of the Roman Church: "from the beginning nature bore free men and the law of nations substituted the yoke of slavery." Since our Redeemer and Creator has taken on flesh to break by divine grace "the chain of slavery by which we were bound," it is "wholesome for us to restore slaves to the freedom in which they were born."

Because of the leadership he exercised in a turbulent Italy as the Roman Empire crumbled, Gregory was known to posterity as Gregory the Great. He was also to be known for the title he assigned to himself as pope and bequeathed to his successors: *Servus servorum Dei,* Slave of the slaves of God. The title reflects his monastic background. Metaphorical as it is, it conveys the sense that Gregory found nothing dishonorable or wrong in the status of a slave. Not only he himself but his bishops and clergy are regarded as slaves of the divine Master. The title emphasizes the pope's obedience and loyalty and, perhaps above all, his humility—he is tops in humility. Slavery for the pope can be, metaphorically, a status of high honor. In actual practice, it is not an intrinsically evil but a usefully available institution. For him, the slaves are not Orlando Patterson's "nothings." The pope is concerned with their spiritual state. His unashamed acceptance of the institution is exemplary. Informed about the Church in the East as in the West, fully cognizant of the tradition of the Church in Rome, himself the grandson of another pope, Felix III, Gregory is not upset by the enslavement of human beings. Buying slaves for low-level work, shipping slaves where he wills to ship them, donating them or emancipating as he chose, Gregory made no criticism of what was part of everyday life.

The pope's position was no aberration. Clement, the wise Alexandrian, had not objected to Christians being slaveowners but to Christians showing off as the owners of many slaves. Saints Ambrose, Augustine, Basil, Gregory of Nazianzus, Jerome, and John Chrysostom had all accepted slavery as an institution. Roman law defined slavery as "an institution of the *ius gentium* whereby one is, against nature, made subject to the ownership of another." The men who became in retrospect the Fathers of the Church did not quarrel with either part of this pronouncement. Slavery was an institution established by a law that was recognized. It was against man's nature to be made a slave. But against nature, *contra naturam,* was not a condemnation of the institution. If anything, the Fathers made the legal institution appear to be according to the will of God. According to Augustine in his magisterial *The City of God,* slavery was instituted by the curse of Noah in response to the sin committed against him. "This sentence [of slavery] is penal and is enjoined in that law which enjoins the preservation of the natural order and forbids its disturbance."

Slavery under a Roman, even a Christian master, could be cruel. Tertullian, expounding on the body's state after resurrection, compares it to a liberated slave no longer subject to scourges, foot-fetters, and brandings. Augustine, expatiating on servile fear in a sermon to his African congregation, noted that a slave feared to offend his master, who "might order him to be whipped or order him to be put in foot-fetters or order him to be ground down working a mill."

The only Father to criticize slavery, Gregory of Nyssa, chose an instructive strategy. In one remarkable sermon he assailed slavery as a sin of pride on the part of the master and as a violation of natural law because human beings were created free by God. "What is such a gross example of arrogance," he asked, "as for a human being to think himself master of his own kind?" Focused on the master's sin, Gregory did not say the slave had a right to freedom. His sermon does demonstrate that the legal and social classification of the slave did not destroy all human perception of the slaves as human beings. In Gregory of Nyssa's homily, as in Gregory the Great's *Pastoral Rule*, the perception is basic that nature has not intended human beings to be enslaved. In neither of the Gregorys does the perception lead to advocacy of abolition.

For that reason, it is hard to invoke Gregory of Nyssa as a dissenter from the acceptance of slavery by the Christian Church. The sharpness of his criticism does underline the Fathers' massive avoidance of the moral issues involving slavery. If Gregory of Nyssa could see the problem so clearly, then the others, too, must have been able to see it. But, as abolition was not advocated by him, Gregory cannot be regarded as holding the institution to be intrinsically evil. He does not even insist that an individual Christian has a duty to be a conscientious objector to the institution and rid himself of his slaves. Some Christians in the Roman Empire were known for their conscientious objection to military service. None were known as conscientious objectors to slaveowning.

Human beings as ware in a Roman marketplace, human beings bought, sold, donated, and transported without the slightest attention to their desires—were not the slaves divested of social recognition? The philosophy that men by nature were free was good rhetoric. The practice of emancipating slaves occasionally put it into practice. Like Paul to Philemon on Useful, like Gregory the Great freeing Montana and Thomas, like Gregory of Nyssa on the pride of the slaveowner, Christians accepted the institution of slavery without wholly denying slaves' humanity. Slaves could attain eternal salvation. Therefore, ran the implicit assumption, it was not wholly bad. The existence of slave saints made this implicit assumption visible.

Human Slaves as God's Slaves

Slaves in Scripture are, in general, either real slaves or God's slaves, but not both. It may be immediately objected that the Hebrews had been made the real slaves of the Egyptians but that as a people they were God's slaves. The double status of the Hebrew slave was carried over to the Hebrew enslaved to a fellow Hebrew and was the basis for the law, not always observed, entitling him to freedom after seven years. An ex-slave, who was a Hebrew, like the Hebrew people as a whole, was not incapacitated or diminished by his former status. Joseph, sold into slavery by his brothers, becomes a superslave in Egypt and is favored by God as well as by the pharaoh, at once a real slave and God's (Gen 41:40–45). He could be seen as a prototype of later Christians. Nonetheless, in the Hebrew kingdoms and in Palestine under the occupying powers, no slave is singled out by Scripture and recognized as God's slave. The slaves named in the New Testament are not named as holy persons.

As slavery in the Roman world was not defined by race or color, an ex-slave could advance without an extra stigma in physical appearance; and so ex-slaves did in Christian communities as in the world. The story of Philemon's ex-slave Useful becoming bishop of Ephesus shows what was thought possible in the first century. Calixtus, bishop of Rome in 200, is said by his opponent

Hippolytus to have once been a slave, and this unfriendly critic associates a ruling made by Calixtus with his former status. In the face of Roman law, Calixtus as bishop of Rome held that the marriage of a free woman with her slave was valid. Here was a direct denial of the legal dogma that a slave had no personality; how effective the ruling was cannot be determined. Despite Hippolytus's indictment, Calixtus enjoyed postmortem recognition as a saint.

Autobiographies by ex-slaves are rare, but one from about 540 is the story of a boy kidnapped at the age of sixteen from his grandfather's home and taken as a slave to a neighboring country. The author describes his work, the tending of animals; his exposure to fog, rain, and snow; and his turning compulsively to prayer and finding strength. At least retrospectively, he does not complain. He had been enslaved "with so many thousands of men according to our deserts, because we withdrew from God." He goes on, "and the Lord laid down upon us the wrath of his anger and dispersed us among the Gentiles." As Patrick's *Confession* indicates, he had not been a devout Christian, and he had committed one major sin which was to haunt him later in life; so he could view the Lord's anger as appropriate. He escaped after four years. His narrative conveys no sense that his personhood was diminished by his experience; rather, slavery was a time of conversion to the Lord. He emerged from enslavement convinced that kidnapping free persons to make them slaves was evil, but evidently with no sense of the intrinsic evil of slavery. It continued to be an institution in the Christian Ireland that Patrick began. In his own life, his enslavement—unlike his major sin—was no barrier at all to his becoming a bishop; still less was it a barrier to acknowledgment of him as a great saint.

A sainted slave story that sounds like romantic fiction is that of Bathilde, a Saxon girl. As her contemporary biographer puts it, "she was, by divine providence, kidnapped from across the seas and sold at a low price." She fell into the hands of the mayor of the palace of the king of Burgundy and Neustria and was promoted by the mayor in service in the royal household to be his cupbearer. Ultimately Clovis II married her. The mother of three sons, she survived her husband and in 657 began to rule during the minority of his heir, her son. A generous patron of abbeys and churches, she was regarded by her biographer as a saint, despite getting a bad press in her native Britain as "a Jezebel." She is remembered as taking two steps reflecting her own trauma: she forbade the sale of Christians within her kingdom and forbade the transportation of Christian slaves beyond it. Of course she did not touch the institution.

Not only ex-slaves were identified as saints. Real slaves, too, achieved this recognition—a recognition that they had been human in the fullest way; by their actions they had demonstrated that they were slaves of God. True, the recognition came posthumously and only by way of martyrdom. But the reverence accorded them after death showed how insignificant their status was in the view dominant among Christians. Three examples may suffice.

The second-century Christian communities in Lyons and Vienne were the object of an outbreak of local persecution that the reigning emperor, the celebrated Stoic, Marcus Aurelius, did not check. First forbidden to appear in public places like the baths, the Christians eventually were dragged to prison, then to the amphitheater. Their pagan slaves, under torture or the threat of torture, accused them of odious crimes like incest. Some apostasized under pressure. In 177, a batch of more than forty persons including the bishop, Pothimus, became martyrs. By letter the survivors, styling themselves "the slaves of Christ," informed "the brethren in Asia and Phrygia" of the "the fury of the Gentiles" against "the slaves of the Lord."

Prominent in their narrative is Blandina, whose "mistress in the flesh" feared that Blandina would not be strong enough to hold out, but who proved to be "the strongest." She endured three days of torture and on the fourth was dispatched by sword. In her, "Christ showed that those things which are so despised among men and held in contempt are led with great glory to God."

A slave become a saint, Blandina was eventually honored with a church in Lyons. Her name graced the martyrologies that Christians began to compile. Eusebius included in his *Historia ecclesiastica* the letter celebrating her suffering. Her feast day is June 2. In passing it may be emphasized how the Christians of Lyons had both pagan slaves and baptized slaves like Blandina. The line of status marked her off in life but not in death. The letter about her makes the catechetical point that the Lord raises up the lowly; it does not otherwise emphasize her servile state.

Aquila and Vitale were martyred at Bologna in the persecution, 302–305, under Diocletian. Aquila was a master, Vitale his slave. In 393, Ambrose, bishop of Milan, brought their relics to a church in Florence and gave a homily in their honor. "The condition of the man," Ambrose said of Vitale, "offers no impediment to his commendation." Vitale died first, with no place in his body "without a wound." The persecutors "wanted to terrify the master by the punishment of the slave." It was a vain attempt. Each stood firm. The slave went first to prepare a place for the master. Once Aquila's slave, Vitale is "now in martyrdom his copartner and companion." A church dedicated to St. Vitale was begun in Ravenna in 526 and completed in 548, a monumental work of architecture in an important imperial city.

Felicity and Perpetua were two of the most famous martyrs of Carthage. Felicity was pregnant, an adolescent, a catechumen, and a slave. Perpetua was a free married woman of twenty-two, who had just given birth to a child. In the persecution of Septimus Severus in 202 they were arrested, together with several men. After examination, they were exposed to the beasts in the amphitheater. Surviving, they were beheaded. A basilica was built in Carthage over their remains. Half a century after their deaths their names entered the canon of the mass at the head of a list of seven female saints. In the story of their martyrdom Perpetua's respectable father urges her to apostasize; Felicity has no relations. She delivers her child before her death. No comment is made on the child's legal status or on the absence of any law permitting Felicity to marry. Augustine, an African brought up on the memory of them, preached several times in their honor. For him, these two women, neither of whom was a virgin, "shone and stood out in the company of martyrs." Uniting them in words, Augustine declared that they "set aside all things in order to glory in perpetual felicity." Is the play on names no more than normal exuberance for Augustine, always a rhetorician, or is it the sign of a certain nervousness as he extolls to the skies two women so far from his view of the Christian virgin? They were "holy slaves of God"—their martyrdom raising both the slave and the free woman to this higher slavery. Mosaics of them ornamented sixth-century Ravenna. Nowhere was a line drawn making Felicity's virtue less than Perpetua's.

Slaves raised to heaven, two slaves honored in the central section of the mass, slaves remembered in churches—none of these facts prevented the practice of chattel slavery by Christians, that is, the use of an institution in which persons were bought, sold, donated, and transferred as tangible pieces of property. The religious honors accorded to slaves did mean that slavery was not seen by Christians as an intolerable condition, an extinction of the person, a wipeout of the image of God in enslaved brothers and sisters. Hypocrisy? Not necessarily. Blindness? All human beings wear blinders. Seeing salvation attainable by slaves, the Church did not condemn the institution.

A Girl Named Zita and Other Commodities

Unchallenged by the theologians of the day or by other moral authority, slavery continued to be a practice in Christian Europe. Its routine character may be suggested by the following document executed on the Rialto in Venice:

> In Christ's name, amen. On November 6, in the fourteen hundredth and sixty-ninth year from His birth, the noble man Lord Jacopo Marcelo . . . , on behalf of himself, his heirs and successors, gave, ceded, sold, and transferred to the distinguished man Sir Bartolomeo Chanedolo . . . , present and accepting, according to the custom of the country, one slave girl of the said Jacopo, by the name of Zita, a Circassian, twenty-five years old, or about, healthy in body and in all her members, hidden and visible, and free from disease. [The price, 65 ducats, is then stated and the fact of its receipt. The seller states that the buyer] may have said slave girl with liberty and power of holding, giving, donating, selling, alienating, and exchanging her, and judging on behalf of her soul and body, and whatever else shall please the said purchaser, his heirs and successors to do in perpetuity as of his own property without any contradiction by the said seller or any other person in the world. [The seller goes on to guarantee the sale under

penalty of double the price and to renounce any privilege he might use to void it.] Done at Venice, on the Rialto at my station. [Two witnesses are listed including a second notary.] I, Bernardo de Ranemis, Venetian, son of Sir Schieti, by imperial authority notary public and regular judge, was present at all the aforesaid and on request have written and published it and affixed my customary seal.

The document is taken from the hundreds of notarial acts assembled by the assiduous historian of European slavery, Charles Verlinden. These documents, along with statutes and governmental registers of slaves, have been used by Verlinden and by students of particular medieval places to establish how, without significant rebuke and without significant hesitation, slaving flourished in a Europe whose public institutions and laws identified themselves as Christian.

The terms of the sale are, in essentials, those used by Gregory I in his notarized gift of the slave John to Bishop Felix. One striking omission in this and other notarial acts: the title of the seller to the slave he is selling is never mentioned. The seller guarantees the sale but not his right of ownership. No one involved is going to ask how the slave came into his hands.

Five points do stand out. First, the elaborate legal language suggests that the form used is a common one, developed to cover two kinds of eventualities: any possible defect in the body of the person sold and any challenge to the sale by the seller or his heirs. Second, the provision that the buyer may judge on behalf of her soul and body (*pro animo et corpore*), a not unusual provision, does convey a slight recognition that a human being is the object of the sale, as does the use of her name, Zita. The name is not Circassian. It is a Christian saint's name, in all probability bestowed at baptism. At the same time the conveyance to the purchaser of power to judge on behalf of the soul of his purchase appears to set aside any spiritual autonomy or privacy in the person purchased.

Third, despite the opening in the name of Christ and the reference to the slave's soul, there is no sense that what is being done is depraved or contrary to any law, divine, natural, or human. The sale of a slave is not a hole-in-the-corner operation but one carried out on the Rialto by a noble lord selling to a distinguished purchaser with an imperial notary drawing up the contract and witnessing the sale. Fourth, the price is a good one, well above average. It may be guessed that it reflects the gender, the age, the skin color, and the reputation of Circassian women. Fifth, no attention is given to Zita's wishes; she is a chattel disposed of as any valuable property would be disposed of. So in this banally routine way, human beings were marketed at a great European capital fourteen hundred and sixty-nine years after the coming of Christ. No Portia protested that you can transfer a body but not a soul.

Slaving in medieval Europe was not a racist enterprise. The slaves' geographic origin, roughly identified, was normally recorded. The slave traders were equal opportunity buyers. Their cargos came from the Crimea and other regions bordering the Black Sea and were labeled Tartar, Mongol, Russian, Caucasian, or identified as coming from even smaller tribes or principalities beyond the Dardenelles. Others were labeled Greek, purchased on Crete for resale in the West or bought from Turks. The practice of buying Greek slaves from Turks was still possible in the nineteenth century when Alexandre Dumas has the Count of Monte Cristo purchase Haydée from a Turkish pasha. Turks themselves were objects of sale at Venice in the fifteenth century. Other slaves were simply denominated Saracens, with religion not nation being the identifier. Others, in small numbers, are "of the race of Serbs" or "of the race of Bosnians." There are also an occasional Albanian, Hungarian, or Georgian, a few Bulgarians, and some Canary Islanders. The whiteness of Circassian girls' skins is sometimes recorded. Slaves are identified as black in a number of notarial documents that also identify them as "Saracen"; others from Egypt or "African parts" are also noted as black.

The generic term for slave is *sclavus* or *sclava,* a gendered noun like classical Latin *servus* and *serva;* in the vernacular it becomes *schiavo* or *schiava* in Italian, *un esclave* or *une esclave* in French, and ungendered "slave" in English. Since the tenth century, the new generic noun had been in use in German lands and its Arabic equivalent in vogue in Moslem Spain. The usage reflected the common perception that the people of Eastern Europe were the most likely human merchandise. They were generically Slavs. Hence, any enslaved human being was known by their name. As early as 1192, for example, a Venetian partnership in the Holy Land purchases an *esclavus* from a seller who had acquired the property as a pledge for a loan to a lord count.

Venetians were early practitioners in the trade, but Venice's role as an important center in the traffic came later, in the fourteenth and fifteenth centuries. By 1359, its mariners had formed a market in Tana, a Black Sea port at the mouth of the Don from which purchases were transported to Venice. By the mid-fifteenth century, Venice furnished not only a market where local nobles, merchants, and even nuns could buy their slaves but "a center of distribution principally across North and Central Italy."

Tuscany was one source of the customers of Venice. A historian of Florence observes that, "at the time of the finest flowering of Tuscan civilization," domestic slavery was brought to Florence. But the institution came after Dante. He does refer to Carlo II of Naples giving his daughter Beatrice in marriage to the marquis of Este for money as

bargaining to sell his daughter,
as corsairs do with slave girls.

Aware of the trade and unsparing in his criticism of his native town, Dante does not see slavery as a Florentine institution. Depopulation due to the Black Death was a factor encouraging it later in the fourteenth century. As the trade continued into the fifteenth century, its success resulted from a match between Florentine prosperity and the markets for human chattels provided by Venetian and Genoese seamen operating in the Black Sea and the Mediterranean. The Priors, the ruling body of Florence, on March 8, 1364, decreed it lawful to import non-Catholic slaves. In the next hundred years slaves became a component of the city. They were owned in some number by nobles and leading merchants. A priest or a nun, a notary or a small shopkeeper, a woolmaker or a carpenter, might have one. Doggerel saluted *le schiavette amorose*, "the amorous little slave girls." The Florentine fashion spread to cities such as Siena, where Ambrogio Lorenzetti put them in his frescoes at San Francesco, and to Lucca, Prato, and Pistoria, until even a country town like San Gimignano had its slaves.

An official registry of the purchases of slaves was instituted in Florence in 1366, but registering rapidly declined after the first three years. Of the slaves registered, the great majority were girls, ranging in age from seven to twenty-seven, with a few older women as well; the small masculine contingent ranged from a boy under seven, to a number of adolescents, to one man of thirty. How much the strong preference for females represented a sexual interest cannot be determined with certainty. In a report to Cosimo de'Medici from his purchasing agent on February 19, 1459, the agent says he has found for him a Circassian slave girl, age seventeen to eighteen, "not too delicate in face, but of good appearance and handy and lively and intelligent." The wife of Francesco Datini of Prato passes on to him, circa 1400, the complaint of another wife that Datini had sent to her husband "a slave girl so young and so pretty." Datini himself instructs his agent on May 12, 1393, to find "a little slave girl, young and sturdy and of good stock to wash the dishes and carry the wood and bread to the oven"—an innocuous set of tasks. Datini, childless by his wife, also had a liaison with a twenty-year-old slave girl whom he freed after adopting their daughter as his own. Florentine fathers worried about their sons having liaisons with slaves. The orphanage founded in 1421 by the Guild of Silk Merchants maintained a register of orphans, "the Books of the Innocents of Jesus Christ." The books identify fourteen percent of the mothers of babies given to the orphanage in the course of the fifteenth century as slaves.

Moral Masters

The *Paradise Book*

Two hundred years before Zita was sold on the Rialto, the commune of Bologna
had celebrated an important event. Paying ten Bolognese pounds for every slave
or slave girl over the age of fourteen and eight pounds for each under that age,
Bologna in 1256 had bought all slaves in the city and within the jurisdiction of
the diocese and liberated them. It memorialized the event in what was called
Liber Paradisus in these terms:

> This is the memorial of the slaves and the slave girls who have been
> emancipated by the commune of Bologna—a memorial that is rightly called
> by the word proper to it, Paradise. The Paradise of pleasure the Lord God
> Almighty planted in the beginning and placed in it the man whom He
> formed, clothing his body with white raiment and giving him perfect and
> perpetual liberty. But that miserable man, unmindful of his own dignity and
> of the divine gift, tasted the apple forbidden to him by the Lord's com-
> mandment. Whence he drew himself and all his posterity and the human
> race into this vale of misery, miserably binding it in the snares of diabolical
> slavery, so that the incorruptible was made corruptible and the immortal

was made mortal subject to change and to the heaviest slavery. But God, seeing that the whole world was perishing, took pity on the human race and sent his only son, born of a virgin mother cooperating with the Holy Spirit, so that the glory of his dignity would break the bonds of the slavery by which we were held captive and would restore us to our pristine liberty. Therefore, it is very useful that human beings, whom nature from the beginning bore and created free and the *ius gentium* set under the yoke of slavery, should be restored by the benefit of emancipation to that liberty in which they were born.

Taking these matters into consideration, the noble city of Bologna, which has always fought for liberty, now recalling the past and providing for the future, in honor of our redeemer, Lord Jesus Christ, redeems for cash all those in the city and in the episcopate of Bologna whom it finds bound in servile condition and decrees them to be free.

After diligent investigation, it legislates that no one bound by any slavery dare to dwell in the city and episcopate of Bologna, lest the mass of natural liberty, which has been redeemed at a price, could be again corrupted by any yeast of slavery; for a little yeast corrupts the mass and the companionship of one bad man dishonors several good men.

The memorial goes on to give the prices and to commemorate the podestà Bonacorso of Soresina, "whose fame shines far and wide like a star," and the judge, Jacopo Gratacelli, under whose auspices the emancipation occurred. The document is duly notarized.

Compactly, the confused medieval understanding of slavery is set out. Slavery to sin is the consequence of Adam's Fall. The law of nations then imposed slavery on men. But, despite the Fall, human beings are born free. Christ freed them from sin. We imitate him in freeing them from human slavery. We can even hope that we are restoring Paradise, where freedom was perfect and forever, and humankind can recall its dignity.

The book records the names of the owners by the four quarters of the city. Beneath each name are listed the names of the owner's slaves and slave girls. Children under fourteen are marked by an "m" for minor. Nothing is said of ethnic or racial stock, the religion, or the work assignments of the slaves. Many of the slaves have recognizably Christian names. Children are often identified as the son or daughter of a named slave or slave girl. Slaves who are married are at least sometimes identified in relation to their spouses. The impression, in short, is not of anonymous tools but of individuals often known in terms of their families. Some owners have only one slave. More common are those having seven to ten. A number own many more slaves. One owner, for example, has about one hundred, forty-four of them under fourteen. According to the book itself, there were "over 6,000" slaves in Bologna; their names are recorded. There were about 250 owners recorded as agreeing to the sale to the commune at the price fixed.

The *Paradise Book* does not say what became of the liberated slaves. The commune was not offering to feed, clothe, and house them. It may be inferred that they stayed where they were, now judicially free but not quite in paradise. Earlier in the thirteenth century, Assisi, Siena, Vercelli, and Verona had effected emancipations. But here was an example set by the center for legal studies. If lawyers riveted the chains, lawyers also showed how the chains should be struck off. What lawyer would not honor the example of Bologna? And it was accomplished at no pope or bishop's instance, at the direction of no church ordinance. It was done under the lay leadership of the podestà and the judge. It was done in emulation of Christ by persons who had accepted the story of man's Fall and Redemption and found that the story provided not a defense of slavery as much as a lesson in how to get rid of it.

Custom

The example of Bologna was prodigious—so prodigious that seven hundred years after the emancipation it was celebrated again in Bologna. It did not catch on as a model municipal exercise. But it may be read as one way Christian consciousness affected the Western European approach to slavery. It is one of several clues to the transformation that occurred earlier, between 900 and 1100, from societies built on slave labor to societies where serfs had replaced the slaves. Three observations made by Marc Bloch on this change should be kept in mind:

> It occurred "very slowly."
> It is "hard to explain."
> It is "one of the most notable facts in our western history."

These observations may be supplemented. The change occurred very slowly because there was no central directive requiring it. Bloch himself is absolutely wrong in stating that "the Church refused resolutely to sanction the enslavement of Christians, true Christians, that is, Catholics." The Church never prohibited the enslavement of baptized Catholics if their baptism followed their enslavement or if they were babies born to slave mothers. No pope or general council laid down as law that Catholic Christians might not lawfully enslave Catholic Christians defeated in battle and along with them their wives and children. In the absence of general marching orders, the change had to be slow.

It is hard to explain, because economists would like to find an economic explanation. Undoubtedly the disruptions of the period, 900–1100, affected agricultural enterprise and made it difficult to run large estates with large gangs of slaves. But economics does not tell the whole story, as a social historian like Bloch acknowledges. The story is difficult to tell because the period is one where documentation is light. Yet there are signs of a change in consciousness, not simply a reflection of economic reality. Here are four examples:

Immediately on taking office, a warrior pope, John VIII, in 872 wrote "the princes of Sardinia" that their countrymen were buying from the Greeks those who had been captured by pagans (the pope means Saracens), and, having bought them, were keeping them as slaves. The pope instructed the Sardinians to free "your own" and receive a reward from Christ; otherwise, the pope told them, "you incur a great sin." The Council of Narbonne in 1054 forbade making "robbery or booty out of any Christian man or woman," under pain of excommunication, but the council's canon is little more than an indication of a new sensitivity confined to a locality. In 1102, a church council in London banned "the wicked trade in which, up to the present, men in England have been accustomed to be sold like brute animals." Presiding over this council was a learned Norman monk, Anselm of Bec, now archbishop of Canterbury, lately returned from exile on the continent. Do we hear his voice reproving the English? A few years later, another French monk chronicling the First Crusade found it astonishing among the Greeks to see "contrary to the custom of the Latins, men and women, although persons of Christian dignity, indifferently bought and sold like brute animals." At this early date the terms "person" and "dignity" stand out in the negative comment on enslavement.

Neither John VIII, nor the councils, nor a French abbot's view of human dignity tell us that the emergent Europe had a general rule against slavery. In the early thirteenth century when the ordinary gloss on Gratian was written, enslaving the enemy captured in a just war was accepted as legitimate. We know from the *Paradise Book* that there were slaves and slave girls in the Bologna of 1256. Sicily, Sardinia, Naples also had slaves in the thirteenth century, as did Scandinavia. Innocent III dealt with aplomb with the case of two slaves referred to him by the archbishop of Lund. But by the thirteenth century slavery had disappeared in England and France.

Reluctant as economists have been to concede the effect of Christian custom, such custom appears to have played a substantial part in the development. The most important custom was that Catholics did not enslave Catholics defeated in war and did not enslave their families. War, the ordinary source of supply, declined as a source of new slaves. That conclusion is stated as a fact by Verlinden. When Christians in Northern Europe no longer fought those who were religiously different, they ceased to enslave the enemy.

The empirical evidence that slavery declined because of the prevailing custom is confirmed by two knowledgeable commentators. Bartolus of Sassoferrato, a leading authority of the fourteenth century on Roman law, notes the Roman rules on enslaving enemies and then observes "according to the mores of modern times and the customs of old observed by Christians, we do not keep the laws of captivity. . . . Captives are not sold nor held as slaves." This achievement in civilization appears to be the work of a new consciousness that found something repugnant in turning a defeated fellow believer into a thing—a consciousness also that, if the battle had gone the other way, the victor would have been in the plight of the vanquished. A rough, illogical line was drawn exempting the defeated French or Burgundian or English or Florentine or Milanese captive from enslavement by his coreligionists.

The observation of Bartolus is repeated in the fifteenth century by Antoninus, archbishop of Florence: it is the custom of Christians not to enslave defeated Christian enemies. Both Bartolus and Antoninus were fierce citers of authority. Neither references a single text justifying the custom. Antoninus does not depend on Bartolus. If neither found an authority on hand to explain a major change in the practices of war, no text existed. The teaching was by deed.

This Christian custom, plus the Christian custom of emancipation, although not on the Bolognese scale, had to have affected European society beyond the Mediterranean where captured Saracens maintained the supply. There was a third Christian factor beyond custom that subtly and indirectly undermined slavery as an institution: the law of marriage.

Law

For Gratian, the master composer, 1120–1140, of the *Harmony of Unharmonious Canons* or *Decretum*, writing in Bologna a century before the *Paradise Book*, slavery was an institution of the *ius gentium* taken for granted. Laconically, he referred to its origin with Noah, adding "if there had not been drunkenness, there would not be slavery today." He did not give it separate examination but thought it worth looking at in connection with marriage. Slaves, Gratian taught unequivocally, were capable of marriage. A free man who knowingly accepted a slave woman in marriage was married indissolubly; so was a free woman who knowingly married a slave. If the slave condition was unknown to the free person at the time of the marriage, the free person could divorce the slave. Two slaves could marry each other with the consent of their owners. Without elaboration, in this peremptory way, Gratian assigned to slaves a right denied them by Roman law and at the same time limited the right so that it depended on the will of the masters. Gratian did not cite the Roman law denying any possibility of marriage. His decisive authorities were local church councils. So, at Bologna, in the book that would be accepted for eight centuries as the law of the Church, a precious human right was claimed, with qualification, for the human beings reduced to servitude. At Paris, Peter Lombard, master of the theologians, agreed.

The English pope, Nicholas Breakspear, Adrian IV, answering the archbishop of Salzburg, ruled that marriages between slaves were not prohibited by the Church. Their marriage held, "the masters opposing and unwilling." As St. Paul taught there was neither slave nor free in Christ Jesus, the sacraments of the Church could not be denied slaves. The pope added, however, that marriage did not free the slaves from their duties. Issued sometime in Adrian IV's short pontificate, 1154–1159, the letter, *Dignum*, led off a short section titled "The Marriage of Slaves" in Gregory IX's definitive decretal collection of 1234. Raimundo of Peñafort, the collection's editor, highlighted with this title the extraordinary step that Adrian had taken—a step not only beyond the Roman law but beyond anything that the canons themselves had dared to declare. Gratian had prepared the way and was surpassed. With the insertion of *Dignum* in Gregory IX's collection it became the guide for the students of the canons at Bologna. It was still sufficiently unfamiliar for Bonaventure, about 1260, to refer to it as establishing "a new right" (*ius*). Slaves with rights! Who ever heard of such a thing? A spouse's condition, if unknown to the other party to the marriage, remained a ground for nullity of the marriage. A mistake as to one's spouse's premarital chastity or wealth did not destroy consent. Slavery was still somehow different. But to acknowledge in slaves any species of right was to undermine the structure of Roman law that denied slaves any recognition.

Particular Christian customs and the law of marriage, not to mention St. Paul, constituted a base from which an abolitionist mentality might have emerged. Would not every decent city-state want to imitate Bologna? It was not to be so. No general law required it. No general council addressed the subject. As we know from the sale of Zita, slavery did not disappear but blossomed in city-states like Venice. Even Bologna came to have slaves again. We can assign some causal force to the Black Death, but there are theologians who may also share responsibility.

Thomas

The most influential of medieval moralists, as the greatest of medieval theologians, was Thomas Aquinas. It is not clear what experience Thomas had of slavery in operation. He knew of it from Scripture, the Roman law, and Aristotle, and in his day, slaves could be seen in Sicily, Sardinia, the kingdom of Naples, and, in numbers, in Bologna. He found no reason to reject or even criticize the institution. He did entertain as an objection that slavery was against nature, quoting Gregory I's statement that "it is against nature for man to want to be master of men" and that, according to natural law, all men are equal. Thomas's answer to the objection was that slavery was "against the first intention of nature," but not against its second. According to nature's "second intention," slavery was introduced as a penalty for sin. This analysis, offered in his youthful commentary on the *Sentences,* made no attempt to show how actual slaves were being punished for their sins or to consider the case of infants born into slavery. Just as the inheritance of original sin was accepted without challenge to the justice of punishing the heirs of Adam, so was the inheritance of slave condition. Slavery was "a corporeal condition," and as offspring had "corporeal substance" from their mother, then, if she was a slave, the offspring were slaves. Thomas did make exception for one kind of *vernaculus* or "home-grown slave," who was Christian but belonged to a Jewish owner: the Church commanded that the child be freed.

In a fuller exposition in the *Summa theologiae,* Thomas asked, "Can natural law be changed?" and noted that Isidore of Seville taught that community of property and individual freedom were both "of natural law." Slavery, like individual ownership, was not "instituted by nature," but both were instituted "by human reason for the utility of human life." Following Aristotle, Thomas noted that it was useful "for this one to be ruled by one wiser and that one to be helped by this one." In this way, natural law "was not changed except by addition." Many things beneficial to human life, he observed, were added to natural law by divine law and human law. Only as to first principles was the law of nature "entirely immutable." He made no reference to the return of Useful by St. Paul. An addition to natural law that cancelled the natural freedom of human beings did not cause Thomas to choke on admitting it.

What the first principles were in relation to slavery was spelled out by Thomas's teaching that a slave's master could not deny him food or sleep or conjugal intercourse and, as a corollary, had no right to deny a slave the right to marry or to preserve virginity. Thomas even added that the duty to pay the conjugal debt to one's spouse trumped the master's command, and that a master should not make slavery heavier by selling a slave to an owner who would put him at a distance from the slave's spouse. Qualifications of this kind on slavery had an unrealistic flavor. Conjugal duty over the master's command—the scenario is one of cruel comedy. It does show Thomas's belief that the slave's natural rights were not extinguished. But those rights for Thomas were entirely the demands of the animal body. He did not for a moment consider any right of a slave to provide conjugal companionship, to educate his children, or to develop his own mind. Spiritual rights were unmentioned. Oddly, it was the body, seen as directed to God, whose integrity Thomas insisted upon. As for pursuing a religious vocation, as that would take all the slave's time, it could only be done with the master's consent. Justice in a proper sense did not exist between master and slave, because "a slave is the tool of the master."

Thomas, in short, took an institution he found described in books and extant in Italy and endorsed it with limitations unlikely to be enforced, with little imagination as to what the life of a slave might be like, and with apparent unconcern for the slave's intellectual and spiritual development. The protection afforded human dignity by the first principles of the natural law was slight. If natural law could be changed by addition to eliminate justice in the proper sense between man and man, to permit the enslavement of infants, and to reduce human rights to bodily functions, natural law provided small guidance. Thomas's perfunctory treatments of slavery reflect not the slightest sense of any evil intrinsic to the buying, selling, breeding, and owning of human beings; and it may be that he neither experienced nor imagined what the institution was like. Any student of Roman law who got into Book I of the *Digest* learned that slavery was against the nature of a human being. Yet, despite abhorrence of sexual acts *contra naturam,* the theologians did not denounce slavery because it was unnatural.

If one stays with the propositions in Thomas on the love of God and the love of neighbor, one could readily conclude that Thomas condemns slavery. For example, treating of the virtue of charity, where by grace God dwells within a person and the person is a friend of God, Thomas notes that such a person loves God for his goodness. One then loves one's enemies because one's friend, God, loves them, just as one loves the children and the slaves of a human friend because they are the friend's. By charity we will the good of other human beings. One could suppose that freedom from enslavement is such a good. But Thomas does not make this application, just as the Fathers of the Church contemplating the two great commandments of love did not make this application. The particular law and customs on slavery trumped these commandments for the scholastic theologians as they had for the Fathers.

It is likely that a sharp distinction Thomas made between "the mind" and "the body" in discussing the love of God played a part in this treatment. "The life of a man is double," Thomas wrote. "One is external according to sensate and bodily nature, and according to this life there is no sharing or intercourse with God and the angels. The other life of man is spiritual according to the mind, and according to this life there is intercourse for us with God and with the angels imperfectly in our present state; hence it is said in Philippians 3:20, 'Our intercourse is in heaven.'" This residual Platonism made enslavement a matter of lesser moment. Natural law was seen as guarding certain bodily needs of slaves, while the mind functioned in a realm beyond the body.

In the course of commenting on Scripture, Thomas came to Paul's letter returning Useful to Philemon. Thomas was moved to strike a new note. "A certain togetherness of mind (*consensus*) exists between master and slave," he teaches, because "a faithful slave passes into a friend," and he should be held by his master "as, in affection, a friend." Visualizing a very transformation of the master-slave relation, Thomas presses further: the slave is brother to the master, even doubly a brother. First, in terms of natural generation, for they are born equally by nature. Then, by grace, for in baptism they are both born of the Spirit.

If taken to the letter, Thomas's teaching here would have done away with the ordinary transactions of the slave market and the ordinary toil of slaves. But his commentary on the letter to Philemon did not have the circulation of the *Summa theologiae* and his transformative inspiration did not become standard theological teaching. Focused on his vision of fraternal affection, Thomas saw no need to teach that Christians should not own Christians or to observe that Paul virtually ordered Philemon to release Useful.

Antoninus

Two centuries later, Antoninus Pierozzi did live in a time and place where the existence of slaves and the practices of slavery could not escape his consciousness. A notary's son who entered the Dominicans of the Strict Observance at sixteen, Antoninus had a career in Rome as a judge of the Rota before returning to Florence to be its archbishop from 1446 to 1459. With the aid of Cosimo de'Medici he built the convent and library of San Marco, an urban jewel. As archbishop, he completed his *Summa of Moral Theology*, published only after his death and still being reprinted in the eighteenth century. The work was a break-through, the first important summa to treat morals as a topic distinct from spec-ulative theology. It was distinguished by consideration of the moral problems of particular professionals, such as bankers, notaries, and pharmacists. Antoninus, it is fair to say, was aware of the problems and vices of his city and he must have observed the slaves of Cosimo and others. He was an austere moralist and a suf-ficiently zealous Christian to be canonized by the reforming pope, Adrian VI, in 1523. Under the heading "The Multiple Kinds of Slavery and Emancipation" he treats our subject.

The first kind of slavery is to the Lord, as the Psalms indicate. The second kind is to sin. The third is to man, where, properly speaking, a slave is defined as one not *sui iuris,* as one without legal standing. As the thirteenth-century Dominican canonist, Raymond of Peñafort, taught, slavery was "inchoately" approved by divine law when Noah cursed Ham. It is today created in three ways: by law, by purchase, and by birth. According to the law of nations, ac-cepted by the gloss on Gratian, those captured in a just war are slaves, and such captives, if they flee their masters, sin. But Christians do not enslave other Christians in war, whether the war is just or unjust, a practice stated as prevail-ing "de facto." For those enslaved by foes waging an unjust war, as Christians may be by Saracens, flight is sinless. Following St. Thomas almost slavishly as it were, Antoninus gives Thomas's rationale why the slave status of a child is determined by the slave condition of the child's mother, as is the case, he says, with the *vernaculi* or home-grown of Florence. Elsewhere, he notes that in "parts of Italy" the male offspring of a free man and a slave girl are treated as free. He raises no questions as to what the character of a slaveowner should be. In this world it was as unthinkable to inquire into the character of the owner of a human being as into the owner of a mule or a piece of furniture. Ever so slightly he amends Thomas to call a slave "a quasi-tool" of his owner.

Slaves have the duty to revere, to obey, and to serve their masters "faithfully and not feignedly," as St. Paul wrote to Timothy. Obedience, Antoninus says elsewhere, "is the most exalted of moral virtues." Slaves may not "ordinarily" make accusations or testify in court, nor can they be ordained, enter a religious order, or make vows without their master's consent. Masters should be humane, not burden them with too heavy burdens, hear their just complaints, give them opportunity to hear mass and preaching, exhort them to prayer and fasting, cor-rect them when appropriate "with words and whips, not mutilating them or breaking a bone," and not feed them delicacies. Slaves are not to be forced to accept the Christian faith or to receive the sacraments. They may marry, as canon law provides, contrary to the will of their owners. A master sins by forcing his slave girl to fornicate and, Antoninus adds cautiously, "I believe that she may lawfully flee him, if she can."

The tidiness of this account is deceptive. Antoninus does not speak of slave trading as an occupation, but when he deals with slaves by purchase, he holds that a Christian "cannot be sold" and that if a buyer, believing he is buying "a Saracen or one of this sort" in fact buys a Christian, he must free him. On the other hand, if he buys "a Jew or a pagan" who wants to become a Christian, he can sell him "although it would be a pious deed to free him." Antoninus has already said at the start of his treatment of human slavery, "In baptism grievous sins are taken away, not the obligations or conditions of men." What Antoninus does not speak to expressly are imported foreign slaves like Zita baptized before resale at a seaport such as Venice; baptized slaves who are not Catholics; and non-Christian slaves bought by Florentines and then, as was customary, baptized at the great baptistery of San Giovanni. In other words, he does not address in so many words what happened in Florence. Taken at the letter, his teaching forbids the enslavement of schismatic or heretical Christians, the enslavement of persons baptized in Venice and sold to Florentines, and at least the resale of those baptized in Florence. But he does not make his teaching confront the common situations.

Why can a Christian not be sold? Antoninus does not say. If Antoninus means to strike down the practice of slavery in his diocese, he is singularly reticent. Even more strikingly, he says nothing about the right to sell any human being as a slave. There is no suggestion that a purchaser has a duty to inquire as to the seller's title. Nor does Antoninus ask how women and children become justly enslaved in a just war. Enumerating the duties of notaries, whose work he recognizes as essential to the public validity of a document, Antoninus speaks of sin in notarizing contracts made by extortion, violence, or fraud or notarizing contracts not understood by women, adolescents, or imbeciles. He says nothing as to notarizing a contract selling a child or selling a Christian. Nor, in recognizing the several areas where divine law or canon law trumps civil law, does he mention Florentine law permitting the importation of non-Catholic Christian slaves.

Under "Avarice," Antoninus denounces usury, simony, and fraud, but has nothing on the slave trade; nor does he mention it under "Restitution." He treats of the morals of tradesmen but says nothing of slave traders. As to the sexual temptations presented by slaves, Antoninus offers no advice to parents or their adolescent boys, no comment on the stream of slave babies being taken to the orphanage. His hesitant opinion—"she may lawfully flee if she can"—cites no law or precedent and is remarkably unrealistic. Where could a runaway slave girl have run?

An absence of the acuteness, the vigor, the realism, and the familiarity with custom that Antoninus brings to banking marks his treatment of slavery. With banking Antoninus enters into the issues of his day and city. He speaks of slavery most of the time with abstractions drawn from old books. Even the common *esclavus* or *esclava* is not used. As far as appears, he never saw a slave sale on the Rialto or on a quay in Genoa. Only the reference to the *vernaculi* and the "flee if she can" point to a man familiar with the poorest of his archdiocese. Under the broad umbrella of "Inhumanity," Antoninus does write something that seems to come from his heart: "To free slaves from slavery, particularly after they have become Christians and it can be believed that they will use their freedom well, is a great mercy just as slavery itself is a great misery." Misery but not sin.

No vocabulary to confess the sin of slaveowning or slave trading existed. Neither Thomas nor Antoninus invented such a vocabulary. Theft, robbery, and usury designated offenses against property. Adultery, fornication, incest, rape, and sodomy designated a variety of sexual offenses. No word designated as an offense the owning of another person.

The sin was unnamed and unknown to be a sin. An unknown sin? The paradox needs unpacking. If the act is not known to be a sin, can it be a sin? One may argue, no doubt, that gross disregard of natural law and the commandment of love of neighbor is itself sinful, and that only by such disregard was slavery seen as a moral institution. One may argue in this way, but to attribute this view of its sinfulness to those who participated in the system is to read back into their consciences our own insights; it is an indulgence in anachronism. As their consciences instructed them, they were not sinners. As the masters of morality taught, the masters of slaves were moral owners of property. As the Americas opened before them, no European was likely to think of slaveholding as a sin.

How the Portuguese Got the Guinea Trade

On June 18, 1452, Pope Nicholas V granted Afonso V, king of Portugal, the right to make war on Saracens, pagans, and infidels; to occupy their dominions; and to reduce their persons to perpetual slavery. On January 8, 1455, Nicholas V issued the bull *Romanus pontifex* confirming the first bull and extending its scope. Drafted with the floridity of a practiced phrasemaker and the care of a conveyancer, the opening words of the bull, constituting its title, emphasized the extraordinary role of the pope in authorizing what was to be done. The most relevant portions of the grant invoked his full authority on behalf of Portugal:

> The Roman pontiff, successor of the key-bearer of the heavenly kingdom and vicar of Jesus Christ, contemplating with fatherly consideration all the climates of the world and the qualities of all the nations that dwell in them and seeking and desiring the salvation of each of them, ordains and disposes with mature deliberation those things which he sees will be agreeable to the Divine Majesty and by which he may bring the sheep divinely entrusted to him to the single sheepfold of the Lord and acquire for them the rewards of eternal happiness and obtain pardon for their souls.

[The pope has learned of the exploits of Henrique, infante of Portugal, who has ventured into lands unknown before, subjugating Guinea and acquiring by force or barter "many Guineans and other Negroes," transporting them to Portugal, where a large number of them have converted. The Portuguese king and the infante rightly fear that other kingdoms, "led by envy, malice or avarice," may intrude into their new domains, with the result that war might break out. The pope has already given], full and free faculty to the said King Afonso to invade, conquer, crush, pacify, and subjugate any whomsoever Saracens, and pagans, and other enemies of Christ wherever established and their kingdoms, dukedoms, principalities, dominions, possessions and all mobile and immobile property whatsoever held and possessed by them, and to reduce their persons to perpetual slavery, and to apply, appropriate, and convert to the use and utility of himself and his successors the kingdoms, dukedoms, earldoms, principalities, dominions and property.

[By this faculty, King Afonso has acquired] islands, lands, harbors and seas. [Now] most fully informed of all and each of the premises, [We] by apostolic authority and out of sure knowledge and from the plenitude of apostolic power [extend the faculty to] whatever can be acquired from the hands of infidels or pagans in the adjoining areas and in more distant and remote parts [and declare that to the king] pertains lawfully and forever what he has conquered from the capes of Bojador and Nam through all of Guinea and beyond toward that southern shore.

This extraordinary legal text (in its verbose entirety running over seven pages in modern print) invites questions. By what authority does the pope dispose of foreign countries and peoples? What occasioned his action? Was the bull an aberration or did it reflect settled policy? What were its consequences? What does the bull show as to the papal view of slavery?

The pope had been born Tommaso Parentucelli, had studied at Bologna, and had tutored the children of two rich families in Florence; he had been bishop of Bologna and a papal legate in Germany. Elected pope at age sixty in 1447, he distinguished himself by his diplomacy, his civic projects, and his book collecting. He was not an ignoramus on the throne of Peter.

The authority he used is identified in the document as "apostolic." Nicholas V appears to believe that God has given to the key-bearer Peter and his successors the authority to rule the world. It is the same belief most famously expressed a century and a half earlier by Boniface VIII in *Unam Sanctam* that "every human creature" is subject to the Roman pontiff. It is the same belief later advanced to dissolve marriage by exercise of the privilege of the faith.

Beyond the assertion of authority, no legal argument is offered. What is being papally authorized is not a crusade to defend the Holy Land or even to retake formerly Christian territory. Saracens, pagans, and infidels are targeted; there appears to be no theological distinction between the latter two; the double reference is lawyerly caution. There is no claim that they are making war on the faithful. Unbelief, apparently ipso facto, makes the unbeliever disposable by the pope and subject to conquest and enslavement by the Portuguese.

The circumstances leading Nicholas V to act were these. The Portuguese for twenty-five years, under the leadership of Henrique, later celebrated as "the Navigator," had been pushing down the western coast of Africa as well as into the Cape Verde Islands. "Guinea" for them, as for the pope, was not precisely defined, just as "that southern shore" referred to by the bull was not clearly identified. The pope referred vaguely to explorations "toward the south and the Antarctic pole." What was clear was that the Portuguese had acquired African possessions and wanted papal sanction, principally with an eye to excluding intrusion by the Spanish, potentially their envious, malicious, and avaricious rivals.

Not especially emphasized in the bull was the Portuguese interest in slaves. Contemporary narratives testify to that interest. "What a beautiful thing it would be," Prince Henrique's captain told his crew in 1441, "if we could capture some people; the Prince would be not a little happy." On his next expedition the captain was instructed "to capture people in any way and the best way you can." When sceptics of the value of the African explorations saw the success of slaving "with homes bursting at the seams with slaves, male and female," they hailed Henrique as another Alexander the Great. The same observer notes, with sympathy for the slaves but without condemnation of their owners, that, once in Portugal, slave husbands and wives were sent to different locations, and children were separated from their parents.

Portugal wanted papal blessing, and Portugal cooperated with the pope. On March 18, 1452, the pope celebrated the marriage of the Emperor Frederick III to Eleonora, daughter of King Afonso. Nicholas V's first grant to Portugal came three months later. After the fall of Constantinople to the Turks in 1453, the alarmed pope tried to rouse the European nations to the danger of Islamic invasion. The response was tepid, except for Afonso. Portugal, which had taken Ceuta in Morocco from the Moslems, was ready to beat back the Turks; so its king declared. *Romanus pontifex* encouraged the king's martial spirit and re-warded his profession of readiness. The bull reads as if its contents were sup-plied by agents of Afonso; its style was that of the Roman Curia; and lawyers for Portugal must have checked every comma and period. The executors of the bull were to be, jointly or severally, the archbishop of Lisbon and the bishops of Silves and Ceuta.

Romanus pontifex was not an aberration. It declared the bull of 1452 to be "inserted word for word in these presents, with all and singular the clauses therein contained in them." Nicholas V died the year it was issued. His succes-sor, Alfonso Borgia, Calixtus III, was a Spaniard, who might have been thought unsympathetic to the exclusive rights of Portugal. On March 13, 1456, Por-tuguese diplomacy triumphed, and in the bull *Inter caetera* ("Among Other Things"), Calixtus III incorporated *Romanus pontifex*. Taking no chances, the Portuguese secured another confirmation of the grant on June 21, 1481, from Francesco Della Rovere, Sixtus IV, and again on November 3, 1514, from Gio-vanni De'Medici, Leo X. Relying on the domains granted them by the bulls, King Manuel in 1501 styled himself "Lord of the conquest, navigation, and com-merce of Ethiopia, India, Arabia and Persia." The Portuguese had not pene-trated all these regions; they rejoiced in the implications of the bulls that they had the right to rule over them. It would be extraordinarily naive to suppose that the curia, engaged in giving away other people's lands, performed this service gratuitously.

As could have been anticipated, what the Portuguese got from the pope, the Spanish wanted, too, and after Ferdinand and Isabella had reported Columbus's discoveries to Rodrigo Borgia, Pope Alexander VI (a native of Valencia), he on May 3, 1493, issued another *Inter caetera* ("Among Other Things"). The pope granted the rulers of Castille and their successors all the things accorded the Portuguese—the same "privileges, favors, liberties, immunities, exemptions and indults . . . as if they were inserted word for word in these presents." This econ-omy of expression was not intended to save paper but to assure the Spanish that they had everything the Portuguese had received. The Spanish right to con-quer and enslave in the New World was to be as good as the Portuguese right in Africa.

Romanus pontifex had referred to the pope's authority as "vicar of Jesus Christ." The authority conferred by this title was given increasing emphasis in the curia as establishing direct papal power over temporal matters. Alexander VI explicitly stated that "by the authority of Almighty God granted to us in blessed Peter and by the vicarship of Jesus Christ that we enjoy over lands . . . we give, grant and assign to you and your heirs . . . all islands and mainlands found or to be found [within certain geographical limits]." The Vicar of Christ acted on the belief that he could give, grant, and assign a large portion of the New World to Spain.

As to enslaving the peoples encountered, *Romanus pontifex* had been explicit but remarkably terse. It could be inferred that the pope thought the right to conquer pagans carried with it the right to enslave them, even though the pope knew next to nothing about their beliefs. Before Henrique's explorations, the bull observed, the land was "unknown to us westerners so that we had no sure information about the peoples of those parts." Nothing in the bull suggested that Henrique had supplied the pope with any information except that the peoples he encountered were not Christian. The bull noted that Henrique had captured some of these peoples and had bought others of them. The pope registered no objection. Henrique's practice was in conformity with the papally granted right to enslave in the future.

Antoninus of Florence, Nicholas V's contemporary, had, of course, listed capture in a just war as giving a lawful basis for enslaving the captives. Nicholas V apparently assumed the Portuguese conquests were and would be just, without bothering to specify this requirement. It was an enormous assumption. By means of it, all the established rights that went with righteous victory were brought into play. The vanquished's wife and child and very person became the spoils of war.

What consequences flowed from the bulls? The Portuguese, it can be argued, would have done what they liked in Africa, whatever the pope said; so too, the Spanish in the lands discovered by Columbus. They were on the scene and had the power. Still, papal approval must have carried some weight for the Portuguese to remain so interested in reconfirmations of their grant and for the Spanish to want the same. The papal pronouncements purported to give their royal recipients legal as well as moral authorization to make slaves. For a pious person like Isabella of Spain the grant "by the Holy Apostolic See to us of the Islands and Terra Firma of the ocean sea" was worth mentioning in her will to confirm its holy purpose of evangelization. The bulls presumably enkindled enthusiasm and stilled doubts at home and put the Portuguese and Spanish on an equal footing diplomatically.

The bulls show that slaving was an enterprise requiring no special scrutiny. Nicholas V and his successors approved the enslavement of whole peoples, virtually unknown to them, and did so incidentally in approving wars of conquest. On the basis of facts presented to them by highly interested parties, without opportunity to check the facts for themselves, and without setting conditions on the right to enslave, the popes, over the critical period 1452–1514 when European expansion south and west began, gave the Portuguese and Spanish the charters that the conquerors sought.

How satisfying those charters could appear to an academic canonist may be gauged by the work of Juan López de Palacios Rubios, canonist of Salamanca and royal counselor, writing between 1512 and 1514. His treatise on Spanish dominion in the New World was dedicated "to the most merciful, the most unconquerable and the always august Ferdinand the Fifth, Catholic King of the two Spains, of both Sicilies, of Jerusalem and of the islands recently discovered in the Ocean and on the continent, glorious and most happy, steady and most spirited Defender of the Church and Dominator of barbarian nations." Palacios Rubios had no doubts about the Defender and Dominator's conquest and the consequent enslavement of the Indians.

Nor were doubts expressed by a more distant and nominally more dispassionate authority: John Major, a thirty-eight-year-old Scottish theologian of some ability teaching at the University of Paris. The first European theologian to address the enslavement of the Indians, Major had nothing but the papal bulls to guide him. In his lectures on Book IV of the *Sentences of Peter Lombard*, delivered in 1508 and published in 1510, he asked if Christian princes could take "any lands whatsoever that Saracens or Gentiles hold?" His answer was a simple affirmative. All power came from Christ. The non-Christians were guilty of *lèse majestié* in not giving way to the Christians. Rule by Christians would, moreover, "increase the worship of the divine name." The Church could make a rational division of the un-Christian lands among Christian princes. Specifically, Major addressed the rights of the Spanish "in the Atlantic Sea" and defended their right to conquest there, adding that the people conquered "live bestially." As Aristotle had said, by nature some are slaves: "it is just for one to be a slave, one to be free." The Aristotelian argument complemented the assertion of Christian supremacy. Paris joined Salamanca in applauding the Spanish accomplishment. Were differences to be heard from the Americas?

If John Major Were an Indian

No Place

Slavery in America had caught the attention of John Major at Paris, and Salamanca focused on it. But it did not become a burning issue for reformers of the Church. The European world and the old conventions held Martin Luther and John Calvin. Each comments on Paul's letter to Philemon. Each reads it as seeking to reconcile the master and the returned slave. Useful, according to Luther, "remains a slave in accordance with the custom of the heathen. Nor does Paul release him from his servitude or ask Philemon to do so. Indeed he confirms the servitude." Calvin declares that from the letter "we learn that the political order is not overturned by the faith of the Gospel, nor is the right and rule over slaves taken from their masters." The care of both Luther and Calvin is to celebrate Paul's skill in seeking mercy for Useful and at the same time to point out firmly that Paul respects Philemon's claim as a property owner. The two reformers took their view of slavery from St. Augustine. As John Calvin told John Knox about the phenomenon of women as rulers: "because it [women as queens] was a bending of the first and authentic order of nature, it should, like slavery, be noted among the punishments inflicted for man's rebellion." With the Fall had come these unpleasant, inescapable, and bearable consequences.

The subordinate status of slavery as a subject of modern morality on the eve of the Reformation is captured in Thomas More's abstract treatment of it in *Utopia*. Slaves in More's imaginary land are won in war, notably persons captured defending cities that the Utopians have attacked. More says nothing of taking the defenders' wives and children as well. Major criminals, including those guilty of adultery, are also made slaves. They are supplemented by foreign criminals who have been sentenced to death. The slaves do the heavy and the dirty work. In particular, they slaughter and clean animals because such work "would gradually destroy the sense of compassion" of the citizens. (This must be irony.) The slaves wear chains and foot shackles, and these are made of gold and silver to teach the citizens to scorn such baubles.

A third class of slaves beyond the prisoners of war and the criminals are the hardworking poor from other nations who come of their own choice to work in Utopia. They are treated decently and not much less kindly than the citizens. They can leave when they want. They are in effect a proletariat that poverty reduces to a state that More recognizes as slavery.

Only one explicit reform marks this regime. Children of slaves are not born into slavery. More does not explain why. In the lightest possible way, enslavement by birth is challenged. His reform would have been a radical restriction on private property rights; but More treats the slaves as public bounty. They are a reward for military success. Otherwise, they are not a source of wealth, but a means of punishing crime more effectively than capital punishment. Enslavement of human beings does not seem to strike More as unnatural. Without emotion, he outlines the rational employment of the slaves for the good of the commonwealth. For this intellectual lawyer, as for John Major, the university theologian at Paris, and for Palacios Rubios, the canonist of Salamanca, the perspectives are different, but in none of them is there a suspicion that there is something intrinsically evil in depriving human beings of autonomy and subjecting their whole lives to the direction of their masters.

When More wrote, he was on a diplomatic mission in Bruges, a city of the Spanish Empire. He had no incentive to be a critic of Spain, but had he heard nothing of the way the Spanish had subjugated the Indians or the way that the Portuguese had for sixty years enslaved the Africans? It is difficult to be certain of More's views of all the institutions of his Utopia (= Good Place or No Place). He plays with possibilities. He indulges irony. Slavery is envisaged academically, without expenditure of empathy for the slaves. The slavery he described did exist in no place.

Voices from the Americas and Roman Echoes

In Europe, the reform-minded did not explore the New World. The corrupt carried on. Johann Tetzel was disgracing the Dominicans by selling indulgences and provoking the indignation of Luther. The papacy focused on the challenge to the unity of the Church and its own position in the Church. The New World remained an unreal world to those who never went there.

Spanish and Portuguese colonists went there and found real gold and silver and Indians to be used as slaves in getting the minerals. Catholic missionaries also went there to minister to the colonists and to convert the Indians. Some religious and responsive men found the Indians worthy of observation, respect, and even understanding. For example, Alfonso de la Vera Cruz, an Augustinian friar, wrote a careful canonistic analysis of marriage in Michoacán; in 1536 it became the first canonical treatise printed in the Americas.

The life of one man above others exemplifies a Christian conscience awakening in America, making mistakes, and developing. Bartolomé de Las Casas came as a young man from Seville to the present island of Haiti–San Domingo, then named Hispaniola by Columbus. Like other colonists, he enjoyed lands, mines, and slaves that fell into his hands. He became a priest without giving up his possessions. He was disturbed by what he saw the colonists doing to the Indians, and he was deeply shaken when he himself was denied absolution by a Dominican. His life did not change until 1522, when he became a Dominican himself and formed the intention of writing what was to be an indictment of his colonial compatriots: *Historia de las Indias*. When he finished the work, Las Casas was learned in theology and canon law; he had not come to these subjects as a naive seminarian, but as a man of experience, able to internalize what was vital; and he applied their teachings with the concreteness of a man who had seen with his own eyes what human avarice, cruelty, and pride could do. No colonial power has ever had to hear such a formidable judgment pronounced upon its treatment of the inhabitants it dispossessed, as Las Casas from observation pronounced in his *History of the Indies*. As he saw it, the Spanish conquest was "opening hell to the Spanish and destroying all Spain, as each day its destruction increases little by little and even much by much."

The difference between the Dominican and the defender of the Dominator has been preserved in Las Casas' annotations on a copy of Palacios Rubios' tract. Where the latter spoke of any jurisdiction exercised by unbelievers in their own lands as merely conceded to them "by a certain silent and precarious consent" of the Church so that the Church appears to be the true sovereign of the entire world, Las Casas wrote, "Absurd." Where Palacios Rubios deduced from his jurisdictional analysis that the pope could judge in any part whatsoever of

se." Where Palacios Rubios citing Hostiensis
apable of jurisdiction when they acknowledge
s Casas wrote, "Heretical."

ere people in Rome who agreed with him. In
ajetan, the master-general of the Dominican
de Peñafiel, O.P., prior of San Pablo in Val-
an an account of Spanish conduct in the Carib-
'And do you doubt that your king is in hell?"

umma theologiae of Thomas Aquinas, published
s the best of a large family of commentaries,
ment of robbery (*rapina*) where Thomas asked
constituted the sin. Thomas answered No, if the
on in fighting was not principally to acquire the
slems inhabiting lands once occupied by Chris-
n of the Church, Cajetan went on as to lands "in
e of Christian." Their lords, "although unbeliev-
e, he answered, "I know of no law relative to their

Against them no King nor Emperor nor the Roman Church can wage war
to occupy their land. No reason for a just war exists; for Jesus Christ, the
king of kings, to whom is given all power in heaven and earth, sent to take
possession of the world not a militarily armed army but holy preachers as
sheep among wolves. . . . Hence we shall sin most gravely if through this
way we should agree to expand the faith of Christ, and we would not be
their lawful lords, but we would commit great robberies and be bound to
restitution as unjust warriors or occupiers.

Cajetan undercuts the argument that the pope as Christ's vicar can authorize
military conquest: Christ did not so proceed, neither can his deputy. He uses
the term St. Augustine used for a state without justice: it is a great robbery or,
we would say, organized crime. He softens the condemnation slightly by using
the subjunctive. But he states plainly the duty of restitution incumbent on those
who are occupiers. He all but names the Spanish and their victims as he goes
on to speak, still conditionally, of those "who may oppress them, despoil them,
scandalize them, subjugate them, and in the manner of pharisees make sons for
a double hell."

In almost the same breath Cajetan made an observation on the nature of
slavery so penetrating and pertinent that, if taken to heart by his contemporaries,

it would have blown up the whole slave structure: "On a living human being, so long as he is held in slavery, personal violence is continually inflicted." The comment is made in the course of explaining why one may lawfully liberate Christians held in slavery by the enemy. The comment, however, is general. Violence, not law, perpetuates the institution.

A cardinal of the curia, the papally picked champion to demolish the errors of Luther, Cajetan stood high in Rome. His commentary was dedicated to Leo X. But the bulls of conquest were neither rescinded nor explained away. Indeed in the whole course of the Fifth Council of the Lateran, 1512 to 1518, no orator and no conciliar document touched on what was happening in the New World.

Within the New World there were avaricious men who contended that the Indians were "beasts and asses." The Dominicans themselves were divided. In Spain, Cardinal Garcia de Loaysa, the president of the Royal Council of the Indies, was committed to the justified enslavement of the Indians. In 1534, Las Casas wrote *The Only Way of Drawing All Peoples to the True Religion*. The only way was not that of war or violence or any coercion. It was the way that God led all creatures "to fulfill their natural purposes—a gentle, coaxing, gracious way": so reason embraced this way. It was the way that Christ "fashioned and prescribed" in preaching and in teaching his gospel. "Learn of me," Christ said, "for I am meek and humble of heart" (Mt 11:29). Christ granted "no power to apostle or preacher of the faith to force the unwilling to listen." Boldly, Las Casas quoted Cajetan: the Roman Church had no right to take away the temporal possessions of the Indians or to authorize war upon them.

In behalf of the Indians, the Dominican Bernardino de Minaya traveled from the Americas to Rome to persuade the pope to intervene. Minaya carried with him the resolutions of a meeting in 1536 of the four bishops and the superiors of the religious orders in Mexico. Responding to this initiative, Alessandro Farnese, Pope Paul III, in 1537 issued *Sublimis Deus,* declaring:

> . . . the Indians are truly men and they are not only capable of understanding the Catholic faith, but, according to our information, they desire exceedingly to receive it. . . . Whatever may have been said or may be said to the contrary notwithstanding, the said Indians and all other people who may later be discovered by Christians are by no means to be deprived of their liberty . . . nor in any way enslaved; should the contrary happen, it shall be null and of no effect.

Sublimis Deus was a strong papal intervention against the enslavement of the Indians. A modern admirer of Las Casas argues for his contribution to the bull and salutes *Sublimis Deus* as "the Magna Carta of the Indians." The bull was not as strong as it might have been or should have been if it were intended to retract the bulls of conquest. Generations late in coming, it avoided mention of the string of papal authorizations of enslavement. The bull's general clause, "Whatever may have been said . . . notwithstanding," was boilerplate. It was not crafted clearly enough to revoke the earlier approvals.

The battle over the evangelization and enslavement of the Indians continued. Las Casas did not have the same academic prestige as a younger Dominican contemporary who in the 1520s and 1530s held a chair of theology at Salamanca: Francisco de Vitoria. In lectures explicitly devoted to questions of justice in the Indies, Vitoria considered and carefully rejected several titles "by which the barbarians can come into the power of the Spanish." Then, after this splendid display of acute reasoning, he considered and accepted "the lawful titles by which the barbarians can come into the power of the Spanish." Among the seven titles justifying conquest was the right of the Spanish as the papally designated "legates of the Christians" to preach the Gospel to the barbarians. If the barbarians resisted hearing the Gospel, the Spanish had just cause to wage war and "despoil them and reduce them to captivity." In a just war it was lawful also to reduce "children and other innocents to captivity and slavery," because liberty is among "the goods of fortune," and the winners of a war may rightly help themselves to the goods of fortune of the vanquished. Vitoria in the academic citadel of Salamanca was faithful to the thrust of *Romanus pontifex* and *Inter caetera*. To his straightforward defense of papal and Spanish policy, Vitoria added a caveat of conscience. Conquest and enslavement were per se lawful, "but I fear that matters go further than law and right permit." Vitoria has enjoyed the reputation of being a founder of international law. The lack of teeth that marks much international law is presaged in this mild comment that does not tackle the realities of the enslavement of the Indians. He leaves in place a justification for making slaves of women and children, a justification treating human freedom as a kind of commodity.

The doctrinal significance of the papal position on conquest played a part in his deliberations. Plainly, the popes thought they possessed the power they purported to exercise. Vitoria explicitly drew the parallel between the power used and the Pauline privilege to dissolve marriage with an unbaptized person. When a sizeable part of a people converted to Christianity, he thought, the pope could change their rulers "in favor of the faith," just as a pagan wife who was converted could be freed from her pagan husband "in favor of the faith." The parallel worked in the sense that the exercise of a power is taken as proof of its legitimacy.

Vitoria was a careful moderate. Other theologians continued in the unashamed defense of conquest and enslavement. Juan Ginés de Sepúlveda, a theologian and a scholar of the classics, followed John Major in asserting that it was in accordance with nature for the strong to rule the weak, and for barbarous and inhumane people to be subjected to those more cultured and humane. Sepúlveda had never been to the New World. But he knew that war against the Indians was justified by their paganism, their abominable licentiousness, and their prodigious sacrifice of human victims. In 1550, now in his sixties, Las Casas engaged Sepúlveda in debate at Valladolid. Since 1544, Las Casas had been bishop of Chiapas (Zacatlán). He returned to Spain with authorization from the Indians there and at Oaxaca to represent them before the Council of the Indies. Emperor Charles V set up a special Council of Fourteen to hear the debate, with eminent theologians such as Melchor Cano and Domingo Soto among its members. Las Casas prepared a small treatise attacking Sepúlveda's defense of war against the Indians and read it, over four days, chapter by chapter to the Council of Fourteen. He dedicated the work to Prince Philip, ruling as his father's deputy in Spain. In his *History of the Indies,* Las Casas had preserved Cajetan's caustic question about the eternal fate of King Ferdinand, but Las Casas himself was a loyal Spaniard, and he saw that the only practical help the Indians could get had to come from the crown. Las Casas wrote:

> Mindful that I am a Christian, a religious, a bishop. . . . I am bound to set myself up as a wall against the wicked for the defense of a completely innocent people. . . .

At the start, Las Casas acknowledged that a prime line of defense for the conquests was Alexander VI's *Inter caetera.* He took the lawyer-like tack that Alexander VI did not mean what his expositors said he meant. The key difficulty was the pope's acknowledgment of the Spanish monarchy's intention "to subject" the inhabitants of the newly discovered lands and "to lead them to the Catholic faith." Sepúlveda argued that the bull authorized wars of conquest. Las Casas argued that it did not: "For how could he [the pope] permit something conflicting with Christ's commandment?" The pope should be read putting a reasonable sense on his words. War would not bring the Indians to the faith but drive them from it. "To subject" the Indians "should be interpreted as 'to dispose' them," to dispose them "in a way in which one should subjugate a most civilized, sincere, naked, docile, decent, and peaceful people." In effect, Las Casas attributed to Alexander VI the thesis Las Casas himself had expounded in 1534 in *The Only Way of Drawing All Peoples to the True Religion,* Christ's way of gentle love. It was an uphill battle to turn Alexander VI's authorization of subjection into a subjection of love. As a trump, Las Casas cited *Sublimis Deus:* "Subject" must refer to subjection born of gentle preaching "even if its literal meaning be opposed to this interpretation, since the bull of the Roman Pontiff, Paul III, expressly forbids these detestable wars that are waged against the Indians under the pretext of religion."

Sepúlveda had also relied on Scripture, citing the fate, divinely sanctioned, of the Canaanites who preceded the Israelites in the Promised Land. He had invoked God's command to the Israelites to destroy the Amalekites and the Midianites. If these were precedents, Las Casas observed, the Spanish would have divine sanction to kill all the Indians and all idolaters everywhere, man, woman, and child, as well as their dogs and beasts of burden. The argument was "completely absurd." Sepúlveda's "shins were showing, as the saying goes."

A secondary target of Las Casas was John Major, the Scottish theologian who had so brazenly upheld the Spanish conquests. John Major had never been to the Indies and knew nothing of the situation. It was "ridiculous that this theologian should say that even before a king understands the Spanish language and even before he understands the reason why the Spanish build fortifications, he should be deprived of his kingdom." Impatiently, Las Casas cried: "Away with John Major and his dreams! He knows neither the law nor the facts." Patiently, Las Casas also used a better approach. He invited John Major to step into the shoes of an Indian and see if he then would submit to an imperious demand from a ruler of whom he knew nothing. "If he were an Indian," John Major would not tolerate it.

It was a delicious hypothetical—"the oracle of religion" in Scotland turned into a naked native of the New World. Who had thought of arguing in this way from the viewpoint of the enslaved? Once the perspective of a European Catholic was surrendered, once one crossed over and looked at the justice of the case from the vantage of the Indian, the outrageousness of the Spanish position was evident.

Vitoria still stood in the way. This "famous and learned father" had refuted seven titles justifying war against the Indians. But Vitoria had been "a little more careless" in putting forward titles that might justify the war. He had "wished to moderate what seemed to the Emperor's party to have been rather harshly put." But he had spoken conditionally, "fearing that he might suppose or make false statements." In fact, Vitoria had supposed circumstances that were false.

A substantial portion of Las Casas' argument was devoted to establishing that the Church had no jurisdiction over unbelievers. Implicitly Las Casas here challenged not only Vitoria but a series of papal assertions of power. His own authorities ranged from St. Paul to Gratian to St. Thomas Aquinas. He did affirm that the Church had jurisdiction over heretics. He could not have thought otherwise in Spain in 1550. But over and over again he denied that the Church or the pope ruled over the unbaptized.

Repentance

In 1516, Las Casas had prepared a memorandum of remedies for the Indies. The Crown should give permission to bring from Castille "black and white slaves." Each Christian on the island should have "two black slaves and two black slave girls." In 1531, he wrote the Council of the Indies and recalled this remedy of replacing the Indians with black slaves. A third memorial in 1541 mentioned the aid to be gotten from black slaves. For twenty-five years, black slaves were in the mind of Las Casas a solution for the oppression of the Indians. Nothing could demonstrate more sharply how slavery appeared to a good, conscientious, and courageous man. Nothing was wrong with slavery. It was the lack of just title that made the Spanish evil kidnappers of the Indians.

Las Casas, however, came eventually to a different view. His *Very Brief Relation of the Destruction of the Indies* had been translated into French and English to become a weapon of propaganda against Spain. For that reason, perhaps, Las Casas prescribed that the full *Historia* should not be published until forty years after his death. It was not completely published until 1951, in Mexico City. In the *Historia* Las Casas confessed he was guilty of serious sin. According to his account, the owners of water mills used for crushing sugar cane needed slaves and sought a royal license to import Blacks. They told Las Casas they would free their Indian slaves if they got the Blacks. Las Casas supported their request for the license. Eventually licenses were obtained on a large scale, the money to the king for granting them going to the construction of the *alcázars* at Madrid and Toledo and nearly one-hundred thousand Blacks being imported by "the islands."

The slaves' source was the Portuguese, who, Las Casas observed, "have had charge of robbing Guinea and with great injustice making slaves of the Blacks." The Blacks themselves, he added, make unjust wars and sell the captives from them to the Portuguese. But it was the needs of the Spanish that drove the business, "so we are the cause of all the sins of the one or the other." As for himself, writing of himself in the third person, he was repentant, "judging himself at fault for inattention, because he later saw and averred that, according to what appeared, the captivity of the Blacks was as unjust as that of the Indians." He now saw his sin and was "not certain that the ignorance he had in this matter and his good will would excuse him before the divine judgment." So the greatest foe of enslavement of the Indians ended judging himself an accomplice in the unjust enslavement of Africans. Was his belated attack on African slavery one reason why the revised *History of the Indies* was not published until 1951?

He cannot be called an abolitionist because he did not believe in abolition. He accepted the institution of slavery. He helped bring Blacks as slaves to the Indies. Yet he worked more strenuously against slavery than any who preceded him. No abolitionist—when abolitionists appeared centuries later—confronted the concrete evils of a slaveholding society with more passion and courage. To a moral challenge that seemed sisyphean he brought what was essential to his task—experience, empathy, energy, and endurance. He put himself in the place of the oppressed. In the history of thought on slavery, Bartolomé de Las Casas towers over other men of his era and most men of other eras.

Conventions, Cries and Murmurs, Repressions

Conventions

Charles Verlinden's comprehensive study of European slavery records slaves acquired for use in Italy in a variety of documents from the sixteenth and seventeenth century: A black woman sold at the Salerno fair in 1527. A purchase of 62 slaves from the collector of customs at Naples by a knight of Malta in 1604. Seventy contracts of sale in the Bari region in the seventeenth century. St. Pius V, the recipient of 558 slaves after the naval victory of Lepanto. (The custom of not enslaving defeated Christians did not extend to defeated Moslems.) Galley slaves obtained from the knights of Malta by Urban VIII in 1629 and by Innocent X in 1645. An inhabitant of Rimini in 1544 buying in Croatia a ten-year-old girl captured in war against the Turks. In 1574, twenty-two shipwrecked Moslems sold at Lucca. In 1677, sixteen shipwrecked Turks sold at Lucca. In 1534, two male Blacks sent by Andrea Doria as a gift to the duke of Mantua. In 1503, the sale in Sardinia of seven Moors captured by corsairs from Trapani. The sale at Cagliari in 1596 of 47 slaves, including two women and three children, seized in a razzia on Barbary. In 1603, the archbishop of Cagliari buying an eight-year-old and a five-year-old Moor out of a lot of thirty-seven, the youngest of whom is eight months. In 1621, the sale of fifty-four Moors shipwrecked in Sardinia. In 1510, the sale of a fourteen-year-old Bosnian girl at Genoa. In 1517, at Genoa the sale of ten men and twenty-three women, including one Russian woman. In 1672, the last sale found in the Genoa records. In 1588, the accounting of a Venetian slave trader buying thirteen men and one woman, all "Turks," in Dalmatia, and transporting them in chains to Genoa, where they were sold. The picture is of an institution that was gradually declining but was at no time classified as criminal or intrinsically evil.

Slavery in the papal states in the sixteenth century was as domestic an institution as it had been in Florence. In *Sublimis Deus,* Paul III denounced the enslavement of Indians. He did not denounce enslavement at home. In 1548, eleven years after *Sublimis Deus,* acting "from his pastoral duty freely procuring with God as far as possible the advantage of each of the faithful," he declared that, "from a multitude of slaves, inheritances are augmented, agriculture better cultivated, and cities increased." By apostolic authority, therefore, the pope decreed that slaves fleeing to the Capitol and there, according to custom claiming freedom, were not freed and were "to be returned to their masters in slavery and, if it is seen appropriate, punished as fugitives." The decree, the pope added, included those slaves who had become Christians after their enslavement and slaves born to Christian slaves. The right of inhabitants of Rome to buy, sell, and contract publicly as to slaves of both sexes was affirmed. Broader, plainer, more matter-of-fact legislation cutting off an escape from slavery could not be imagined.

The catechism based on the decrees of the Council of Trent dealt with slaves under the commandment against theft, mentioning there the sin of kidnapping, defined as taking place "if a free man or the slave of another is led away into slavery"—a succinct statement simultaneously condemning the enslaving of a free man and affirming the property rights of a slaveowner. These rights were further fortified under the commandment against coveting a neighbor's goods. The catechism said that the neighbor's slave and slave girls that the commandment prohibited one from coveting are "to be understood as captives as well as the remaining kind of slaves, whom, like the other goods of another, we ought not to desire." "Whom," not "which," but they were like other property. This slight expansion of the law from Mount Sinai seemed meant for the inhabitants of a place like Portugal where captives could be seen enriching one's neighbor. Nothing was said in the catechism about enslaving free Indians or buying Blacks unjustly enslaved. These problems of the present were not addressed.

Giovanni Botero, secretary of Carlo Borromeo, the reforming archbishop of Milan, wrote *The Reason of State* as an anti-Machiavellian work. In his dedication to the archbishop of Salzburg, Botero proclaimed the supremacy of conscience over all the concerns of humankind, public as well as private. He observed that there was "nothing to which the ruler should pay more attention than usury, for usury means robbery or, rather, worse than robbery." In contrast, Botero's conscience was at ease with slavery, commenting that slaves could carry out projects of public work without great expense and noting the Portuguese trading their goods in Guinea for "thousands of slaves," who were put to work "in the sugar plantations of the Cape Verde Islands, St. Thomas and Brazil" or who were else sold to the Spanish, "who use them in the same way in Hispaniola and the rest of the New World." Botero's book, published in 1587, ran through four Latin editions, six Spanish, and ten Italian during his lifetime.

Murmurs

Three different voices can be detected with doubts. The first is Tomás Mercado, the author of a treatise addressed simply to "contracts." Unlike Gregory I or Thomas Aquinas or Antoninus, Mercado focuses on the title of the seller: by what right does he own the slave he sells? Writing in Spain after experience in Mexico, Mercado recited the titles by which slaves could be acquired but went on to say "many or almost all" of the titles by which slaves were sold as captured in war were unjust titles, and that the slaves were condemned to slavery by false witnesses. As for selling children as slaves, it was "brutal" and "bestial." The traders themselves engaged in cruelty. The trade was "lawful," but "infamous." In a word, it was "mortal sin," abominated by God, who saw to it that the prosperity of the slave traders did not last; and to God they must account for their conduct. Published in Seville in the middle of the sixteenth century, this work by a Dominican theologian singled out and condemned what even in conventional terms was the morally vulnerable component of slavery as an institution— the trade. If the royal legislators or the popes or all Christians had responded to his analysis, the trade would have been stopped and the institution would have withered.

A voice in a different key is that of Jean Bodin (1537–1596), a Catholic believed to come from a Jewish heritage, who first tried his vocation as a Carmelite but then turned to law and held minor legal positions in the provinces. Georges Goyau, a perceptive critic, describes him as "more or less openly hostile to the existing ecclesiastical order," but he was buried in the Franciscan church at Laon.

Bodin's major work, *Six livres de la République* (1577), was an essay on political theory in which, among many other topics, he addressed slavery. "The general consent of almost all people" excluded slaves from the citizenry. "And yet the question remains undecided. . . . If referred to me, I should like the right and liberty of the city to be left open." Why, Bodin asked, "enforce so divine a creature, having his liberty shamefully taken from him . . . to make no more of him, yea and peradventure less too, than of a very beast?" Aristotle said some were naturally slaves. "But lawyers, who measure the law . . . according to the common sense and capacity of the people, hold servitude to be directly contrary to nature, and do what they can to maintain liberty." Bodin cited the case of a German merchant who had bought a slave in Spain and was bringing him through France to Italy, but was stopped in Toulouse and compelled by a magistrate to emancipate his purchase.

Bodin goes through a pro and con on slavery, where the strongest argument for slavery is that it has always existed and that, in particular, the West Indies "have always been full of slaves." Contra, he observes that an evil custom can last a long time without making it right. As for the argument that a victor in war could justly kill his prisoner and therefore does him a kindness by enslaving him, Bodin observes that wars for the most part are unjust. Then he makes an even more sweeping response: to enslave instead of killing is "the charity of a pirate."

In the end, Bodin is not an abolitionist but a cautious critic. He opts for what he calls "the law of God," i.e., the seven years term of slavery prescribed as the maximum for Hebrews in the Hebrew Bible. His instincts, very different from those in the rut of the theologians, are those of a French lawyer in a nation whose new colonies might still find slavery useful.

Another fresh, different, and tentative voice is heard in Shakespeare's *The Merchant of Venice*. Shylock, accused by the doge of hardness of heart for demanding the pound of flesh for which he has bargained, replies:

> What judgment shall I dread,
> doing no wrong ?
> You have among you many a purchas'd slave,
> Which, like your asses and your dogs and mules,
> You use in abject and in slavish parts,
> Because you bought them. Shall I say to you,
> "Let them be free! marry them to your heirs!
> Why sweat they under burdens? Let their beds
> Be made as soft as yours and let their palates
> Be season'd with such viands!" You will answer,
> "The slaves are ours." So I do answer you,
> The pound of flesh which I demand of him
> Is dearly bought: 'tis mine and I will have it.
> If you deny me, fie upon your law!

The underlying assumption of the speaker and his audience is that slavery is lawful. The argument follows: if human beings can be treated as property in this way, why not in Shylock's? Under the surface of the speech is a counterargument: if it is monstrous to demand a pound of human flesh, as the play's audience will think, a parallel reduction of human beings to property is also monstrous. The analogy asks to be recognized. Shakespeare does not dwell upon it. Usury, not slavery, is the center of his drama. The human trade on the Rialto remains background.

Nuance

In terms of the professional teaching of moral theology, Shakespeare and Bodin meant little; Mercado left a challenge. It was taken up by the most capable casuist of the seventeenth century, justly celebrated by Paul V as *strenuissimus* or extraordinarily vigorous in morals: the Spanish Jesuit Tomás Sanchez. His *consilia* or opinions were collected and published posthumously in 1635. Among them were his views on the trade as practiced by the Portuguese.

Following Mercado, Sanchez said that there were four bad titles to ownership of a slave. The first was an unjust war, in particular a war made in order to obtain slaves to sell to Portuguese merchants. The second was sale of children by their parents who were moved to make the sale "by light anger," rather than by "grave necessity." The third was condemnation to slavery by a tyrannical law. The fourth was self-sale by one who didn't understand what he was doing or who was married and therefore not free to dispose of himself. On the other hand, there were four good titles to ownership: enslavement in a just war; sale of children by parents in serious need; penalty for crime; and self-sale by one who was free and of sufficient judgment to know what he was doing. A fifth title was conferred by "Ethiopians," that is Africans, who had been captured by cannibals and preferred to become slaves to being eaten. Some doubted that the Africans' preference gave their new owner a good title; but Sanchez, citing Navarrus, accepted it.

In sum, there were good titles and bad. What was a trader to do if he was unsure whether a seller of slaves had good or bad title? It was, as Mercado had pointed out, morally impossible to examine each title. Naturally, men were free. That presumption held here. In doubt as to whether the seller of slaves had good or bad title to them, the purchaser committed mortal sin in buying and was bound to make restitution of those unjustly bought.

Sanchez's conclusion is a clear condemnation of the slave trade as practiced by Portuguese traders buying en masse from African sellers. But Sanchez adds a qualification. If one buys one or two slaves from a trader, one is not bound to inquire as to the trader's title: the trader is in possession, and, as the old legal maxim runs, "the condition of the possessor is better." Even if the purchaser develops doubts about the trader's title, the purchaser is not held to restitution; he now enjoys the status of a possessor.

On a variety of other topics touching the emancipation of slaves, Sanchez sustains his unsentimental and unempathetic posture. Is it sinful for one captured in a just war to flee? The more probable opinion is Yes, it is sinful. May a slave girl flee if her owner seeks to abuse her shamefully? Yes, and the bishop may emancipate her. Is it a work of piety to free slaves? Today, it is neither pious nor useful unless the slaves are honest and can sustain themselves by their own industry; otherwise, they will become idle and thieves and end in jails and fetters. No strenuous emancipator here!

Sanchez's opinion muffled Mercado's condemnation, leaving an opening for buyers at retail. It was an exacting exercise in casuistry. A conscientious slave trader, on learning of it, would have given up his work. The probable effect on a buyer in the New World is not so evident.

Repressions

The golden age of casuistry was also the age of absolutism. Sanchez's subtleties were overridden by a clearer, more consistent upholder of the ways of the Iberian monarchies: Juan de Lugo, S.J., a cardinal under Innocent X. On subjects like usury that excited his attention, Lugo was marvelously acute and flexible. Slavery, which now predominated in Latin America and was still encountered in the Mediterranean, was treated by him, by and large, in cut-and-dried fashion. The standard titles to slave property—war, punishment, self-sale, and birth—were set out. Most slaves today were captured from "a hostile commonwealth" or were descendants of such captives. He did ask why it was lawful to enslave prisoners of war and answered only that the right to make use of a prisoner came along with the right to kill: by long custom, Christians held Christian prisoners for ransom rather than enslavement. He did ask why infants captured in war could be enslaved. He replied, "They are part of the hostile commonwealth." Similarly, although it would not be lawful to kill them, it was acceptable to enslave women "captured at sea or elsewhere" who were of "a hostile commonwealth." Children born to a slave mother were rightly enslaved because slavery, like infamy, was a penalty that embraced descendants. In short, as part of a Latin treatise entitled *Justice and Law*, as part of a section entitled "The Methods of Acquiring Ownership of Things," the subsection "Whether and How One Man Acquires Ownership of Another Man" explored few problems and gave short answers. Slavery, Lugo observed, was "not against the prohibition of nature but beyond the intention of nature."

In this way he followed Aquinas, as he did in enumerating the rights of slaves—to the integrity of their members; to marry and to have sexual relations with their spouses; and not to be forced to sin: "in these matters, he is not considered a slave but a man." A slave girl solicited to sin by her owner or threatened by him with prostitution had the right to flee. Galley slaves, justly condemned to this punishment, still had the right to escape, since to deny the right would be "very hard and beyond the common condition of men." Some moralists—Luis Molina, S.J., Navarrus, and Sylvester da Prieras, O.P., were named—held it to be sin for a slave captured in a just war to escape. With Soto, Lugo held the contrary. Successful escape dissolved any obligation.

In this fashion, not obliterating entirely the humanity of the slave, broadly asserting the justice of enslavement, and showing no curiosity about the ways slaves were procured or the ways they lived, Lugo left the system, except for very modest qualifications, untouched.

For Jacques Bossuet, bishop of Condom, later bishop of Meaux, and spokesman for the militant Catholicism of France under Louis XIV, a "sure sign of falsity" was change in doctrine: "What has been believed everywhere and always and by everyone"—the old criterion of Vincent of Lérins—was for him "the absolute criterion of Catholic truth." He had no difficulty in deducing from it 'the immutability of morality or dogma.'" In 1688, he wrote with relish the *Histoire des variations des églises protestantes*. When a Calvinist theologian, Pierre Jurieu, replied, Bossuet pounced upon him, and among other palpable absurdities denounced Jurieu's argument that all relationships, including slavery, were "established upon mutual obligations." How wrong that was, said Bossuet. Slavery is founded on victory in a just war. The victor, who could take the life of the vanquished, spares him. To think that a contract results "goes directly against the nature of slavery. For one, who is the master, makes the law as he wills; and the other, who is the slave, receives it as the master wills to give it." There is no contract: the laws say "that the slave has no status, no head, *caput non habet;* that is to say, he is not a person in the State. No good, no right belongs to him. He has neither voice nor judgment nor action nor force more than his master permits."

Bossuet capped this especially enthusiastic celebration of slavery by saying he knew that Jurieu did not want to go so far as to condemn slavery, a posture that would be *outré*. Why, to condemn slavery would be to condemn the law of nations, which admits slaves. Worse, "it would be to condemn the Holy Spirit, who orders slaves, through the mouth of St. Paul, to remain in their state and does not in the least oblige their masters to emancipate them."

On account of his style Bossuet has a place in French literature. Ferdinand Brunetière observes: "In his sermons as in his writings, it would be impossible to deny that Bossuet has an imperious and authoritative style. He counsels nothing which he does not command, or which he does not impose." Making any challenge to slavery a sin against the Spirit the grand Gallican orator outdid himself.

By mid-eighteenth century, the moral issues arising from slavery aroused even less attention among those working in the main tradition. Alfonso de'Ligouri completed his magnum opus on moral theology in 1755, when the Atlantic slave trade was flourishing and slavery existed not only in Africa, the Americas, and Asia but in Italy. He showed extraordinary reserve on the subject. He did not discuss it at all in setting out how ownership was acquired. He discussed the mutual obligations of masters and servants (*famuli*), but not of slaves. Only as an add-on to that discussion he asked, "May slaves captured in a just war lawfully escape to their homes?" Molina and others answered No, their owners "justly possess them." Lessius and others answered Yes. Alfonso pronounced the Yeses to be "the more common and more probable opinion," proved by Justinian's *Institutes* 2.1.17: "Those who escape our power and return to their homes regain their former status." Relying on Roman law, Alfonso left a slaveholding society free to follow the less common and probable opinion and hold a fugitive slave to be a thief. He did ask if captives of the Turks could steal from them to get what was needed to ransom themselves. Here he simply threw up his hands. The question had generated "a mighty confusion." The doctors spoke too obscurely. "I myself dare to decide nothing." Such taciturnity was not how Alfonso earned his reputation.

From the brevity of his treatment, one might infer that Ligouri had no experience of a slaveowning society. Au contraire, he was born in 1696 in Naples, a seaport of 214,000 inhabitants, of whom about 10,000 were slaves. Generically referred to as "Turks," some of them rowed in the royal galleys, where Ligouri's father was a captain. For domestic services in his own home, his father used "a good number" of other slaves, among them one Abdallah, a teenager from Rhodes. This slave was presented by his father to Alfonso, aged about eighteen, as a personal slave. Impressed by his master's kindness, Abdallah took the step, not usual among the Moslems, of seeking instruction and baptism. Baptized Giuseppe Maria at age eighteen, he almost immediately died. No trace of his experience with this slave or with the galley slaves or with the slaveowners of Naples appears in Alfonso's exhaustive analysis of virtues and sins.

Voices had been raised which, if heeded, would have been enough to bring down the institution of slavery. Cajetan had challenged the title conferred by conquest of the innocent infidel and remarked on the perpetual violence to which a slave was subject. Mercado and Sanchez had challenged the titles acquired by traders buying en masse. Ligouri must have been aware of these authorities. But in his treatise, the cries and murmurs against the institution have disappeared.

What was taught in Europe continued to have its greatest impact in the non-European world where slavery existed and Catholic missionaries evangelized. What word did they bring?

Advice to the Missions

Goa, Angola, Cartagena

Home customs did not weigh heavily on colonists: most Englishmen and
Frenchmen took to owning slaves in their respective colonies without batting an
eye. Accustomed to slaves at home, Portuguese and Spanish religious were even
less likely to be scandalized by slavery in the colonies. For example, in 1635, the
one hundred Augustinian nuns of the convent of Santa Mônica in Goa com-
plained to the local authorities that they were restricted by an ordinance to a total
of one hundred and twenty slaves. Any unmarried European in this Asiatic out-
post of Portugal was permitted to have fifteen or twenty slave girls. Why should
the nuns be limited?

The nuns' complaint is one small sign of the quotidian prevalence of slaves
among the religious orders as they traveled in the wake of Portuguese and Spanish explorers and conquerors. On a large scale, the whole economy of Angola
was geared to the slave trade. Among those enriched by the business were the
bishop, other ecclesiastical officials, and even the Santa Casa da Misericórdia.
For the Portuguese, African slaves were "Black ivory," sellable to the Spanish
or to the Portuguese in Brazil to be the workforce of plantations. Why should

the religious orders or the bishop or the Holy House of Mercy not get a piece of a profitable and legal trade?

By the will of María Barros, dated March 25, 1609, the discalced nuns of Our Lady of Mount Carmel in Cartagena, New Granada, received a gift from the charitable lady who had founded their establishment in the New World. The gift consisted of fifteen slaves. These bore Christian names and must therefore have been baptized. They included both men and women as well as three children aged seven, six, and three. Cartagena was the emporium for all slaves imported for Spanish South America. The nuns belonged to the branch of the Carmelites reformed by Saint Teresa. No one thought it surprising or improper that religious distinguished by the austerity of their lives should become, collectively, the owner of a dozen adult Christians and three Christian infants.

Also living in Cartagena, from 1610 to 1650, was Pedro Claver, a Jesuit from Catalonia who made extraordinary efforts to instruct slaves in the Christian faith and to baptize them. Meeting the carracks as they arrived from Africa loaded with their shackled cargo, Claver would greet his fellow creatures in kindly fashion and offer what was for them a luxury: fresh water. When they were housed in slave sheds ashore, he undertook to impart to them the essential truths of the faith. When he was sure that they understood and accepted his teaching, he would baptize them. In over thirty years of such work he believed that he baptized over three hundred thousand. His devotion to this apostolate was such that he described himself to be "ever the slave of the Africans." But to carry out his catechetical tasks he had to communicate in the slaves' tongue. He learned rudimentary Angolese. There were at least fifteen other languages spoken by the arrivals from Africa. To speak to them, he had to use interpreters. Owners of slaves who could have served this function were unwilling to let them be employed so profitlessly. To obtain what was indispensable to his work, Claver had no option but to buy slaves himself. According to testimony in his canonization process, he paid a ship captain to identify and bring back from Africa the native speakers that he needed; the captain carried out his order to acquire the useful slaves. One could believe that Sanchez's opinion on buying slaves retail was designed to accommodate this kind of single-minded purchasing.

The Brothers Cibo in Rome

In the 1680s, Lourenço da Silva de Mendouça came to Rome from Brazil. Of mixed African and Portuguese origin, he identified himself as a descendent of the kings of the Kongo and as the current procurator of the Confraternity of Our Lady, Star of the Blacks. Lourenço protested the perpetuating of the slavery of black Christians and of their children of mixed blood and the cruelty of the treatment to which they were subjected. His petition was referred to Propaganda, whose secretary, Archbishop Eduardo Cibo, confirmed the truth of the charges after consulting both Portuguese and Spanish missionaries. On March 6, 1684, the cardinals governing Propaganda condemned both the torture of slaves and the sale of Christian children. The papal nuncios to Portugal and Spain were informed of the decision.

Emboldened by this initiative, the procurator-general of the Capuchins in the Kongo protested to Cibo about the way the Blacks in the Kongo were sold or traded. Cibo drew up a set of propositions putting baldly without qualification the position of the slave traders. He referred to the Holy Office of the Roman and Universal Inquisition the correctness of these theses:

> It is lawful to capture by force or fraud Blacks and other forest creatures harmful to no one.

> It is lawful to buy and sell and make other contracts in respect to Blacks and other forest creatures, harmful to no one and captured by force or fraud.

> Since the Blacks and other forest creatures who have been unjustly captured are mixed in with other justly salable goods, it is lawful to buy all of them or, as they say, the good and the bad alike.

> Buyers of the Blacks or of other forest creatures are not bound to inquire as to the title of their enslavement, that is, as to whether they are justly or unjustly slaves, although the buyers know many of them have been unjustly captured.

On March 20, 1686, the Holy Office replied simply and tersely as to each proposition: "It is not lawful."

Cibo sent the condemnations to the bishops of Angola, Cadiz, Seville, Valencia, and Malaga and to the nuncios to Portugal and Spain, with orders that the condemnations be enforced. Clearly the Holy Office rejected razzias or raids undertaken to procure slaves by kidnapping and did not countenance buying slaves without inquiring how they had been procured. The Roman decisions did not treat enslavement itself as the unlawful treatment of human beings; but these model instructions, if carried out, would have made a substantial dent in the slave trade.

In the background there was a memorandum in Cibo's file, apparently from his brother, Alderano, Innocent XI's secretary of state, dated at the time of the

March 6, 1684, decision and entitled "Instructions for Monsignor Cibo." These instructions noted "America's great need for Blacks, whether for cultivating the land or for work in the mines, for no other people could survive that work or that labor." Evidence exists that in practice the condemnations were not enforced by the ecclesiastical authorities, and the secular authorities were not informed of them. "Don't sell slaves to heretics" was as far as some churchmen would go.

Cambodia and Korea

On September 12, 1776, the Holy Office responded to this question: "May Cambodian Christians buy Laotians even if they have a founded doubt, or know certainly, that these were stolen by theft in their own country?" Giovanni Angelo Braschi, Pope Pius VI, as president of the Holy Office, gave this response: "No, if they were stolen by kidnappers from their lawful owners, for it is wrong to buy stolen property." But the pope went on to say that it was different if the kidnappers had made slaves of free persons. In that case also, the Laotians could not be bought, unless, "fully informed" of their right to freedom, the Laotians preferred slavery under Cambodian Christians to slavery with the kidnappers. If the Laotians so preferred, the Christians could lawfully buy them "at a just price" and keep them in slavery with the intention of bringing them to the Catholic faith; this course, the pope suggested, was defensible "in favor of the faith." Pius VI did not indicate how enslaved Laotians, having been informed by someone—perhaps the would-be Christian purchasers—that they were unjustly enslaved, would be in a position to prefer the Christians as owners. The scenario had the flavor of a strained academic hypothetical. Referring to the favor of the faith, a phrase which seemed to have almost magical power, Pius VI did not explain how the intention to make converts gave the Cambodian Christians the right to keep as their slaves the Laotians who were the victims of kidnapping.

On April 29, 1840, the Holy Office responded to missionaries in Korea with a phrase that had come into use in 1830 when questions about usury were raised in Rome. Here the question was, "May a Christian sell a slave who is of bad character and wants to hear nothing about our holy religion?" The answer: "Provided that he [the slave] is not baptized, he [the Christian] is not to be disturbed." *Non inquietandum* dodged a definitive resolution.

On November 29, 1854, the Holy Office dealt with questions that combined the rules on usury and slavery. The question came from Cambodia, a country where it was reported that the missionaries had long labored to keep Christians from the stain of usury but where "almost one quarter of the population" were enslaved and where the faithful often failed, lending usuriously and taking as security the body of the debtor or that of his wife or the bodies of his children. The questions and answers, here paraphrased, assume the unlawfulness of usury and the lawfulness of slavery:

Question 1: May a Christian lend money and get his debtor's labor as a slave until the debtor has paid the principal? Answer: The Christians should count toward payment of the debt the value of the debtor's labor, less the Christian's expense in maintaining him.

Question 2: May a Christian keep the children of the debtor born during the debtor's slavery and sell them "exactly as if they were born to parents who were true and proper slaves?" Answer: Negative.

Meticulously, the Holy Office rebuffed the thought that the lender could make a profit out of the security and the lender's effort to turn the security interest of a slave's body into more permanent property through selling his offspring. Enslavement itself was uncriticized.

Chattels in Maryland and Louisiana

Around the world, slaves were used by religious orders as labor. Here, for example, is an excerpt from the account given by William Hunter, the Jesuit superior, to the provincial, John Dennett, on the seven principal Jesuit missions in Maryland as of July 23, 1765. Each mission was reported on in Latin in this form:

Mission St. Francis Borgia, popular name White Marsh. Two missionaries. Plantation 1,900 acres, adjoining tracts 700 ditto; distant tracts 700 ditto; Slaves 65, of which 29 working hands viz. 3 within doors, 26 in the fields, the rest children or superannuated.

Collectively, the seven missions owned 192 slaves, of whom 101 worked. The rest were children or too old. Slaves were referred to as "which," not "whom." Field hands greatly outnumbered those working indoors. The report was sent to Father Hilton in Rome. A note in the provincial archives states that there it was "much approved of."

In 1792, six French Sulpicians arrived in Maryland, and one of them, Ambrose Maréchal, leased a former Jesuit parish in Bohemia, where among other business in 1793 he sold "Philis and her infant 3 weeks old" for thirty-five pounds, and a month later sold "Clara, Philis's other child, 4 years old" for five pounds. Maréchal thought the proceeds belonged to the Sulpicians as "profits of the estate," like the crops, the increase of stock, and firewood not fit for building. The Jesuits (organized as regular clergy since their suppression by the pope in 1773) objected: like timber, the Negroes belonged to the landlord. No objection was registered as to the sales, not even that separating Philis and Clara.

In the background was a growing Northern belief in emancipation. Pennsylvania, guided by the Quakers, had started to limit slavery in 1780. In 1814, two Irish Dominicans, who had served in Philadelphia, informed the first archbishop of Baltimore, John Carroll, that the clerical slaveholders of Maryland were "stumbling blocks in the way of their Quaker brethren and of thousands besides among their fellow citizens." The Dominicans carried their complaint to the Congregation for the Propagation of the Faith, then in charge of affairs in the United States. The congregation did nothing.

In time, Maréchal became archbishop of Baltimore and quarreled with the Jesuits over what was diocesan property and what belonged to the Society of Jesus, now restored after its suppression. Maréchal reported to Cardinal Giuseppe Maria della Somaglia, secretary of state and prefect of Propaganda, on January 15, 1826, on "the movable property" of the Jesuits. "They have about 500 African men bound in slavery to them, of whom the mean price is about 200 *scudi*. Therefore their total value is 100,000 *scudi*." Maréchal's next sentence notes the large number of "horses, cows, sheep, etc., etc., etc." on their farms. The number of slaves was disputed by Anthony Kohlmann, S.J., who stated that he could swear the Maryland Jesuits had no more than 240 or 250 slaves, a number appropriate for the number of farms, "since the farms without them are worth nothing." Neither Kohlmann nor Maréchal suspected that there was anything wrong in owning human beings as chattels that had a market price; and neither of them expected the authorities in Rome to be concerned with more than an accurate valuation.

The moral criticism of slaveholding became more public. In 1832, 124 ministers, most of them Congregationalist and most of them in New England, issued a manifesto denouncing slavery as "a great and crying national sin." They called for abolition now. The movement that would end in the Thirteenth Amendment had begun. In the 1830s it consisted of only a small and zealous clerical minority. The Maryland Jesuits, who may have heard of it or felt some criticism generated by it, were no more converted than other Southern slaveholders. They did not believe that slaveholding was a sin.

It was eventually agreed that the Jesuits owed the archbishop of Baltimore a pension of $800 per year, which the Society of Jesus in Rome began to pay. But the Maryland Jesuits were informed that their Dutch General, Johann Philipp Roothaan, wanted them to settle accounts by a lump sum payment. This instruction, converging with other factors, led them to consider selling their slaves. A minority composed of Jesuits mostly from European countries objected: "the blacks . . . are our sons." They were outvoted. Familiarity with the institution bred acceptance, however regretful, of its ways of distributing humans as property.

In 1836, Roothaan sent the rules that should govern the sales. The purchasers must give the slaves free exercise of the Catholic religion and the opportunity of practicing it. Husbands and wives, parents and children, were not to be separated from each other, "to the extent it can be done." It took two years to find buyers because what was looked for was a way of disposing of such a large quantity. Finally two Louisiana planters, Dr. Jesse Beatty and Henry S. Johnson, were found; the latter was a former governor of Louisiana, who had married Elizabeth Key of Maryland. In all, 272 slaves were sold for over $422 per head, a total of $115,000. The down payment was $25,000; the remaining balance was secured by two mortgages on the slaves themselves. Of the cash, $8,000 was paid to the archbishop of Baltimore, $17,000 went to pay off the debts of Georgetown College. The remaining $90,000 was intended to provide an income for the training of young Jesuits. Johnson got into financial trouble and sold his slaves. Both mortgages were still being paid off as late as 1860; it is not clear that they were ever paid in full.

The aversion of the slaves to being sold into the Deep South was known to their masters. The superior, Thomas Mulledy, visited the farms in company with Johnson and the local sheriff to round them up at each location. Approximately a dozen escaped into the woods and were not removed. The rest were sent in three shiploads to New Orleans and from there to Ascension and Iberville Parishes and distributed to two or three big sugar plantations about seventy miles north of New Orleans on the Mississippi River. Their emancipation ensued only with the enactment of the Thirteenth Amendment. At no point had the Congregation for the Propagation of the Faith found any problem in the use, purchase, and sale of human beings by the missions to satisfy an American diocese then under the congregation's direction.

Only if Christianity Is a Lye

On August 8, 1693, at the Monthly Meeting of Friends in Philadelphia, George Keith presented a reasoned and impassioned "Exhortation & Caution." Commonly, the Negroes sold to white men had been kidnapped. To buy "Souls and Bodies" of men for money was "a great hindrance to the spreading of the Gospel." As Revelation 18:13 put it, "Slaves and Souls of Men" were the merchandise of Babylon drawing down God's judgment. Every Christian was implored not to transgress "the Golden Rule and Law, *To do to others what we would have others do to us* and so not to buy Negro slaves" and to keep none "in perpetual Bondage." In this nutshell, a Christian case against slavery was made. The Quakers came to take it up. It took a century to become a force affecting English politics.

Remarkably, it was in the culture of late eighteenth-century England that Jesus's great commandment of love proved victorious over an institution hitherto impervious to its implications. To a casual reader of history and to the larger segment of modern secularists devoted to finding intellectual ancestors, the dates alone proclaim the victory as won by the Enlightenment. But if this superficially solid noun is dismantled and representative persons of the period are examined, the phrase "era of the Enlightenment" fragments into different countries and different men with different ideologies and motivations. As far as slavery is concerned, John Locke, as it were the first philosopher of the Enlightenment and the prime champion of "natural rights," was also a defender of slavery imposed on the aggressors captured in a just war and had no objection to it in the plans for South Carolina of which he was the draftsman. Thomas Jefferson, the most prominent figure in America to bear the burden of Enlightenment, deplored slavery but kept slaves and drew up the Virginia legislation that governed slavery when the colony became a state. James Madison, the enlightened Christian who became the effective champion of religious liberty, was a slaveowner contented to leave the institution as he found it. "Enlightenment" alone did not equate with abolitionism.

Neither England nor France at the time of their colonial expansion in the Americas were slave societies. Their legal structures were not set up to accommodate transactions involving slaves. Yet both England and France had easily accepted slavery in their colonies and formed the legal institutions that would facilitate and govern it. Nonetheless, the homelands, receiving an occasional slave from the Americas, did not turn into slave societies. As empires, each was half free and half slave. It is useful to compare the course of abolition in each.

In the Caribbean, Guadeloupe, Martinique, and Saint-Domingue (all of the present Haiti and the Dominican Republic) had more slaves than colonists. Marseilles and Bordeaux were slave trading posts; Nantes on the western banks of the Loire as it opened into the Atlantic was the French equivalent of Liverpool as a center for capital invested in the trade. The *négriers* ("blacksters" or slave traders) of these towns were men of commercial importance, and commerce with these Caribbean colonies was a large part of France's external entrepreneurial enterprise.

In this context, in 1748, Montesquieu addressed several chapters of *The Spirit of the Laws* to slavery. Speaking first in terms of the types of government, he found slavery compatible with despotism but contrary to the spirit of aristocratic, democratic, and monarchial government. He followed Bodin in rejecting the Roman rationalizations for slavery. He expressly addressed the reasons why the blacks might be enslaved, reciting absurdities and stating with matchless irony: "It is impossible that we should suppose those people to be men, because if we should suppose them to be men, we should begin to believe that we ourselves are not Christians." Yet a certain detachment went with Montesquieu's stance. He did not present himself as an abolitionist. A student of mankind who stressed the influence of climate on manners, he turned to "countries where the heat enervates the body." In such climes, slavery was "against nature" but "may be founded on a natural reason," namely, that difficult work there would be performed only from fear of punishment. The *négriers* could read *The Spirit of the Laws* and believe that climate was their ace of clubs.

A decade later, in 1758, Voltaire placed the protagonist of *Candide* in Dutch Surinam, where he encounters a black man missing his right hand and his left leg. Candide is appalled and asks the explanation. "It's the custom," the Black replies and goes on to say that in a sugar mill, if a finger is caught, the hand is cut off, and, if one flees, a leg is cut off. "It's the price that you may have sugar in Europe." The bland acceptance of the custom of course accentuates the horror of the business, carefully set in a non-French colony. Voltaire does not go beyond standard Christian exhortation against the mistreatment of slaves. A Catholic priest, the Abbé Raynal, had already produced a large geographic history that provided numerous instances of the intolerable cruelties of slavery in the New World.

In his contribution on slavery to *A Philosophical Dictionary* (1765), Voltaire found slavery to be as natural to humankind as war; mocked the Jews as many times slaves; and denied that there was a word of criticism of slavery in the New Testament. His tone accords with that in most of *Candide*, where the hero's beloved Cunegonde is taken captive as a slave by the Bulgarians and is later sold to a Jewish merchant, while her friend, "the old woman," is enslaved by Moslem warriors and repeatedly sold. Slavery is the way the world is organized. Voltaire in his garden is not about to destroy it.

Rousseau wrote against slavery but also against property. His anti-slavery polemic was swallowed up by his general blast at the overarching institution. Kings and priests could become targets of revolution. Property remained sacred. In contrast, the *Encyclopédie* edited by Diderot carefully distinguished property in things from property in persons, found no justification for the latter, and denounced it as "against the rights of peoples and nature" and "repugnant to our religion." In a country where Catholicism was still the state religion, the criticism of slavery drew on natural law, the Gospel, the sixteenth-century critique of Bodin, and anecdotal evidence of the cruelty that marked the system. No practical program of abolition was championed.

In 1788, an attempt was made to meet this lack. Jacques-Pierre Brissot founded La Société des Amis des Noirs, whose principal aim was the abolition of the slave trade. By 1789, it had 141 members, including Lafayette. The Marquis de Condorcet became its director. An English model was in mind but no national campaign was launched. Brissot, idealist, hack writer, and police spy, was executed in 1793 as the Revolution devoured its children. The revolutionary National Assembly—led in this instance by a Catholic priest of Jansenist inclinations, Henri Gregoire—freed the slaves in the colonies in 1794; but the slaves in St. Domingue were already in revolt. The legislature's gesture—dare one say characteristically?—was grand, but no better than a gesture. A decade later, Napoleon rescinded the decree of emancipation. No mass movement against slavery developed in eighteenth-century French political life. France did not finally abolish slavery in its colonies until the revolution of 1848. The French case demonstrates that something more was needed than "the rights of man" to produce the antislavery movement that effectively affected English politics under Pitt.

Daniel Defoe's famous novel conveniently lets the English change be measured: Robinson Crusoe, half German, half English, but the embodiment of English enterprise, is "set up for a Guiney Trader," until he is captured by a Turkish raider and made a slave himself. Escaping, he takes with him as his own slave Xury, a Moorish boy. Rescued by a kind Portuguese captain, he makes his way to Brazil, where he sells Xury to the captain on the understanding that the captain will free the boy in ten years if he becomes a Christian. Crusoe then acquires a small plantation, "a Negro Slave and an European Servant." His neighbors, excited by his tales of trading for Negroes on the Guinea coast, persuade hm to be the supercargo on a 115 ton vessel they outfit to go to Guinea and buy slaves. En route, in September 1659, a storm takes the ship off course and leaves Crusoe on the island where his ingenuity assures his survival. Friday, "my man" or "my servant" as Crusoe sometimes calls him, owes his life to Crusoe and so begins his service by acknowledging himself to be Crusoe's slave and learning to call him "Master." A pious master, Crusoe catechizes Friday. No one in 1719, when the book was published, thought it odd for the hero to be a Guinea trader, a buyer and seller of slaves, and the owner of them. Robinson Crusoe's image was that of a bold, resourceful, admirable entrepreneur. As late as 1919, Virginia Woolf could see the tale as "one of the anonymous productions of the race itself," and few readers have puzzled over its hero's view of slavery. But by the end of the eighteenth century his slave trader past would not have been so prominently presented.

Multiple causes were at work in England. The religious sceptics of the age loosened old assumptions and at the same time challenged Christians to show the sincerity of their convictions. The emphasis of philosophers such as Francis Hutcheson on benevolence was fertile soil for the antislavery evocation of the sufferings of the slaves. The emphasis of empiricists such as David Hume on facts prepared minds to be receptive to investigative journalism. The Industrial Revolution gave increased strength to a middle class sensible to appeals to feeling. It has been argued that when English elites accepted the abolition of the slave trade and, in the next generation, of colonial slavery, they solidified English institutions of social control and the exploitation of free wage-earners—institutions made to look good in comparison with the condition of the unfree. The imputation of self-interest is plausible and difficult to disprove; it has the color of political correctness and the appeal of cynicism. English and Scots self-esteem and the world reputation of Great Britain did benefit from the country's stance on emancipation. Self-interest alone does not explain what happened.

Three observations made in 2001 by the dean of American historians of slavery, David Brion Davis, are pertinent. First, there was nothing unique in New World chattel slavery with one ethnicity enslaving another ethnicity; since the beginning of recorded history, that is the way the world had run. Second, the Atlantic slave trade and the social system it fed "had never appeared so prosperous, so secure, or so full of promise." Third, what was without recorded precedent was "the emergence of a widespread conviction that New World slavery was deeply evil and embodied all the forces that threatened the true destiny of the human race."

No English institution was more jealous of property than the courts. The law was not an invention of the Enlightenment. Yet William Blackstone, publishing in 1765 his great treatise on the common law, declared that English law "abhors and will not endure the existence of slavery within this nation." Although his treatise did not speak of English colonies, his rhetoric reflected detestation of the institution; and he attacked the justifications provided in Roman law. What for centuries had been accepted as obvious by jurists, moralists, and theologians he followed Bodin in denying to be true. War did not create a right to enslave the enemy in perpetuity. "Much less" did war justify the enslavement of the captive's offspring into succeeding generations. War only justified disabling prisoners from "doing harm to us." In 1772, Blackstone's position was strengthened by Lord Mansfield in a case before King's Bench giving James Somerset, a slave brought by his owner from Virginia, his liberty in England when his owner sought to return him to America. An institution whose existence depended on law was now being attacked by those shaping the legal culture of England. In America in 1776, Thomas Jefferson drafting the Declaration of Independence singled out the slave trade as an evil that the Crown had foisted on the colonies—an evil whose denunciation he could suppose would win support in England.

"How is it that we hear the loudest *yelps* for liberty among the drivers of negroes?" Samuel Johnson asked sarcastically of the American revolutionaries; and in July 1776, Johnson became actively interested in the case of Joseph Knight, an African bought in Jamaica and brought to Scotland by his owner. Knight sought his freedom in the Scots' Court of Sessions. Johnson reviewed his advocate's argument, authorized James Boswell "to contribute, in my name, what is proper," and was pleased when the majority of the court held Knight to be free. Johnson thought the case more significant than the case of Somerset, described by him as only holding "that a negro cannot be taken out of the kingdom without his own consent." Johnson's own reflections on the subject were that a human being is naturally free; to prove him a slave you must prove that in some way he forfeited his liberty; that slavery cannot be entailed on a slave's children; that the right of a merchant to sell a slave "never was examined"; that the positive law of Jamaica was "apparently injurious to the rights of mankind"; and that Joseph Knight in Jamaica was "certainly subject by no law, but that of violence, to his present master." Holding this view, he once startled some very grave gentlemen from Oxford with the toast "Here's to the next insurrection of the negroes in the West Indies."

The Oxford startle at the idea that slavery is wrong anticipates Newman by nearly a century; Oxford was conservative by conviction. On the violence that was the law of slavery, Johnson spoke two and a half centuries after Cajetan and two centuries before Orlando Patterson. Each expressed the same judgment.

Boswell recorded Johnson on slavery with the remark "perhaps, he was in the right," but went on with little regard for his mentor to defend the slave trade "so very important and necessary a branch of commercial interest." The trade, he wrote, involved "immense properties" and introduced "African Savages" into "a much happier state of life." Publishing his *Life of Johnson* in 1791 Boswell was reacting to the political efforts then under way to abolish the trade. No doubt he expressed sentiments he thought necessary to mollify some readers of his book. He did not deny or disguise his master's Catonian conclusions. The difference between Boswell's misgivings and Johnson's unqualified condemnations points to the audience abolitionists had to persuade—men of property ready to believe soothing myths but open to considering blunt presentation of the case against slavery made by a master moralist who was at once deeply conservative and deeply Christian.

Central to the English openness to emancipation was the judgment made by the English and Scots legal establishments that slavery was incompatible with the air of a free country and the rejection of the standard centuries-old titles justifying the institution. Add the radical judgment of Dr. Johnson that the slave in the colonies was subject by no law but that of violence and the old legal-moral rationalizations were shattered. Beyond these judgments, energy and zeal were necessary to challenge the bankers and merchants of slave-trading Bristol and Liverpool and the wealthy absentee owners of the slaves in the Caribbean. That energy and zeal came from Christianity.

The Obstinate Hill, Climbed

In 1785, a twenty-five-year-old deacon in the Church of England, a recent graduate of St. John's College, won the Latin Prize of the University of Cambridge by an essay on the question "Is it lawful to enslave the unwilling?" To answer the question he plunged into the work of the American Quaker, Anthony Bezenet, and soon found himself overwhelmed by the horrors of the slave trade. He not only won the prize but found a life vocation, to work for the abolition of the trade and of slavery itself. For the next sixty-one years Thomas Clarkson made this "the business of his life." He did not work alone. Another Anglican, Peter Peckhard, had set the essay question that had set off Clarkson, and Peckhard himself had preached a university sermon entitled "Am I Not a Man and a Brother?" The words were put on a medallion from Josiah Wedgwood's factory as if spoken by an enchained African. The image was eventually distributed by the thousands in Britain as the symbol of the antislavery movement and was even reproduced on snuffboxes, bracelets, and hairpins, ornaments of the prosperous who became converts to the cause. John Wesley was also stirred by Bezenet in 1774 to recognize the evils of slavery. The Methodists, a larger religious minority than the Quakers, were ready to be enlisted by their awakened leader. Evangelical Anglicans, Nonconformists, Quakers provided the political base for the movement that William Wilberforce led in Parliament.

A week before his own death in 1791, Wesley expressed his sense of the mission God had given Wilberforce:

> Unless the divine power has raised you up to be as *Athanasius contra mundum,* I see not how you can go through your glorious enterprise in opposing that execrable villany which is the scandal of religion, of England, and of human nature. . . . Go on, in the name of God and in the power of his might, till even American slavery (the vilest that ever saw the sun) shall vanish away before it.

When Wilberforce and Clarkson began, slavery was lawful in every British colony. As the driving force of the Quaker-organized Committee for the Abolition of the Slave Trade, Clarkson gathered the evidence to move Parliament and did the investigative journalism that reached voters. Before he was done, first the trade, then slavery itself had been abolished in the empire, and Britain had become the moral leader against the international trade throughout the world. For Emerson, with his great man theory of history, the Reformation was "the lengthened shadow" of Luther, "Abolition, of Clarkson." When in 1807 the trade was banned, Wordsworth saluted him:

Clarkson! it was an obstinate hill to climb:
How toilsome—nay, how dire—it was, by thee
Is known; by none, perhaps, so feelingly:
But thou, who starting in thy fervent prime
Didst first lead forth that enterprise sublime,
Hast heard the constant Voice its charge repeat . . .

The trade had been engaged in by Englishmen for two centuries. Slave-produced sugar was the foundation of the prosperity of England's West Indian colonies. The English elite deprecated revolutionary enthusiasm and excesses. Clarkson climbed against this mountain of selfishness, greed, and indifference, attentive to the voice within. The first doctrine of Christianity was brotherly love. Only if "Christianity is a lye," he wrote, could slavery "be acceptable." There could not be "any property whatever in the *human species*," Clarkson stated in his first book. Christianity bound every human being to account to God. Only the free could be accountable. The demonstration was euclidian. When Clarkson committed himself to the cause, he thought: "Never was any cause, which had been taken up by man in any country, or in any age, so great and important . . . never one in which the duty of Christian charity would be so extensively exercised, never one more worthy of the devotion of a whole life towards it." He devoted his whole life to the cause. His devotion showed Christianity to be no lie.

The Pope Is Prompted

The Checkered Continent

Slavery continued to exist in the Papal States into the early nineteenth century. From 1600 to 1800 a total of two-thousand slaves, almost all Moslem, manned the galleys of the pope's navy. As late as 1800–1807 in the troubled papacy of Barnaba Chiaramonti, Pius VII, four privately owned slaves and eleven slaves of the state were registered in Rome at the Casa dei Catecumi. In Lisbon, in 1808, an inquisitor-general defended the justice not only of slavery but of the trade.

Pushed by the British in 1815, the restored French monarchy had taken steps to stop the trade, but public opinion "was sharply divided even among Liberals." Enforcement was spotty. In the fall of 1821, for example, *La Jeune Eugénie,* a slaver registered in Guadeloupe, turned up in Boston, Massachusetts, a prize captured by the navy of the United States. In Paris in 1823, the French Academy made abolition of the trade the subject of its poetry competition—a sign that it was still an issue. Working from an English painting by George Morland, Théodore Géricault prepared a sketch *African Slave Trade,* that, if turned into a finished work, would have equaled his *Medusa* in emotional power. He was an unlikely ally of the Société de la Morale Chrétienne, which also worked against the trade. Emancipation was not on the table.

In the German states, which owned no part of the New World and no longer enslaved the Slavs, a different spirit was abroad. Philosophy was being refashioned by Immanuel Kant. In the light of his fundamental principles, Kant wrote scathingly of the injustice of the Europeans who had taken over "America" and "the lands inhabited by the Negro" as though the lands were without owners and there carried their injustice "to terrifying lengths." In particular he marked the hypocritical piety of the European nations that owned "the Sugar Islands, that place of the most refined and cruel slavery." Persons—never to be used as mere tools or things—had "inborn rights which are inalienable and belong necessarily to humanity."

Some German Catholics were captured by Kant. In Bavaria, Johann Sailer condemned slavery as contrary to "the foundation of all morality," because it made a human being into a means, whereas a human was an end. Slavery made into "a mere thing" one who is a person. The freedom of a person was inalienable. A man could not be sold. On these firmly Kantian principles, Sailer in 1818 went on to say that Christianity "makes it necessary to remove, without revolution, the essence of slavery"; so Christians, following the example of St. Paul, were to treat slaves as brothers. The letter to Philemon became for him a moral precept.

Not coming to grips with the Christian moralists who permitted the buying and selling of human beings, Sailer presented a position easily accepted in a country where there was no slavery. Independent enough in his theology to have his orthodoxy doubted by conservatives, he taught at the Ludwig Maximilian University and was in 1829 made bishop of Regensburg. He wrote in terms so far removed from the tradition of the scholastic moralists that his rejection of slavery was passed by unnoticed by them and by the Roman congregations. It was all the easier for them to ignore because Sailer wrote in German.

Analogously, Catholic laymen like the young Charles de Montalembert were against slavery without changing the theological manuals and curial responses. Most notably, Daniel O'Connell, the champion of the freedom of Ireland, was equally for freedom of Blacks. By his advocacy of abolition, he alienated many of his supporters in the United States. Neither he nor Montalembert carried weight as moral mentors in Rome. Inspiration there was needed from outside the fold.

The British Bid

As early as 1814, in preparation for the Congress of Vienna, Castlereagh, the British foreign secretary, had pressed Cardinal Ercole Consalvi, the pope's secretary of state, to obtain a papal prohibition of the international slave trade. Pius VII responded by writing personally to the monarchs of France, Portugal, and Spain deploring the trade, but published nothing. Consalvi is not recorded as speaking on the subject in 1815 at the Congress of Vienna.

In 1822, the Concert of Europe met to deal with revolution in Spain. A new occasion was provided for British overtures, this time from Foreign Secretary Canning to Secretary of State Consalvi, who referred the matter to the secretary of the Congregation for Extraordinary Ecclesiastical Affairs for examination. The report back was not favorable. True, there was suffering caused by the trade, but abolition was a notion of the antireligious philosophers of the eighteenth century. The most competent theologians and canonists held slavery to be not contrary to natural law and to be approved in principle by the Old Testament. A papal prohibition would please the British, who oppressed Catholics, and it would compromise the colonial interests of France, Portugal, and Spain. Pius VII did nothing.

A Capital Bull

By 1839, Great Britain had extended abolition to its colonies. The country was beginning to shine as the champion of human liberty. Freetown, Sierra Leone— its foundations going back to Granville Sharp in 1787—was now a port where the British navy set down hundreds of slaves liberated from slavers. The cause was not only good domestic politics but a source of prestige and an element of foreign policy. Spain was pushed by Britain into a treaty outlawing the trade. Portugal remained adamant against renouncing it. The British foreign secretary, Henry John Temple, Viscount Palmerston, made suppression of the trade his personal cause. In 1839 the Palmerston Act, passed by Parliament, authorized the British navy to stop all slavers carrying the Portuguese flag, deposit their crews in Portugese territory, and take the rescued Africans for care by British authorities. Palmerston was also pressing the duke of Tuscany not to permit Tuscan transport of African slaves from Tunis to the public slave market of Constantinople. Against this background of vigorous diplomacy and naval intervention, Palmerston thought of the pope.

Thomas Aubin, chargé d'affaires in Rome under the direction of Henry Edward Fox at the British legation in Tuscany, was directed to sound out "the court of Rome" on whether it would cooperate in a move against the slave trade. On May 23, 1839, Aubin reported that he had spoken to Monsignor Capaccini. Francesco Capaccini was a key contact. He had been for nine years of his career the favorite *minutante* or minute-taker of Consalvi, who referred to him as Pupo ("little fellow"). He had advanced to become inter-nuncio to England and Holland and was stationed in London when Bartolomeo Cappellari took office as Gregory XVI. "Papa Cappellari," Capaccini confided to a friend, "loves me as a son," and the pope promoted him to undersecretary of state, Capaccini taking care to stipulate that he be provided a pension lest the pope die before he did. The English request could not have been put in friendlier hands. Consalvi's Pupo was an obliging and reliable man.

Capaccini told Aubin that "the Pope would accede to our wishes with regard to the slave trade but the thing must be brought off in a natural manner (those are his words). He means that some cause should be given to show why the Pope's taken a part in the matter." There would be an objection if it were done "at the request or invitation of a Protestant Government alone." Capaccini suggested that France and particularly Austria be asked to join in the request. Capaccini also looked into canonizations scheduled for the end of the month to see if any of the new saints had helped to liberate a slave, so that the pope could refer to the trade in his allocution; "unfortunately he found none." (Alfonso de'Ligouri, to be canonized May 26, apparently did not furnish the right occasion for a pronouncement on the trade.) Capaccini emphasized that what he told Aubin was his private opinion only, without consultation with the cardinal secretary of state, Luigi Lambruschini; but Aubin was sure that he had cleared what he said with Lambruschini.

On receipt of this intelligence the Foreign Office drafted a note for Aubin to present to Gregory XVI. It asked the pope's aid in "suppression of the African Slave Trade, an object which the British Government is most anxious to accomplish and which is of great importance to all Christendom." The note delicately alluded to "the Christian Church" being "mainly instrumental" in ending slavery as it once existed in the Roman Empire. Modern slavery was much worse. It began with "unprovoked Aggression upon innocent people" and was "undertaken from the cold blooded calculation of gain, the basest motive which can tempt to crime." It inflicted "sufferings of Body and of Mind" beyond the power of tongue to describe. Unfortunately certain governments "in spiritual communion with the See of Rome" were either delaying (Spain was meant), or refusing to cooperate (Portugal) with the British government in suppression of the trade.

The pope was asked for "some further Declaration of the just abhorrence with which His Holiness regards this abominable Crime." Such a declaration would redound greatly to his honor. If it were successful, "the Holy Pontiff would have the unspeakable satisfaction of reflecting that he had rescued from indescribable misery the Hundreds of Thousands of Africans who are annually Victims of this Piratical Trade." It would bring peace to Africa itself; permit normal trade with Europe; end the descent on African coasts of "the fiend-like destroyer," the European slave trader; and open the interior of Africa to the light of Christianity. The note concluded, "Can there be any object more worthy of the Solicitude of the Spiritual Chief of a large section of the Christian community?"

The note was dispatched on June 28, 1839, to Fox in Florence and sent on by him to Aubin in Rome. Aubin translated it into Italian, explaining to his superiors that the cardinal secretary of state did not read English and that Aubin wanted no mistakes in translation and no delay in getting the message before the papal government. On July 12, 1839, he presented it to Lambruschini.

Palmerston appeared to have hit a bull's-eye. With signs of his own agreement, Lambruschini told Aubin that he would bring it before the pope the next day. The receptivity of the cardinal was remarkable. Austria and France had not joined in the request. The Foreign Office had failed to furnish any plausible reason for the pope to be suddenly concerned about the trade. True, the Holy See was at odds with the anticlerical governments of Portugal and Spain, so their influence was at a low ebb. True, the pope, precariously ruling his secular domain, could value the British government as a friend. Still, the sudden willingness to intervene was startling.

The pace then slowed. On October 18, 1839, Fox was told to instruct Aubin to press for an answer. Palmerston also decided to send reinforcements in the person of England's leading abolitionist, Thomas Foxwell Buxton. The British government thought it desirable not to publicize Buxton's mission, and it was cloaked as a trip for the health of Buxton's wife.

On December 12, 1839, Buxton arrived in Rome. Asked by customs to declare his purpose, Buxton imagined that an honest answer would have been:

> If the truth I must tell, I came here in the hope
> Of curing my wife and converting the Pope.

But the curia had not been inactive. Unlike previous occasions, the full membership of the Congregation for Extraordinary Ecclesiastical Affairs considered the request. The *ponenza*, the rapporteur's statement of the question for the cardinals, reported that "the most competent among the authors and theologians" refuted the arguments in favor of slavery and the slave trade. But the pope was not about to become an abolitionist. It was only one year since the Jesuits had sold their slaves in Maryland to the buyers from Louisiana, so even some commerce in human beings was acceptable. Still, the pope was not insensitive to the role Great Britain invited him to play and to the power of Great Britain in public affairs. With Capaccini and Lambruschini already aboard, the pope thought that he could say something on the trade. The cardinals focused on what form the prohibition should take. There was agreement that it should not appear to be done on the initiative of the British. A public declaration, addressed to no one in particular, was decided on.

On November 3, 1839, Aubin saw Lambruschini again, who told him that "circumstances he could not prevent" had stalled the pope's response. Now everything was decided except the form and the wording. On December 6, 1839, Gregory XVI issued *In supremo Apostolatus fastigio*—"At the Supreme Summit of the Apostolate," opening words calling attention to the pope's authority rather than to the subject under scrutiny. Published in Rome as a pamphlet, the document was given a title that tried gamely to find a Latin equivalent of the standard European term for the international traffic out of Africa, "the trade" or "la traite"; the editor could do no better than *De Nigritarum Commercio non exercendo*—"On Not Exercising the Trade in Blacks." The pope wrote to unspecified addressees to dissuade the faithful "from the inhuman trade in Blacks or any other kind of men." The early Christians, the pope declared, treated their slaves as brothers. Eventually several Christian nations had no slaves. But some of the faithful, led by filthy lucre, reduced Blacks and other poor folk to slavery or did not hesitate to help the crime of trafficking in them. The pope mentioned measures of Paul III, Urban VIII, and Benedict XIV against enslaving the Indians, the letter of Pius II against enslaving Christian converts on the Canary Islands, and Pius VII's letter to the three European monarchs on the trade. Christians, however, still engaged in "that inhuman traffic." Gregory XVI strictly prohibited it and ordered the prohibition to be posted in Rome.

As a commentary on a commerce still alive in Portugal, thriving in Brazil, and widespread in Africa, the pope's letter furnished none of the gruesome detail that Clarkson or contemporary missionaries might have supplied. It gave an unrealistic account of early and medieval Christianity. It referred to papal actions without acknowledging their limited scope. The prohibition, when it was announced, was not anchored in natural law or in the Gospel. A theologically literate reader would see that with these remarkable omissions there are what a modern observer accurately notes as "ambiguities and silences." The pope stigmatized the trade as "inhuman" without developing an argument. As a performance, *In supremo* can profitably be compared with *Mirari vos*, an encyclical discussed below in chapter 21, in which Gregory XVI warmed to the task of denouncing liberties he saw as perilous. Yet the letter satisfied Buxton—"a capital bull hurling the Vatican thunders in excellent style"—and it enraged the Portuguese minister to the Holy See, who without waste of time blamed the British.

No one in the papal government expressed surprise or regret that it had taken a Protestant power with a highly pragmatic foreign minister to lead the pope into repudiating a traffic that had flourished since the fifteenth century. At the Foreign Office *In supremo* was received with satisfaction: "My dear Aubin, You have done very well and we are extremely satisfied with the Wisdom and Goodness of His Holiness on this occasion." The Foreign Office was happy not to take credit. If the apostolic letter were "too openly shown to be the consequence of Protestant application," this knowledge "might sensibly weaken its effect." The Foreign Office thought it might have to take the initiative in disseminating it in Spain and Portugal, nations with which the Court of Rome was not on terms. In South America, especially in Brazil and Mexico, the Foreign Office trusted it would be sent to the bishops and the clergy and have an impact. In the United States, "a strong and salutary effect" was expected.

The Qualified Reception

In supremo did cause minor ripples in the United States. It was read aloud by abolitionists in Faneuil Hall, Boston, and Gregory XVI was cheered—probably the first cheers for a pope in Boston. During the presidential campaign of 1840, Secretary of State John Forsyth, writing on behalf of the Democrats to his old constituents in Georgia, linked William Henry Harrison, the Whig candidate, to abolitionism and to the Catholic Church. Forsyth cited Gregory XVI's pronouncement as a condemnation of the sale of slaves in America. He was answered by John England, bishop of Charleston, the leading Catholic prelate in the United States, an immigrant from Cork and bishop of a see embracing North Carolina and Georgia as well as South Carolina. Bishop England indignantly noted that the pope had in view only the international trade; he quoted Gregory XVI himself as telling him in person in Rome that the Southern states "have not engaged in the negro traffic." Bishop England went on in a series of articles in his newspaper, the *Catholic Miscellany*, to show that the Catholic Church had always accepted domestic slavery; it was "not incompatible with the natural law"; and, when title to a slave was justly acquired, it was lawful "in the eye of Heaven."

In 1843, in his treatise on moral theology, Francis P. Kenrick defended the institution of slavery in the United States, going so far as to argue that any defect in title to slaves in this country was cured by prescription: the passage of time made it too late to challenge the owner's assertion of ownership. Commenting in 1851 on Scripture, Kenrick came to St. Paul's letter to Philemon, always a litmus test for detecting the commentator's true view of slavery. For this commentator, it was not a summons to Christians to back emancipation but "evidence that the Gospel is not directed to disturb the actual order of society by teaching men to disregard their obligations, however severe their enforcement may appear." In a footnote, Kenrick acknowledged there "may be an intimation of the hope that Philemon may manumit Onesimus." Kenrick's main point was that the Gospel "does not indulge vain theories of philanthropy to the prejudice of the social order." So difficult it was to comprehend the Gospel's message of love; so difficult to see the slave as made in God's image and a brother.

Kenrick was a secular priest from Ireland, educated in Rome twenty-five years earlier at the college conducted by the Congregation for the Propagation of the Faith. His *Theologia moralis,* written in Latin and evidently designed to educate seminarians, was the first textbook on Catholic moral theology produced in the United States; he was bishop of Philadelphia when it appeared. He commented on the letter to Philemon in the year Pius IX promoted him to be archbishop of the primatial see of Baltimore, and he presided as apostolic delegate at the First Plenary Council of the bishops of the United States in 1852. His views were those of his colleagues and of the Roman authorities. The trade out of Africa was one thing; slavery as an institution was quite another.

Gregory XVI's letter had no obvious impact on the two nominally Catholic countries engaged in the slave trade, Portugal and Brazil, nor on seminary teaching in France. Three years later, under the pressure of the effective enforcement of the Palmerston Act, Portugal by treaty with Great Britain abolished the trade. Earlier, in 1830, Britain had also persuaded Brazil to abolish the trade, but Brazilian cooperation was so uncertain and sporadic that in 1845 Lord Aberdeen obtained a law, modeled on the Palmerston Act, authorizing the royal navy to seize Brazilian slave ships, with the result that the Brazilian slave trade came to an end in 1850–1851. *In supremo* had taken away any claim to moral legitimacy. It was British resolution and sea power that brought a stop to the business.

Emancipators' Éclat

Berlin

Islam condemned neither slavery nor the slave trade, and slave trading and slavery continued in Africa. The Anti-Slavery Society in London kept itself and the issue alive. When, in 1884, Bismarck called a conference of European powers to deal with the Congo, the British saw a new opportunity to burnish their reputation and to do good. Sir Julian Pauncefort, permanent undersecretary of state for foreign affairs, wrote George Granville, the foreign secretary:

> This country is not likely to gain or lose anything by the Conference. The 'éclat' of it, such as it is, will appertain to Germany. It has occurred to me that G. Britain might carry off all the honors of the meeting by being the first to propose (on so fitting an occasion) an international Declaration in relation to the *traffic in slaves* (la Traite) as distinguished from the institution of Slavery, making it a crime against the *Law of Nations*.

Pauncefort continued:

> "If the Powers sh obj to the generality of that Declaration, we might propose to restrict it to Africa. . . . the honor and credit of proposing either

Declaration . . . should be reserved to this country—and . . . no time sh be lost in apprising Prince Bismarck of our intention to propose such a Declaration otherwise we may be forestalled.

Great Britain took the initiative and succeeded in securing a declaration that the maritime slave trade be forbidden by international law and that operations on water or on land which furnished slaves for this commerce be also forbidden.

The Perspective of a Poet

The Foreign Office's perspective was not shared by all educated Englishmen, not even by the finest poet in the British Isles. In 1885, Bede's perspective on Gregory the Great's reaction to Anglo-Saxon slaves was retained by Gerard Manley Hopkins, who celebrated the scene in the slave market at the beginning of the papal mission to England. The encounter of Gregory and the beautiful boys is described in these lines that betray no uneasiness about slavery except a desire to see it as serving God's plan:

> Master more may gaze, gaze out of countenance
> Those lovely lads once, wet-fresh, windfalls of war's storm.
> How then should Gregory, a father, have gleaned else from swarm-
> ed Rome? But God to a nation dealt that day's dear chance.

Hopkins's lines answer the question posed in the title of his poem—"For What Serves Mortal Beauty?" The enslavement of the English was part of Providence's design for the evangelization of the English. Gregory was a father, not a market browser or buyer. What was not known as a sin in the Rome of 590 was not known as a sin to an Oxford-educated English Jesuit of the second half of the nineteenth century. Like Newman, Hopkins had no notion that he was looking at an intrinsically evil institution.

A Great Crusade

The Berlin Conference had taken no notice of the pope. But the British example was not lost on Charles Martial Allemand-Lavigerie, the French archbishop of Algiers. Lavigerie was the founder of the White Fathers, who had established missions near Lakes Victoria and Tanganyika and had seen the work of the Arab slave traders. As early as 1878 Lavigerie had addressed to Rome a memoranda on this evil, calling for "a great crusade of faith and humanity, which would reclaim honor for the Church" and "crown the immortal papacy of Pius IX." Rome made no response. But in 1882, the new pope, Gioacchino Vincenzo Pecci, Leo XIII, made Lavigerie a cardinal, and Lavigerie dreamed that the new pope would see the opportunity for action.

In 1888, Leo XIII agreed that a suitable occasion had arisen. In 1888, Brazil, the last theoretically "Catholic" nation in which slavery was legal, abolished the institution. On May 5, 1888, the pope issued *In plurimis,* addressed to the bishops of Brazil, congratulating them on "this happy event," which was "so full of the spirit of Christian mercy." Quoting Gregory I and Augustine, the pope observed that God created human beings free, but that, as a penalty for sin and by the law of nations, human beings had been enslaved. The Church ameliorated the condition of slaves by Paul's teaching that in Christ Jesus there was neither slave nor free and by "clearly defining and strongly enforcing the rights and mutual duties of masters and slaves." The pagan attitude toward slavery was "marked by great cruelty and wickedness," the Christian attitude "by great gentleness and humanity." The Church had deprecated "any precipitate action." But "with what prudence the Church cut out and destroyed this dreadful curse of slavery!" The popes, beginning with Gregory I, "did their best for the slaves." Near the end of the fifteenth century "the base stain of slavery had been nearly blotted out" in Europe, and the Apostolic See "took the greatest care that the evil germs of such depravity should nowhere revive," especially not in Africa, Asia, and the Americas. In contrast to the Catholic record, the Moslems even today were engaged in the slave trade in Africa, so that "each year 400,000 Africans are regularly sold like cattle." Apostolic men were urged to work for the liberty of these slaves and to take as their model the Jesuit canonized by Leo on January 15, 1888: Pedro Claver, the missionary who had labored at Cartagena, the principal slave market in South America.

Leo XIII offered no evidence that Christian slavery was different from pagan slavery. He cited the *Institutes* of Justinian to show that slaves were in the power of their masters, without observing how Justinian proclaimed his devotion to Christianity. He noted that slaves had duties to masters, an implicit acceptance of the institution. He accepted the patristic teaching that slavery was a penalty for sin without explaining how the penalty was visited upon the innocent upon birth to a slave mother. He cited letters of the popes rebuking isolated instances of slave trading without mentioning the popes who authorized the kings of Portugal and Spain to invade and enslave the unbelievers. He held up Pedro Claver as a model identifying him as "the Apostle of the Moors," a phrase quaintly marking as Moors the slaves brought from Africa. Leo did not remark that St. Pedro criticized neither slavery nor the slave trade. Picking up Lavigerie's information on the Moslem slave traders, he commented caustically on them without conceding that his own predecessors, including Gregory I, had bought human beings as slaves. Leo wrote without regard to past involvement in the institution by Christians, the religious orders, the bishops, and the popes.

Describing the decline of humankind into the practice of slavery, Leo spoke of men "keeping no account of their common nature, nor of human dignity, nor of the divine likeness expressed therein" and making war, from which there resulted two parties, "the conquered slaves under the conquering masters." It has recently been argued that this passage was a denunciation of slavery in principle. The passage did open the way to this development. By the time of the Second Vatican Council, "human dignity" was a powerful criterion. But in the context of the encyclical, this passage read as historical narrative about the evils that sinful human nature brought about. It was not read by the moral theologians as a radical rejection of an institution accepted for over eighteen hundred years. Leo labeled the institution "base" and "cruel." He did not condemn it as intrinsically evil.

Two weeks after the issue of *In plurimis,* Lavigerie presented to the pope a group of Arabs and Blacks who had been rescued from enslavement by being purchased from their owners and freed. In a private audience that followed, Leo XIII, according to Lavigerie, authorized him to preach a Christian crusade against the horrors of the slave trade. Lavigerie committed himself "to give a great cry," a cry which would reach "anyone still worthy of the name of human being and the name of Christian."

The Anti-Slavery Society in London was the only existing organization in Europe concerned with the topic. The society and Lavigerie made contact, and he spoke in London, Paris, Brussels, Fribourg, and Naples and took the lead in organizing seven local antislavery societies, aided by a gift on October 17, 1888 from Leo XIII of three hundred thousand francs. In a letter to Lavigerie accompanying the gift, the pope congratulated him "on safeguarding in so many of our brothers the dignity of the human person." The last six words struck a note that was to become, in the twentieth century, a central theme of Catholic theology.

In September 1890, a meeting of the antislavery societies in Paris led Lavigerie to present their resolutions to the pope, who responded on November 20, 1890, with a new letter, *Catholicae Ecclesiae,* addressed to Catholic missionaries in Africa. The pope announced a collection to be made annually on the feast of the Epiphany to raise money to help missions "primarily to eliminate slavery in Africa." He noted cautiously that "even if the collection is small, the burden spread among many people will make it lighter for all." The call for the collection was a pledge of papal support. The main thrust of the letter was announced in its opening words by which it would be known: it trumpeted the role of the Catholic Church as "from the beginning having sought to eliminate slavery completely." Twelve popes were named as applying "every effort to eliminate the institution of slavery wherever it existed." No citations to their efforts were supplied. Leo XIII did not see the need to establish the truth of what he so triumphantly and so inaccurately claimed.

As matters turned out, neither pope nor cardinal did very much more against slavery. Leo went on to use Lavigerie chiefly as his agent in persuading French Catholics who were monarchists to accept the Third Republic. Leo himself found his words on slavery a bridge to a subject where his contribution was more substantial: the rights of labor. Addressing a letter to a Swiss society of workers in 1893, Leo evoked his image of the antislavery activity of the Church as an augury of what the Church could now do "to rescue workers" from exploitation.

Gordian Knots Cut

Neither *In plurimis* nor *Catholicae Ecclesiae* appeared to have any effect on the Roman congregations dealing with slavery in Africa and Asia, nor on the moral theologians who analyzed the morality of slavery. Rulings judged pertinent to the missions were published in 1907 by the Congregation for the Propagation of the Faith, the Roman bureau in charge of missionary activity. The collection went back to the founding in 1622 of the congregation. The collection was not intended as archival material contributing to the historical record. What was published, the preface said, was information that "laborers for the Gospel should find helpful, indeed powerfully helpful." The rulings, the preface suggested, "cut Gordian knots" and dealt with difficulties ignored by learned treatises. The collection, in fact, had something of the flavor of an advice column in a newspaper, the identities of the parties being replaced by conventional names and the advisor putting brevity and firmness of advice over elaboration and reasoning.

The collection included the responses on slavery already noted as given from the seventeenth through the nineteenth century. Without exception, the Roman congregations had assumed that slavery in itself was a morally acceptable institution. On June 20, 1866, about the time of the Thirteenth Amendment and shortly after Father Newman's exchange with Thomas Allies on the intrinsic evil of slavery, the Holy Office answered a variety of questions raised by Guglielmo Massaia, vicar apostolic to the Galla in East Africa. The questions as to slavery were preceded by Massaia's observation that slavery among these people was so related to social status that "it is almost impossible to create and maintain a household without slaves" and that slaves "serve as a principal material of commerce" and "as currency," in that, by law or by order of the ruler, slaves had to be accepted like money in payment of a debt. The Holy Office replied with the general reassurance that, although the popes had left nothing untried by which slavery might be abolished, slavery per se was not repugnant to natural law or to divine law, and it answered several questions along the lines it had already done in 1776 apropos of the Cambodians, including the remarkable proposition that victims of kidnapping could be kept as slaves if, advised that they were rightly free but unable to free themselves, the victims presented themselves for sale to Christian masters who might evangelize them; again the Holy Office judgment was reached "with respect for the privilege of the faith." I select and paraphrase several of the new queries and replies:

Question 1: What is the status of a fugitive slave? Answer: If the slave was unjustly enslaved or is inhumanly treated, the slave may escape. If the enslavement was just, all profit from the slave's labor belongs to the slave's master, and the fugitive slave is guilty of theft. Christians, including the missionaries, may pursue fugitives from enslavement that was just and may return them to slavery.

Question 2: The laws of the Galla give the master power of life or death over a slave. May a Christian or a Christian missionary kill his bad slave? Answer: Sell him, don't kill him. If he's baptized, don't sell him to infidels. And, as an aside from the Holy Office, it causes wonder that a missionary would think of killing his slave.

Question 3: What should a Christian owner do about a male and female slave who live together in a sexual relation and cannot contract marriage for life, as they are at any time separable by their masters by reason of their slave status? Answer: Don't be sure that it's not a true marriage; but if it's not, and they refuse to marry, separate them by force. That goes for infidels, too, for fornication is forbidden by the natural law.

The firmness on fornication made a nice contrast to the Holy Office position on profit from labor of a slave. The Holy Office also noted that one should not sell a slave to a trader in "that most iniquitous commerce" especially denounced and strictly prohibited by Gregory XVI.

Two responses of the Holy Offices relative to the Pauline privilege, one response made before Leo XIII issued *In plurimis* and one issued thereafter, reflect the matter-of-fact way the Roman Curia encountered social situations in countries where slavery existed. In the first response, November 22, 1871, for Siam, the case presented two pagans, Titius and Lola, who were married and divorced. Lola then married Brutus. Titius married Fotilla. Later, this couple were baptized. To establish his right to exercise the Pauline privilege, Titius had to ask his first wife, Lola, if she would be willing to live peacefully with him; he discovered that Brutus had sold her as a slave. Lola informed Titius that if he redeemed her from slavery and took her back, she would become a Christian. Titius represented that he was too poor to buy Lola, as well as unwilling to give up Fotilla. Must he remain unmarried? No, the Holy Office answered, he can use the Pauline privilege and marry Fotilla. Implicit in the decision was the assumption that Titius was not bound to his first wife because he could treat her enslavement as equivalent to her refusal to return.

In the second answer, for Victoria in Nyasaland dated July 8, 1891, three years after Leo's *In plurimis* and one year after *Catholicae Ecclesiae,* the Holy Office was asked about a pagan husband who himself had sold his first wife as a slave. He was now baptized and wanted to marry someone else. He represented that he was unable to obtain his first wife's freedom. Was he eligible to use the Pauline privilege and take a second wife in Christian marriage? The answer was Yes, as long as it was clear that he had sold his first wife before he was baptized.

It would be difficult to discern in these phlegmatic administrative rulings any sense that slavery in itself was an affront to human dignity or that Christians should not be enslavers. The Congregation for the Propagation of the Faith in 1907 apparently thought the teaching still relevant and useful.

The moral theologians were equally unaware that *In plurimis* marked a change in the centuries-old position of the Church on slavery. Near the start of the twentieth century Arthur Vermeersch published in Bruges his treatise *Quaestiones de iustitia.* Vermeersch, then a young Jesuit, was to become in time *the* Jesuit moralist in Rome, a man of intellectual penetration and moral weight. In his youthful analysis of questions of justice, he discussed the right of a workingman to be paid enough to support a family. After defending "the family wage," he raised a problem: "You ask, How slavery by which human work is done for nothing, is not strictly repugnant to nature?" Surely a slave was denied a family wage. Vermeersch's answer: Nature "has not neglected to provide for the slave; because the slave is co-opted into the family of the owner, the latter is compelled to provide fit food for his children and wife." The answer, perfect in its ignoring the legal and economic realities of slavery, made sense only for an author who did not care to disturb the moral theology of his predecessors.

The new *Code of Canon Law*, published in 1917, maintained the positions set out in the old law that a free person contracting marriage with one believed to be free but in fact a slave contracted invalidly; and that slavery was an impediment to the reception of holy orders. The law establishing slavery in the regions where it still existed was still strong enough to trump a Christian's reception of the sacraments of matrimony and orders.

In 1960, on the eve of the Second Vatican Council, Tommaso Iorio, an Italian Jesuit, published in Naples the fifth edition of his *Theologia moralis*. Tract X treated "Justice and Law." Iorio defined slavery as "a state of perpetual subjection in which one is bound to furnish all his work to another in exchange for support." Was it against the law of nature? No. As Lugo had explained in the seventeenth century, there were four ways one was justly enslaved: by contract, selling oneself; by the law of war; by condemnation for a crime; and by birth from a slave. *Per accidens*, slavery was unlawful if it separated spouses, and today, generally, it was unlawful by secular law and, "the Church agreeing," has "on account of innumerable abuses" been abolished. Iorio found no text by which the Church or any pope condemned slavery outright or proclaimed its intrinsic evil.

Also close to the era of Vatican II, Karl Rahner, the preeminent Jesuit theologian, published the thirtieth edition of "Denzinger." This authoritative and convenient handbook, first produced in 1854 by Heinrich Denzinger, S.J., bore the title *Enchiridion symbolorum definitionum et declarationum de rebus fidei et morum* and contained the teaching of popes and councils from Clement I in the first century to the date of the edition. It presented, for example, ten distinct condemnations of usury or usurious transactions up to the "*non inquietandum*" of 1830. Not a single word repudiating or condemning slavery occurred in the collection. The éclat of fostering emancipation had not generated enough papal activity to warrant a citation. *In plurimis* and *Catholicae Ecclesiae* were unmentioned; so was *Sublimis Deus*. No antislavery legacy was significant enough to be recalled by Rahner.

Two leading American Jesuit moralists, John C. Ford and Gerald Kelly, did publish in Maryland in 1963, as the Second Vatican Council was in progress, the second volume of their treatise on moral theology in English. They characterized "chattel slavery" as "utterly repugnant" to natural law. Apparently by qualifying slavery as "chattel slavery" they intended to distinguish what they condemned from the slavery accepted by their predecessors. They did not, however, cite the earlier authorities, nor did they define chattel slavery to show it did not exist in first-century Rome or fifteenth-century Florence or nineteenth-century Maryland. They did not remark that their position marked a major mutation in moral doctrine. They were revolutionaries without knowing it. Their unawareness of any change made a striking contrast to John Ford's resistance to any development of doctrine on contraception, a resistance fueled by the conviction that major mutations in moral theology could not occur. It would not have been likely to occur to these two authors that the council was about to seal, without palaver, the change that they had unwittingly endorsed.

The Sin Perceived, Categorized, Condemned

Vatican II did make the mutation, but not with fanfare and trumpets, not after a bitter theological battle, not as a conscious correction of the old theology. By 1960, everyone knew that slavery was bad. When the term was applied to European conditions it referred to the Nazis' enslavement of persons in the countries they had occupied or to the Soviet Union's gulags. The evils of these institutions and of the practice of slavery in the few corners of the world where it existed were not controversial issues. In the preparatory work for the council, no text was prepared addressing the Church in the world; a fortiori, no text dealt with slavery. Only after the first session of the council, on January 30, 1963, was a committee set up to draft teaching on the Church's promotion of the social good. At the end of the second session, there was no satisfactory draft. A subcommittee charged Bernard Häring, C.SS.R., and other experts on morals to take on the task. Their text was presented to the fourth session as *Gaudium et spes,* a "Pastoral Constitution on the Church in the World of This Time." The document listed as "shameful" (*probra*) "whatever is hostile to life itself, such as any kind of homicide, genocide, abortion, euthanasia and voluntary suicide; whatever violates the integrity of the human person, such as mutilation, physical and mental torture and efforts to coerce rational minds themselves; whatever is offensive to human dignity, such as subhuman living conditions, arbitrary imprisonments, deportations, prostitution, trading in women and children; and degrading conditions of work which treat laborers as mere instruments for profit and not as free responsible persons." "All these things," the draft said, "while they infect human civilization, stain more those who carry them out than those who suffer the injury; and they especially are contrary to the honor of the Creator."

Slavery was not among the offenses denominated. On the initiative of nine Fathers, an amendment was proposed that added it. The drafting commission adopted the amendment, placing "slavery" (*servitutis*) without definition, elaboration, or explanation after "deportations." The amended text was distributed to the council on December 2, 1965, six days before the end of the fourth and final session. The whole amended text was adopted by a vote of 2,391 to 75 and promulgated by Paul VI on December 7. In the context provided by some of the other evils enumerated, such as "arbitrary imprisonments" and "deportations," it was modern state slavery that was in the draftsmen's minds. But along with slavery were condemned three other accompaniments of any slave system—prostitution; the trading of women and children; and the treatment of laborers as mere instruments for profit and not as free responsible persons. All such acts were reprobated as offenses to human dignity.

"Shameful" was not the strongest of theological epithets. It was weaker than "evil" and much weaker than "intrinsically evil." Nonetheless, put in the same box with homicide and genocide, slavery was comprehensively condemned.

Still in the twentieth century there was a problem of vocabulary. Unlike "murder" or "adultery," which describe identifiable actions, *servitutis* in Latin or "slavery" in English is ambiguous. It indicates a state in which a person is held or the rule of those holding slaves. It is an odd ambiguity, designating both the condition of subjection and the practice imposing the condition. "Enslavement" embraces the initial act of aggression against another person but it does not encompass habitual ownership. "Slaveholding" can be used as a noun to describe the action of ownership in a phrase such as "He engaged in the sin of slaveholding." The phrase lacks the pungency packed into "murder" or "adultery." The Latin equivalent is not evident.

The council's action was the first categorical condemnation by the Church of an institution that the Church had lived with for over nineteen hundred years. The development of doctrine, John Courtney Murray wrote at the time, "is *the* underlying issue of the Council." No one at the time marked the development accomplished by the condemnation of slavery.

The teaching of the council was completed, in time, by the *Catechism of the Catholic Church,* a compendium of doctrine prepared by a committee of seven diocesan bishops under the supervision of a commission of fifteen cardinals, chaired by Cardinal Josef Ratzinger, the head of the Congregation for the Doctrine of the Faith. The work began in 1986, and the draft was commented on by "numerous theologians, exegetes and catechists" and submitted to all the bishops of the world before being formally approved by John Paul II on June 25, 1992. Under the heading "The Doctrinal Value of the Text," the pope declared it "a sure norm for teaching the faith."

The plan of the catechism required various virtues and vices to be treated under one of the Ten Commandments, thereby tying Christian moral life to its Hebraic roots and God's covenant with Israel. Under which commandment did the prohibition of slavery fall? It was not an easy question to answer. In the end, the catechism chose the seventh commandment as follows in a teaching numbered 2,414:

> The seventh commandment forbids acts or enterprises that for any reason—selfish or ideological, commercial or totalitarian—lead to the enslavement of human beings, to their being bought, sold and exchanged like merchandise, in disregard of their personal dignity. It is a sin against the dignity of persons and their fundamental rights to reduce them by violence to their productive value or to a source of profit. St. Paul directed a Christian master to treat his Christian slave "no longer as a slave but more than a slave, as a beloved brother . . . both in the flesh and in the Lord."

Paul's letter to Philemon, sometimes in the past used to justify slavery, was now given paradigmatic force against slavery. The commandment against theft, once used by some theologians to forbid a slave to escape, was now treated as the most relevant commandment against slavery. The text condemned acts that led to enslavement, thereby staying within the commandment against theft and using language that did not address enslavement by the state. Unconscious irony abounded, as did awkwardness. Protection of property was enlarged to protection of the person. Awkwardness was hardly avoidable when support for the condemnation of enslavement was sought among commandments two of which had given divine approval to the institution.

A Better Comprehension

On February 2, 1992, on the island of Gorée, Senegal, where France once collected slaves for its Caribbean colonies, John Paul II was received at the former "House of slaves." The pope spoke these words:

It is fitting that there be confessed in all truth and humility this sin of man against man, this sin of man against God. How long is the road the human family has to run before its members learn to regard each other and respect each other as the image of God, so that they may finally love each other as the sons and the daughters of the heavenly Father.

What this confession did not remark was how recently the sin had been discovered.

In 1993, in *Veritatis splendor*, John Paul II saluted the *Catechism of the Catholic Church* as "a complete and full exposition of Christian moral teaching." In the same encyclical he used Vatican II's list of offenses against human dignity to illustrate the intrinsically evil, the acts incapable of being ordered to God. In the pope's presentation an offense to human dignity was intrinsic to the act of slaveholding. As already seen in chapter 1, the pope's teaching was that always and everywhere slavery is sinful.

The old teaching of the Church on slavery taught that masters should allow their slaves the opportunity to practice religion and to marry and to perform the sexual duties of marriage. The Church taught that manumission was an act of charity so that being free was better than being slave. The offenses to human dignity that the Church did not condemn included the buying, selling, hypothecating, inheriting, and owning of human beings; the use of slave labor without any measure of just compensation; the denial to slaves of education, including instruction in reading and in writing, and the denial to slaves of the right to educate their children; the denial to slaves of any right to a religious vocation or to the sacrament of holy orders; the denial to slaves of the full range of conjugal companionship and protection; the denial of any right to personal development; and the complete exclusion of the slave from the political community. According to the teaching of John Paul II, all these denials and exclusions would be serious sins today. They were not denominated so by any magisterial document before the recent development of doctrine.

No special consciousness of the development in this matter was shown by the pope, who cited none of the old authorities approving the institution. Of moral theologians after St. Thomas, the pope mentioned only Ligouri, and then only peripherally. On the obligation to seek the truth he quoted Newman, "the distinguished defender of the rights of conscience," so Newman, the defender of development, was in his mind. John Paul himself spoke of the popes' efforts in the nineteenth and twentieth centuries to expound moral doctrine. "Fortified by the help of the Holy Spirit to a better comprehension of moral requirements in sexual matters and in familial, social, economic, and political matters, they have spoken. By their teaching, the continuous investigation of moral knowledge belongs to the tradition of the Church as it belongs to the history of the human race." Not in specific re-examination and reprobation of the old doctrine on slavery but in the broadest terms, the papal message endorsed the deepening of doctrine in morals. No better example was provided than the new teaching of the council, the new catechism, and the pope himself on slavery.

Neither the action of Vatican II, nor the teaching of the *Catechism,* nor the encyclical of the pope occasioned surprise or scandal among Catholics. The Church had always been against slavery. So thought that improbable stereotype, the average Catholic. No doubt most Catholics had been against slavery for a long time—at least since 1888 in Brazil and since 1865 in the United States and longer still in parts of Europe. In the recent formal condemnations the magisterium came into harmony with the thinking of the body of the faithful.

Only among persons with reason to be specially concerned with the legacy of slavery was the change remarked. Notable among them were the Spiritans, the French missionary congregation that had labored in Africa and Cambodia. Their journal in 1999 published a special issue on the Church and slavery. As to the Church's past condemnations mentioned by Gregory XVI, an article asked, "What condemnation?" The issue as a whole bore the title *L'esclavage négation de l'humain*—Slavery, the negation of the human. Neither Leo XIII nor Gregory XVI, neither St. Thomas Aquinas nor St. Augustine, not even St. Paul himself would have dared to define the sin so powerfully and so exactly.

INTRINSIC EVIL

Unnatural Reproduction

The Triple Contract

On June 22, 1573, a commission of Jesuit provincials and theologians, meeting in Rome, issued a decision to guide all Jesuit confessors, preachers, and moralists in their treatment of the so-called "German contract" or "5 percent contract," whereby five percent was charged on money advanced to another person. Generically, the contract was a loan from which profit was made; as such it was usurious and therefore morally unlawful, the commission ruled. Analysis showed that there was a way of looking at it that made it right. A contract of partnership in which the capitalist got a return on the capital he invested was perfectly legitimate. Say he could reasonably expect 10 percent. Then suppose he entered a contract of insurance guaranteeing the return of his principal and surrendered 3 percent of his expected 10 percent in exchange for the guarantee. Again, it was perfectly legitimate. Suppose he surrendered another 2 percent to be guaranteed his profit—also legitimate. Then suppose he entered these contracts of guaranty with his partner, so that 5 percent of the expected return on the capital went to his partner, and he was guaranteed the return of his capital and 5 percent. The three contracts were all lawful. What was wrong with collapsing them into a single contract, "the triple contract"? What was wrong with finding the triple contract not spelled out but implicit in every contract at 5 percent where an investor intended to act lawfully?

Nothing was wrong, concluded the commission.

We seem to be in the world of Enron's financing where loans are packaged as sales and insurance companies guarantee the interest. How did such intricate lawyerly analysis come to occupy the attention of the most acute moral theologians in Europe? What development of doctrine was represented by this decision of 1573, which was reaffirmed by another Jesuit commission in 1581 that at the same time taught that a loan at 5 percent was "intrinsically evil?" To answer these questions it is necessary to look at Scripture and fifteen hundred years of reflection on Scripture.

Scriptural Texts and Their Interpreters

The parable in Matthew 25 is the story of the property owner who, going on a journey, distributes cash to his slaves according to the ability of each, five talents to the first, two talents to the second, one to the third. Each of the first two doubles what's given, the third buries his one talent in the earth. Much later, their master returns and gets an accounting. The first two are congratulated and promoted. The third, returning only what's given, is denounced by his master as a "bad and lazy slave." "You knew that I reap where I do not sow and gather where I have not threshed. Then you ought to have put my money with the bankers, and on my return I would have received what is mine with offspring" (Mt 25:26–27). With minor variations, and the same demand for offspring, the story is told in Luke 19:12–27.

The master stands for God or for Jesus as Lord of his followers, from whom much is demanded. What is striking for our consideration is the master's view that his money should have been multiplied—not by interest as in some tame English versions, but by *tokos,* offspring or fruit. The observation that money breeds money is founded on the use of *tokos* as the term for the return paid on a loan. The observation undergirds Aristotle's famous objection to profit on a loan that it is against nature for money to breed. The argument has a popular appeal. It puts in terms of nature what is in fact an objection to the human use of a human invention.

Offspring, *tokos,* would be born at the "bankers." Is it not implicit in the parable that breeding money cannot be an ugly form of exploitation? If money-breeding were a sin, could the figure standing in for God or Jesus recommend it as a good way to invest? Expressly the wretched slave is told he should have gone to the professional moneylenders, *trapezetes,* to get a good return. If breeding money is a metaphor for action approved by God, one might infer that money-breeding is good.

Another parable suggests that the inference is simplistic and unjustified. Jesus in Luke presents the story of a judge "who did not fear God or respect man" and who is plainly described as an "unjust judge" (Lk 18:2–8). Yet this judge is put forward to show how God will respond to persistent prayer. No one is asked to assume that the unjust judge is good. Could one not say the same of the master who recommends money-breeding? The meaning of the parable would lie in his high expectations, not in the method used to meet them. May not moneylending still be bad?

The answer is not entirely clear. Hebrew law dealt with money-breeding by forbidding it where it was done by a loan to a fellow Hebrew (Lev 25:36; Dt 23:19). The Greek I have translated as "fruit" or "offspring"—a neutral translation—is used in the Septuagint to designate a disapproved or sinful return on money, to mean usury. The prohibition of taking usury from Hebrews in Leviticus and Deuteronomy was made universal in Psalm 15 (Psalm 14 in the Vulgate), which asked:

> O Lord, who may lodge in thy tabernacle?
> Who may dwell on thy holy mountain?
> The man of blameless life who does what is right . . .
> Who does not put his money out at usury
> and takes no bribe against an innocent man.

The psalm of course was familiar to Jesus, and the evangelist putting the parable into Greek must have known that *tokos* was the term chosen by the Septuagint to translate the psalm's reference to usury. The psalm's teaching and repudiation of *tokos* is repeated in Ezekiel 18:8. It seems possible, then, that the parable in Matthew is parallel to that of the unjust judge as a type of a fortiori: God will do more, or expects more, than an unjust human being. In the event, the image of the master who sought usury did not operate in later developments as a defense of professional moneylenders.

Money-changers, as distinct from moneylenders, appear once in New Testament narrative. It is in the dramatic scene where Jesus drives from the Temple those "buying or selling things in it" and upsets "the tables of the money-changers" (*kollybistes*) (Mk 11:15; Mt 21:12; cf. Jn 2:13–16). I follow Daube in not identifying the money-changers with bankers. They were there to facilitate the purchase of sacrificial offerings, as the Temple accepted only the Tyrian half-shekel. They are condemned because they have made the Temple a place of business (Jn 2:16). In the Synoptic tradition, they "have made it a cave of rob-bers" (Mk 11:17). But the money-changers are not differentiated from the bird and animal vendors. No sin of usury is charged against them.

What caught the attention of patristic commentators as decisive on lend-ing were two lines in a series of teachings presented by Luke, who begins with "Blessed are you who are poor" and goes on:

> To the man who strikes you on the cheek turn the other also. . . . Treat oth-ers as you would want them to treat you. . . . Again, if you do good only to those who do good to you, what merit is that for you? Even sinners do that. And if you lend only to those from whom you hope to receive, what merit is there in that for you? But love your enemies and do good to them and lend despairing of nothing, and there will be a great reward for you. (Lk 6:21–35)

What was to become key was the second reference to lending, Luke 6:35. As the Greek puts it, and some versions of the Vulgate translated it, what it appeared to say was, Lend [to your enemies], despairing of nothing, i.e., not despairing of being repaid—in Latin, "*mutuum date, nihil desperantes.*" But other versions of the Vulgate translated the Greek as "*mutuum date, nihil inde sperantes*"—introducing an *in* and detaching the *de* from *sperantes*, so that the half-sentence ran, "Hoping nothing therefrom." This Latin half-sentence capped the prohibition of usury in the Middle Ages. The version in Matthew's parallel and earlier collection of Jesus's sayings was milder: "If one wants to borrow from you, do not turn away" (Mt 5:42).

The Fathers—Tertullian, Jerome, Ambrose, and Augustine in the West, Basil, Gregory of Nyssa, Gregory Nazanien, and John Chrysostom in the East—condemned the taking of *tokos* or *usura* as a grave sin. They saw it as a way of oppressing the poor. Strikingly, they condemned it as causing indebted-ness leading to slavery, while they did not condemn slavery itself. Basil, for example, wrote, reproaching the borrower as much as the lender:

> I have seen a piteous sight: free sons dragged to the marketplace to be sold because of their father's debt. If you are not able to leave money to your sons, do not deprive them of their dignity.

In his in-depth treatment of usury in his homily on Tobias, Ambrose adapts this passage from Basil.

As such rhetoric suggests, the majority of the Fathers focused on the con-sequences of usury and lamented its effect upon the poor. Jerome went further.

An unabashed rigorist, he brushed aside the objection that the borrower might be a successful businessman and use a loan to make a profit; the lender charging for the loan still committed usury. All the Fathers relied on the Old Testament texts, with the Greeks, followed by Ambrose, also borrowing from Aristotle to deny that money was fruitful and could yield offspring or *tokos*. The Latin equivalent of *tokos* is *foenus*, plausibly supposed to be derived from *fetus*—a shamed stammer acknowledging something incongruous in money bearing money. The Fathers agreed that the forbidden offspring was anything beyond the principal. Basil and Chrysostom, Jerome and Ambrose also read the two verses of Luke 6:34–35 together as a fulfillment of Mosaic law by way of expansion; the Christians were to love their enemies and to lend without seeking any benefit.

These teachings of the Fathers may have impacted individuals. They had no effect on public justice. Basil and Augustine contrasted imperial law permitting profit with the Christian rule denying any return to the lender. Augustine wanted judges to order the restitution of usury to the borrower; he noted that no judge would do so. Book 22, chapter 1 of the *Digest* had a title that began *De usuris et fructibus*. It bore on the rate and payment of interest. *Usura* in the Roman law contained no connotation suggesting foul and unnatural transactions. The Christian emperors—the consciously Christian emperors proclaiming the empire's support of the Catholic Church—did not change imperial law permitting the payment of interest on loans and treating banking as an honest profession. If the message of Jesus was read as forbidding profit on any loan, as Jerome read it, the message was too muted to alter the pattern of financial practice in the empire.

It was different when the empire dissolved in the West and the barbarian kingdoms began to take shape. The *Hadriana*, a collection of canons for Charlemagne's empire, contained a decretal of Pope Leo the Great forbidding usury to clerics and describing usury taken by laymen as *turpe lucrum*, shameful profit; and the secular legislation of Charlemagne, guided by churchmen, contained a flat prohibition of usury, comprehensively defined by the Fathers as "where more is demanded than is given." In a largely agricultural economy, one may infer, the moneylender, making money whatever the weather, was an unpopular figure, and money breeding money was perceived as a social evil. Biblical teaching, patristic commentary, and social hostility to moneylenders united to form an intellectual milieu in which usury was seen as intolerable. Development of the doctrine by acute legal minds had to await the flowering of a culture cultivating canon law.

In Your City You Say It Often Happens

At the end of the evolution that began with Charlemagne there came the teaching of Gratian's *Harmony of Unharmonious Canons*. *Causa* 14 set out these facts and two questions:

> The canons of a certain church raise a question as to their endowment. . . . They have loaned money to businessmen in order to obtain compensation from their goods. . . . Is that to demand usury? Is it lawful for clerics or laymen to seek usury from anyone?

Citing Augustine, Jerome, Ambrose, and a statute he attributes to a church council, Gratian answered the first question:

> Behold, it is evident, whatever is demanded beyond the principal is usury.

In response to the second question, Gratian cited fourteen authorities, identified as popes, councils, or church fathers, whom he interpreted as forbidding usury to everyone. Gratian was an author familiar with Scripture and not backward in citing it as a source of doctrine. Neither he nor his authorities quoted a single word of Jesus on lending.

The Second Lateran Council under Gregorio Papareschi, Innocent II, forbade usury to everyone, declared usurers to be infamous in law, and announced in *Porro detestabilem* that usury was reprobated by both the Old Testament and the New. The council provided no gospel reference, and the council stretched to find usury reprobated in the New. Gratian's *Harmony of Unharmonious Canons* was begun before the council met in 1139. The work was revised to incorporate canons from the council. The revision did not include *Porro detestabilem* or supply the lacuna as to the New Testament.

Gratian's work used as a framework a question about investments by a church. Earlier in the Middle Ages the monasteries were the institutions apt to have accumulated capital and be in a position to lend. By the middle of the twelfth century Gratian saw urban churches to be in a similar position. Contemporaneously with Gratian, Pietro Paganelli, Pope Eugene III, once a Cistercian monk of Clairvaux, legislated against a favorite practice of monasteries—lending upon a pledge of land and retaining the fruits of the land without counting the fruits toward payment of principal. The teaching of the Church against usury was here forcefully applied to the Church's own economic detriment.

With Gratian accepted as the law book of the Church and studied by all students of canon law at Bologna, the campaign against usury intensified in the twelfth century. Rolando, Pope Alexander III, attempted to close an obvious loophole—the sale of goods on credit with a charge for the credit extended. "In your city you say it often happens," he answered the archbishop of Genoa, "that pepper, cinnamon or other wares, not worth more than 5 pounds, are bought in public documents promising to pay 6 pounds at a fixed date." In form, the pope noted, the contracts were not usurious—there was no contract of loan; nonetheless the sellers incurred the sin of usury unless there was a doubt what the goods would be worth at the time of payment. Part of the old loophole remained if the commodity sold on credit was traded in a volatile market. But the thoughts of men, the sellers should remember, "cannot be hidden from Almighty God." In this tightening of the usury prohibition by what became the decretal *In tua civitate* one can observe legal minds at work, making logical inferences and deductions, and combining them with religious exhortation. A legal enterprise has its own momentum and its own logic. To ban profit on the extension of credit in a sale seemed logical.

Alexander III informed the archbishop of Palermo that usury could not be taken for the pious purpose of raising money to ransom captives of the Saracens; nor could the pope dispense from the sin: "since Sacred Scripture prohibits lying to save the life of another, much more is it prohibited that anyone be involved in the grave offense of usury, even to redeem the life of a captive." Usury, he noted, was "detested by the pages of both Testaments." At the Third Lateran Council, which he convoked in 1179, the pope joined the council in speaking of the spread of usury, "with many giving up other businesses, practising usury as if it were lawful and never attending how it is condemned by the pages of both Testaments." Still no New Testament verse was cited. The council decreed the excommunication of "manifest usurers," the denial of Christian burial to them, and the rejection of any offerings they made. In this way, as an urban economy developed in Italy, the battle against usury became more intense. Not as much a priority as the battle against simony in the sale of church offices, the campaign against usury was on the agenda of reform.

Two years after the Third Lateran, a new pope, Uberto Crivelli, Urban III, reached for the words of Jesus. The pope was asked if, in the judgment of souls—that is, in confession—one who, without any contract, loaned money with the intention to receive more than the principal, "must be judged as if a usurer." The pope answered that what was to be held "was manifestly known from the gospel of Luke, in which it is said, 'Lend, hoping nothing therefrom.'" Having the "intention of profit," such men "acted evilly and in the judgment of souls they are to be efficaciously induced to make restitution of what they have received." Without reference to the context in Luke, without quotation of more than the half-sentence mistranslated from the Greek, the words of Christ were set out as a commandment that governed lending. At the same time, the idea implicit in *In tua civitate* was made explicit: the intent to profit from lending was sinful; anything beyond the principal was made subject to the obligation of restitution. Interestingly, no use was made of the line in Matthew's version of the Lord's prayer, "Forgive us our debts, as we forgive our debtors" (Mt 6:12). In Luke, the pope had found all he needed. Fastening upon it, he had a text that united a rule of zero gain to a rule extending the prohibition to an intention to gain. Potentially, a comprehensive coverage of all credit transactions had been designed, making them all gratuitous.

The scriptural injunction was reinforced by an argument from the nature of things. In its crudest and most popular form, the argument was a mere restatement of Aristotle: it was not natural for money to bear money. In more refined form, in the hands of Aquinas, the argument ran that in fungible things, use and value could not be distinguished; so the value and the use of one dollar was one dollar, just as the value of one hairpin and the use of one hairpin was one hairpin. Whatever may be thought of the truth of such an argument if fungible goods are thought about in abstraction from any context, the argument made the enormous assumption that time should not enter the valuation. Even more surprisingly, perhaps, the builders of the natural law case against usury put it forward as a teaching of nature that usury was unnatural. They did so resting on the proposition that money and like fungibles were intrinsically sterile. They must have been aware that, when they dealt with slavery, they started with the proposition that men were born free and ended with the proposition that the law of nations had added slavery to what was natural. But the analogy was not drawn, that the law had added something to nature by recognizing rates of interest. Instead, the improbable position was defended that a highly human invention—money—was subject to natural law, and that usury was intrinsically unnatural.

I will not set out here the immense legal and moral structure that was then developed on the basis of the usury prohibition. For a very long time, at least until the partial withdrawal of the teaching that occurred in the nineteenth century, the flat prohibition of profit on a loan appeared to be an essential moral precept of the Catholic Church. It was an injunction based on nature itself, because for money to reproduce itself was unnatural. The evil was intrinsic. The injunction was confirmed by the teaching on lending of the Lord himself: it was a dominical precept. So taught a series of popes; so taught three general councils of the Church; so taught all the bishops. Everywhere and at all times usury, the making of profit from a loan, was condemned as sin.

At the same time that profit on a loan was banned, the Church was not hostile to profit from the investment of capital where the capitalist shared the risk of the investment. *Societas,* partnership, was such an arrangement if one partner put up the capital, the other the labor. The capitalist ran the risk of losing his capital and so was treated as its owner, entitled to profit from it. The inability of money to bear offspring was *not* used as an objection. Capital was treated as productive. Partnerships thrived in seafaring ventures and other commercial operations. Capitalist enterprise characterized the emerging city-states of Northern Italy.

Another contract formally distinct from a *mutuum* or loan was the *census* or annuity. In its basic form a *census* was the purchase of a return from a field for a fixed number of years—say one-thousand florins for so many bushels of grain for the next ten years. The contract was analyzed by the commentators as a straight purchase of the crop, on which it was lawful to make a profit. Credit, of course, was involved. The buyer of the annuity was putting up present cash and getting a return over time. The price of the annuity reflected the deferred payment. The *census* could have been denounced as a disguised loan in the same way that Alexander III had treated sales on credit as loans. But it was not. It became a common device in the financing of cities—a city, for example, selling the revenues from its tax on salt for twenty years to an investor who provided cash on the spot. Annuities were pushed even to the point of resembling personal loans when a buyer bought the return from a man's labor for the next five years in return for present cash. Debate over what was a true loan and what forms of credit might be legally distinguished from a loan went on for centuries.

I stress the legal character of the distinctions because the usury prohibition of the Church was developed by lawyers—canon lawyers or theologians sensitive to the canons. The usury prohibition affected every corner of European economic life—the financing of nations, international trade, local business, agriculture, and personal borrowing. The usury prohibition went hand-in-hand with commercial enterprise. Prohibition of profit on partnerships and some types of sale was not the rule of the Church; profit on a loan was sin. Lawyers drew the lines.

Difficult as it is now for us to imagine the importance of the usury rule in the economic life of an earlier Europe, we can get some sense of the problem by looking at Moslem culture today, where the Koran's prohibition of profit in lending affects banking and finance. Different Moslem countries take the prohibition with varying seriousness, but the prohibition is never denied, and where *sharia* law is enforced by the state, the prohibition is controlling. The chief judge of the *sharia* court in Pakistan told me that my own book, *The Scholastic Analysis of Usury,* was for him "a very practical book," in setting out ways that the scholastic theologians developed for accommodating credit transactions to a rule forbidding profit on a loan.

For four centuries, from 1100 to 1500, the theologians tended to rigorism in rejecting profit from lending. In the fourteenth century in the hands of a great preacher like St. Bernardino of Siena the usury rule convicted a large part of his commercial city of mortal sin. Not only did its merchant bankers practice usury, but the bankers' wives lived on it, and their children inherited it. Yet usury was like theft, a sin against justice, and until the stolen property was returned, the sin was not remitted, and the dependents and heirs of usurers were as guilty of living on stolen property as the usurers themselves. Not only their families but all cooperators in usury—lawyers making, and judges enforcing, usurious contracts; princes protecting usurers; heads of hospitals and spiritual houses receiving gifts from usurers—partook of the sin. Bernardino acknowledged that it was common belief that the state could not exist without usury, that, in effect, God had placed people under an impossible precept. But that, Bernardino said, was blasphemy. He stuck with the commandment.

St. Antoninus, archbishop of Florence and friend of the Medici, wrote his fifteenth-century *Summa theologiae moralis* in a city even more a center for banking than Siena. In this pioneering work taking up in some detail the practices of a variety of trades and professions Antoninus came to the *campsores,* the exchange bankers, who provided cash at Rome in exchange for a note payable, say, three months later in currency in London. Short-term credit, of course, was involved. But it was argued that the transaction was a sale of coins at a profit and so perfectly legitimate. The exchange bankers took one more step—the bill of exchange on London was paid by a three-month bill of exchange drawn on Rome; no coins were actually sold; the transaction had the effect of a six-month loan at a profit. This was "dry exchange," said Antoninus, a fictitious loan, and the profit was usurious. But, its defenders replied, it was the practice of the exchange bankers tolerated by the Roman Curia. It was in fact the way bishops financed the charges put on them by the curia for their appointments. The exchange bankers were part of the financial operations of the Holy See. It made no difference, wrote Antoninus, who had lived in Rome as an auditor of the Rota: the curialists keep concubines, too; that did not make whoring right.

The strictures based on the usury rule had, I have suggested, their own momentum. In place in canon law, expounded by generation after generation of canon lawyers, theologians, preachers, and priests hearing confession, the usury rule was engrained in the European consciousness without explicit reference back to Jesus. Dante puts it as a puzzle to Virgil in *The Divine Comedy:* "'Go back a little,' I said, 'to where you said usury offends the divine goodness, and untie the knot.'" Virgil's explanation is in terms of the nature of money. Yet it is impossible to comprehend the impact of the usury rule without taking into account a European culture built on the ideal of taking seriously the teachings of Jesus as the culture understood them. Without the motivation of heaven and hell, without the awareness of judgment by God, without some sense of a Christian community as an organic whole in which charity was the lifeblood, the usury rule would have been without effect.

Those who really needed cash, St. Bernardino argued, could be helped by charity, if usury did not exist. In the late fifteenth century, the *montes pietatis,* backed by the Franciscans, attempted to meet the need for small cash loans by being public pawnshops where no profit was sought, but interest to meet expenses was charged. Dominicans claimed the charge itself was usury. But by 1500 there were eighty *montes* in Italy, and the Fifth Lateran Council in 1516 upheld them as praiseworthy. The Monte di Paschi, the bank in Siena, has its name from this old experiment, one of several signs that the old, rigid rule was cracking and new approaches would soon blossom.

The Custom of the Country

Acceptance of the *montes* was part of the turning in the sixteenth century from the rigor of the medieval period. In part, this turning was due to the commercial prosperity of Europe attendant on the European discovery of the Americas and the expansion of European trade; opportunities for the investment of money increased. In part, the turning was brought about by new analyses of credit transactions—analyses made by innovative moralists and maintained by them in the face of stubborn conservative reluctance, often papally supported, to accept analyses which subverted the old prohibition. In part, the turning was due to a change in the attitude of theologians to lenders; a far greater willingness was now shown to recognize the good intentions, honesty, and social utility of the bankers. The customs of the business community were powerful support for any approach that permitted moderate profit from the extension of credit. Between 1450 and 1750, the rules changed so that only the simulacrum of the prohibition remained, even though papal authority was unwilling to admit as much until the nineteenth century, when confessors were instructed by Rome as to penitents asking about usury, "Do not disturb them."

The Jesuit decisions of 1573 and 1581, set out in chapter 18, were key episodes in the shift. The background of the decisions was a strenuous effort to maintain the old prohibition of profit on a loan—an effort made by three reformers later recognized as saints, Carlo Borromeo, Petrus Canisius, and Michele Ghislieri reigning as Pope Pius V. In 1565, Borromeo had become archbishop of Milan and found prevalent the practice of deposit banking, exchange banking, and business investments where the investor was guaranteed his capital and a return. The diocese, as he informed Rome, was "full of usury and usurious contracts." It was time for the pope to speak.

Meanwhile, the Jesuits were at work in Augsburg, trying to win over Protestant merchants, but finding that the German or 5 percent contract was in general use. The common defense was that it was not a return on a loan but a payment of a *census* or annuity, an annuity that was founded on the business or labor of its seller and redeemable on demand or after a term by the buyer. A personal, redeemable annuity at 5 percent looked very much like a loan at 5 percent. Petrus Canisius, the Jesuit provincial, informed the canons of the cathedral that lawyers could not disguise the usury. This battle also was referred to Rome, where Pius V set up a commission to advise him. Finally, after over two years of consultations, the pope issued the bull *Cum onus.*

The opening words referred to "the burden of apostolic slavery" that compelled the pope to judge "the innumerable contracts of annuity" that were in contempt of divine law. The personal annuity, redeemable by the seller and paying a fixed return, was offensive to the law of God. Such was the pope's flat conclusion. On its face, *Cum onus* was the end of the 5 percent contract. Waiting until Pius V was dead, the Jesuit commission of 1573, described in chapter 18, held an implicit triple contract could justify the 5 percent. *Cum onus* was not as decisive as it appeared to be.

Controversy continued. In 1581, Wilhelm, duke of Bavaria, wrote Borromeo asking help from the pope about what seemed to be usury "everywhere" but as to which the theological advice he got was conflicting. The pope, Ugo Buoncompagni, Gregory XIII, consulted a new Jesuit commission, which in 1581 returned the verdict, already noted in chapter 18, that money advanced to a merchant, to the owner of fruitful lands, or to a working person, taking account of the person's status, could be interpreted as a lawful triple contract of partnership or a lawful real or personal annuity. The commission did not mention *Cum onus.* Gregory XIII ignored the Jesuits' advice and wrote Duke Wilhelm, upholding a ban on the 5 percent contract. Popular outcry was enormous. By 1583, the duke was obliged to turn to the Jesuits. They followed the decisions of their 1581 commission.

In 1586, Felice Peretti, Pope Sixtus V, in the bull *Detestabilis avaritia,* condemned the triple contract. The "decent name of partnership was being used as a pretext for usurious contracts." Persons enforcing such contracts were to be regarded as manifest usurers, excommunicated, and denied Christian burial. The bull seemed to be the death sentence of the triple contract. But it was not. The theologians took two paths in limiting its application. Some, such as Cardinal Lugo and Alfonso de'Ligouri, held it applied only to contracts that were "naturally usurious," that is, where the rate of return did not take into account the discount due for the guaranteed return of the capital invested. Others, such as the Jesuit moralist Leonard Lessius, taught that the bull set out pure positive law. To be binding, positive law had to be "accepted," that is, recognized in some public way as being the law. *Detestabilis avaritia* was accepted nowhere and therefore was nowhere binding.

Rejection of *Detestabilis avaritia* and *Cum onus* and another papal bull, *In eam,* on the exchange bankers, meant that the extension of credit at a profit could be made without much of a moral problem except as to excess in the rate of interest charged. What completed the transformation was the general availability of extrinsic titles to interest. *Damnum emergens* or emergent loss had been recognized even in the thirteenth century. It embraced the loss a lender actually incurred in making or collecting a loan—the cost, for example, of going to court to collect. Compensation for such loss could not be considered profit. *Damnum emergens* was what justified the charges of the *montes pietatis. Lucrum cessans* or profit ceasing was a little harder to justify: it was the loss a lender suffered by pulling his money out of a lawful, profitable investment in order to make a loan. To defend *lucrum cessans* one had to assume that the original investment would in fact have been profitable, and that the profit received from the loan that took its place was no more than the profit one lawfully would have had if the loan had never been made. *Lucrum cessans* easily crossed the line drawn against expecting profit from a loan. It came into its own when there was a market in capital, as Antwerp was in the seventeenth century; then it was possible to calculate the normal return on partnerships and so to estimate what compensation should be paid when money went not into a partnership but a loan.

A third extrinsic title to interest was recognized only in the late seventeenth century: the risk of not being repaid. Every loan, of course, carries the risk. For a long time it was thought that the risk was intrinsic and could not be recognized without destroying the intrinsic gratuitousness of the loan. The risk was carefully distinguished from the risk run in a partnership by a capitalist, who did not relinquish ownership of his capital and so was entitled to profit from it. Eventually, in the face of testimony from missionaries in China, that the risk of non-repayment was unusually large there, the Holy Office gave way and held that, under the circumstances stated, the lender could be compensated for the risk he ran. The way to more general acceptance was open.

The retreat became evident in a series of responses from Rome to questions posed by scrupulous French priests confronted with penitents making money from loans. In 1822, under Pius VII, the Roman reply was simply, "A response will be given at a suitable time." In 1830, during the brief pontificate of Francesco Xaviero Castiglione, Pius VIII, a formula emerged: *"Non esse inquietandum"*—the penitent who was profiting from a loan was "not to be disturbed." The formula became standard in the 1830s under Gregory XVI. Struggling to recover from the French Revolution and the Napoleonic invasion, without benefit of any first-class theologians, the papacy had no appetite for renewing the old strictures. The intrinsic evil of money reproducing itself no longer seemed so plain.

In the case of slavery, the extrinsic titles to owning a human being justified the institution. As these titles were challenged, the justification for slavery disappeared. In the case of usury, the extrinsic titles destroyed the intrinsic gratuitousness of the loan. The usury prohibition in its old form was dead.

Express Gospel texts were not a major influence on this development, except in one respect. Theologians eventually challenged the interpretation that Luke 6:35 was a commandment of Christ forbidding usury. The Spanish Dominican, Domingo Soto (1493–1586), professor of theology at Salamanca, was the first, contending that the popes who used the text in condemning usury did not mean to canonize their interpretations, but simply found the text apposite. The words of the text, he argued, did not attempt to decide the justice of lending at a profit. Moreover, as the laws of the Old Testament did not bind unless renewed by Christ or unless they were part of natural law, the only objection to usury was one that must be based on natural law. The same position was taken by a leading Spanish Jesuit, Luis Molina (1536–1600). In the same period John Calvin (1509–1564) dismissed the appeal to Luke 6:35 and argued that usury be determined only by the Golden Rule. It was not profit from a loan but profit from a neighbor's loss that was usury. It was only in the twentieth century, however, that the insistence on Luke 6:35 as a strict precept was abandoned by Catholic theologians as a whole. In modern Catholic exegesis, Luke 6:35 tells Christians to lend expecting no repayment; but this austere advice is a counsel not a commandment.

In the rise and fall of the usury rule what might be called a fundamentalist reading of a single Gospel text played a part in a moral structure that for four centuries influenced European commerce and for another four centuries offered resistance to complete dismantling. Even in modern times Dorothy Day's

The Catholic Worker with columnist Peter Maurin invoked the old anathema against usury; but this cry was an anachronism without reverberations. Objection to profit from a loan was still heard as to loans between countries. John Maynard Keynes, acting as advisor to the Exchequer, actually described the American demand for the payment of any interest on postwar loans to the exhausted English as "usury"; but he was told that Congress would never approve loans that were interest-free. The developed nations have been papally encouraged to be generous in their treatment of the debt of Third World countries. In preparation for the millennium, John Paul II suggested "giving thought" to "the reduction, if not the entire forgiveness" of the international debt borne by Third World nations. But the old strictures against usury were not applied or even mentioned. The *Catechism of the Catholic Church,* like the Second Vatican Council, did not mention the sin.

From 1150 to 1450 the usury rule had a bite because it was appreciated in a largely agrarian economy. It was, I venture to speculate, a useful rule. It was supported by a theory of money that was in itself misleading but fortunately not extended to partnerships and annuities. It was maintained by lawyers making fine, sometimes hairsplitting distinctions. It was possible only in a society that trusted the Bible as a principal source of wisdom and accepted the rules of the Church invoking and interpreting the Bible. That money should not reproduce itself was a slogan easy to popularize and difficult to dislodge. Even in the twentieth century the aged Jacques Maritain wrote that the Church with wisdom had infallibly condemned "the principle of usury"—that "money itself and by itself should give a yield or make offspring." But the slogan did not withstand scrutiny. The simple rule proclaimed by popes and council and taught everywhere by the magisterium turned out to be adaptable, open to multiple exceptions, not the master rule of credit. In the exceptions to the prohibition, the true principle had been hidden.

FOLLY, CHAMPIONED

TWENTY-ONE

The Future Is Put Off

In October of 1830, a new newspaper appeared in France. Its editors accurately described it as "the first daily newspaper in Europe to be devoted to the interests of Catholicism." Its appearance was a recognition of the new power of the press in a France moving slowly toward representative government. The Orléanist revolution of July had replaced an old regime Bourbon with a more politically astute cousin. The Catholic Church, hated by some for its association with the old monarchy, looked as though it had a brighter future free of the connection. The new paper was named *L'Avenir*—"The Future." After being ravaged by the Revolution of 1789, after being made to serve Napoleon, after being resaddled by the restored Bourbons, the Church could now look to different and better days. The future was for the revitalized Church to seize.

The editor-in-chief of *L'Avenir* was Félicité de Lamennais, a Catholic priest and the most respected, if controversial, champion of the Church in France. He was the author of a massive defense of Christianity entitled *Essai sur l'indifférence en matière de religion*. No reasonable person could be indifferent to the question of faith, he argued; how could anyone shrug off his destiny after death? He was controversial, for two reasons. He was ultramontane, that is, he rejected the nationalist Gallican tradition of the French bishops and looked to the leadership and authority of the pope. He was a democrat. He said that the future of the Church lay with the sovereign people; with the right of revolution against a tyrant; with a free press where the state would not censor Catholic books; with the Church separated from the State and able to have its own schools; with religious liberty for all and the freedom of each one to form his own conscience. "God and Liberty" was the motto of *L'Avenir,* whose thought was to be echoed later in the 1830s by Alexis de Tocqueville's *Democracy in America.* The example of the constitutional freedoms of the United States was, not incidentally, brought to the pope's attention when Lamennais made his case in Rome. Lamennais' ideas were powerful enough and concrete enough to influence the constitution of Belgium, just freed from Dutch oppression.

The bishops of France did not welcome *L'Avenir;* some of them were outspoken in their criticism. Lamennais decided to disarm his local critics by going personally to the pope. In September 1831, he shut down his paper and set out for Rome, accompanied by two idealists, Henri Lacordaire, the future restorer of the French Dominicans, and Charles de Montalembert, the future leader of French Catholic liberals. These two young men were to persevere even as their leader fell.

The French writers had not paid close attention to the signals from Rome. A scant six years before *L'Avenir* began publication, Annibale Della Genga, Pope Leo XII, had issued his encyclical *Ubi primum,* a shocked survey of the evils of the day. Among them was *tollerantismus,* a Latin neologism meant to describe the notion that everyone had full freedom from God to join the religious sect of his choice—a folly (*deliramentum*) against which St. Paul had warned in Romans 16:17–18 when he spoke of "the smooth and specious words" of those evil teachers who seduced the innocent. Why, this tolerance was even extended to deism and naturalism! The mystery of evil was abroad. A flood of pernicious books hostile to religion was capped by the Bible Society putting out the Bible in the common tongues. "May God rise up and restrain, destroy and reduce to nothing this unrestricted license in speaking, writing and distributing what is written." So had publicly prayed Leo XII in 1824.

The pope when the trio came to visit was Bartolomeo Cappellari, Gregory XVI. He had been a Camaldolese since the age of eighteen; abbot of a Roman monastery; and secretary of Propaganda. Elected pope in February 1831 at the age of sixty-five, he chose the name Gregory in memory of Gregory VII, who had brought the emperor to penance at Canossa. He was a man of the eighteenth century or earlier, without the intellect or the intellectual training or the experience to deal with fresh ideas from France; but he was the pope to condemn the international slave trade at Palmerston's request.

A small sign of the trouble in store was the extravagant epistolary courtesy of the curia that called for even a routine note to the pope from a cardinal to be closed by the cardinal "very respectfully kissing your most holy feet." Style of this sort was a convention without significance it could be thought. It betokened an attachment to a vanished world. Lamennais' little company adapted to this posture, closing their own presentation to Gregory XVI: "The sovereign pontiff will judge in his wisdom; and now, full of love for him and docile like small children to his voice, we prostrate ourselves at his feet and implore his paternal blessing."

Larger signs of trouble were the length of time they had to wait for a papal audience and what happened when they had it. They had come to Rome not only to see the pope but to make their case to the pope. They waited from the end of December 1831 to the middle of March 1832 before the pope agreed to receive them. When he did, it was for fifteen minutes. The talk was of people they knew and Michelangelo, not a word on their opinions, which they were too childlike to bring up. The pope offered them each a pinch of snuff. The offer was an insubstantial act of politeness.

If the trio had known of the intracurial correspondence and what Gregory was getting from outside the curia, they would have been seriously unsettled. Luigi Frezza, titular archbishop of Chalcedon and secretary for Extraordinary Ecclesiastical Affairs, the congregation in charge of the case, reported on it forgetting Lamennais' first name and calling him "François"—his Frenchness stood out in the secretary's mind. For Frezza it was no merit but a black mark that *L'Avenir* was "no stranger to the revolutions of Belgium, of Poland, of Ireland, of the Rhine provinces, and even of Italy." As one of five experts asked for their opinion on the views of the group, Frezza noted that *L'Avenir* admitted a right to resist the Prince, "a criminal act, for he who commits it resists what God has ordained"; that, further, the paper backed freedom of the press, separation of Church and State, and freedom of religion, "an absurd and shameful system." Recent authority had already expressly condemned the error of religious toleration. Frezza meant Leo XII's *Ubi primum*. Frezza was wholly for condemnation again, advising only not to make it a personal judgment of Lamennais but a general rejection of his bad ideas.

Meanwhile Metternich, the chancellor of Austria, on whose troops the stability of the Papal States depended, was writing his ambassador in Rome to put under the eyes of the pope the dangerousness of the liberties championed by Lamennais. The ambassador himself, Count Lützow, employed agents to intercept Lamennais' correspondence to friends in France, and he himself read damning tidbits from these stolen letters to Cardinal Luigi Lambruschini, who passed them on to the pope. Gregory XVI supinely received the fruits of the Austrian's underhanded enterprise.

When, in July 1831, the pope broke the hearts of the Poles and denounced their resistance to the Russian domination of eastern Poland, the French trio finally understood that all was lost. On the promise of help from Russia, the pope obeyed the czar, so Lamennais thought. As the official paper of the papacy mocked the defeated Poles, Lamennais imagined the czar's command to the pope: "You want to live? Stay there, near the scaffold. As its victims pass, curse them." The French left Rome. The condemnation of their own cause came on August 15, 1832, the feast of the Assumption of the Virgin Mary, who was saluted by the encyclical "as patron and as saviour," whose "heavenly breath" was asked to inspire the Christian flock.

The encyclical, entitled *Mirari vos* ("You wonder"), addressed the bishops of the Catholic Church in a world where "unrestrained wickedness, a science without shame, a license without limit, triumph." The obedience owed to princes was under attack. Celibacy was under attack. The rights and the authority of the Church were under attack. "Academies and schools resound" with open war on the Catholic faith. The bishops must "keep the deposit of faith in the midst of this great conspiracy of impious men." As the Church was "taught by the Holy Spirit, which unceasingly suggests every truth to her," it was "totally absurd and maximally injurious to her" to contend that the Church needed "restoration and regeneration," as if she "could be judged exposed to failure, to becoming obscured, or to other inconveniences of this nature." What the innovators wanted was that "she, who is of divine matter, become a human Church."

The pope moved on to the need to instruct people on the sacredness of Christian marriage (not Lamennais' problem) and then to "another fecund cause of the evils at which we groan," to wit, "*indifferentism,*" the italicized notion that all could achieve eternal salvation provided their morals were good. On the contrary, "they will perish eternally if they do not hold the Catholic faith." From "this most foul font of *indifferentism,*" the pope continued, "flows that absurd and erroneous teaching, or rather that folly (*deliramentum*), that it is necessary to assure and guarantee to whomever it may be *the liberty of conscience.*" Some—who else but Lamennais could be meant—said that freedom of opinion was advantageous to religion. But take away restraints, "and *the pit of the abyss* is open," into which, human nature, "inclined to evil," will fall. The pit of the abyss, an unexpected scriptural phrase, was a compact allusion to the Apocalypse 9:2, where "a star fallen from heaven to the earth" opened a smoke-belching pit obscuring the light (a poetical anticipation of the dangerous Frenchman who believed in a free press). "What worse death of the soul than freedom of error!"

Freedom of conscience, *Mirari vos* added, was related to "that worst freedom, which one could never hate and detest enough," freedom of publishing, a freedom that some—who else again?—"dared to seek and to extol with so much noise and enthusiasm." Its supporters said it would permit a book defending religion to be published. But what man of reason would say that it is necessary to let poisons be freely sold because there is a remedy among them by which one might sometimes avoid death? The discipline of the Church was very different. Even in the time of the apostles "we read of a great quantity of books being burned." Gregory XVI cited the Acts of the Apostles for its account of the converts who had formerly practiced "magical arts" burning their old books worth fifty thousand pieces of silver (Acts 19:18–20). The Fifth Council of the Lateran, the Council of Trent, and Clement XIII had all legislated against "dangerous books." Rightly they sought "to deliver to the flames the culpable elements of evil."

Was it with deliberate irony that the drafters of this lugubrious document derived Lamennais' errors from a doctrine against which Lamennais had devoted a four-volume attack? Or were the drafters simply confused as to where Lamennais stood on religious indifferentism? It is hard to say. What is incontestable is that in absolute terms, without qualification as to context, the pope pronounced freedom of conscience and freedom of religion to be pernicious errors.

Lamennais was driven out of the Church, but his ideas were not. It was necessary for Maria Mastai Ferretti, Pius IX, a former liberal disillusioned by revolt in the Papal States, to attack them again. He did so in the Syllabus of Errors that culminated in condemnation of the proposition, "The pope could and should accept modern civilization," and he did it in the encyclical letter *Quanta cura*, issued December 8, 1863. The encyclical repeated Gregory XVI's condemnation of "the folly that freedom of conscience and worship is the proper right of every human being." In 1885, Leo XIII endorsed his predecessors' teaching in the encyclical *Immortale Dei*, devoted to "the Christian constitution of States." His precedents stretched back to the Roman Empire and to the great moral teacher of the Western Church, St. Augustine. The overwhelming weight of authority restrained any advance to the future.

With Words for Infidels, with Fire for the Faltering Baptized

When Christianity was a minority religion and after it had been persecuted by the Roman state, the fourth-century convert Lactantius wrote, "Religion cannot be compelled. The whole thing must be done with words, not whips, so that it be voluntary." Here was a classic defense of freedom of conscience by a Christian; and Christianity asserting a faith and a power separate from the State created a zone in which conscience could operate—a zone without parallel in the ancient world.

Separation of Church and Empire was too countercultural to be comprehensible when the emperors became Christian. The idea that Catholicism be established by law became irresistible. The idea implied coercion of Christian dissenters. Augustine and the other African bishops sent a delegation to Ravenna to ask the emperor not to legislate against the Donatists. The delegation came too late; the laws had been enacted. Augustine now discovered that persecution worked. Such "medicinal harassment" as beatings were necessary "for the hardness that could not be changed by words." Insidiously, the mind-set of the slave-owning class offered Augustine an analogy. Unselfconsciously, he adopted it. The heretics were like "bad slaves" to be called back to the Lord "by the lash of temporal scourges."

Not only did persecution work, but Augustine found scriptural warrant for it. "They are accustomed to cry. 'To believe or not to believe is free. On whom would Christ use force?'" Augustine's answer was: St. Paul. Christ had knocked Saul from his horse on the road from Jerusalem to Damascus and blinded him for three days (Acts 9:2–9). The result was to make the new man, Paul, a fervent convert. Moreover, Jesus told the parable of the unwilling dinner guests to show what had to be done by his followers: "Go out into the highways and hedges and whomever you find compel to enter" (Lk 14:23). Scripture reminded the rulers of the earth to serve the Lord (Ps 2:10–11). How else should they serve but by their laws enforcing the faith? Scripture provided an example of the use of force and the Lord's authorization to use it.

The texts invoked by Augustine would have authorized the use of force to make Christians out of Jews and pagans. But the Roman Empire had been made by pagans and had tolerated many Jews. These customs were not changed by Augustine's development of Christian doctrine to favor using force in behalf of faith. Among the Christians the belief held that faith was a gift and that the act of the will accepting faith could not be compelled. Persecution was reserved for the baptized, a result reflecting psychological and sociological realities. Those closest in belief who in some respect fell short were the most galling. They were also the ones easiest to corral and coerce.

Augustine defended correction, not destruction, of the heretic. In the fierce struggles of the twelfth century against the Cathars, in a Europe in which the popes enjoyed political power, death became the penalty for obstinacy in heresy. *Ad abolendam,* a decree in 1184 of Ubaldo Allucingoli, Pope Lucius III, intended "to abolish the wickedness of a variety of heresies," was one of sixteen papal ordinances against heretics given special status by incorporation in the title "Heretics" in the *Decretals* of Gregory IX. *Ad abolendam* directed that a lapsed heretic be "left to secular judgment." Any unrepentant heretic should receive from the secular judge "due punishment in proportion to the nature of his crime." *Ad abolendam* did not state that the secular punishment was death. The decretal adjoining it in Gregory IX's collection was Innocent III's *Vergentis,* which noted that secular crimes of lèse-majesté were punished by death and added that "it was far more serious" to offend God.

Reflecting theologically on the development, Thomas Aquinas, in the middle of the thirteenth century, asked, "Should heresies be tolerated?" He answered, No, after the first and second correction, enunciating a third strike rule taken from Titus 3:10. Recidivism was intolerable. True, the Lord had said to let the tares grow up with the wheat, Matthew 13:25–29, but that was to be understood to mean only if the tares could not be extirpated without extirpating the wheat. True, the Lord commanded Peter to forgive his sinning brother not seven times but seventy times seven (Mt 18:22). But to the contrary the decretal *Ad abolendam* required handing over a relapsed heretic to the secular arm. True, God was always ready to forgive. But God knows who is truly repentant. "The Church cannot imitate this"—perhaps the most chilling line in Thomas. As the Church cannot imitate her Lord, the Church presumes that the relapsed did not truly repent and therefore "does not safeguard them from the peril of death." Forgers, Thomas added, were put to death. A fortiori, death was a fit punishment for those who counterfeited faith in God.

With the popes leading the way, with the greatest theologians of the Western Church endorsing the use of force, the machinery of the Inquisition went unrebuked. Priests themselves were forbidden to shed blood. The problem was not addressed that they were cooperators in the shedding of blood when, as ecclesiastical judges, they judged a heretic to be relapsed and turned him or her over to the secular power. Astute as the canonists and theologians were in denouncing cooperation when it was sinful, they avoided speaking of blood guilt when condemnation by priests led to the death of those they condemned.

Zeal to preserve orthodoxy was joined with opportunity to use the machinery of death for purely political ends. Jan Hus, Jeanne d'Arc, Girolamo Savonarola were executed as the machinery clanked into the fifteenth century. The Inquisition did not involve mass murder on the scale of Nazi or Communist atrocities. It was reasonably selective. It sometimes led to the deaths of persons whose positions, by the criteria of the day, were formally heretical. Sometimes it led to the execution of the actually innocent. Always it put terror at the service of truth. Always it assured unity of faith by suppressing those who challenged the Church.

When Martin Luther defied accepted doctrine on indulgences, Leo X in 1520 in the bull *Exsurge Domine* denounced forty-one propositions attributed to Luther as pestiferous or pernicious or scandalous or subversive of pious and simple minds or against all charity, reverence, and obedience—scattershot condemnation that did not measure the precise degree of each error; each was poisonous, some more so than others. Within sixty days Luther was told to renounce and to burn the writings containing these teachings. If he did not repent, he and his collaborators were excommunicated, and all ecclesiastical and secular authorities were told to capture them and send them to the pope. Luther could have had little doubt as to his destiny if he had been captured and sent to Leo. With this mighty salvo, the wars of religion were begun. Among the condemned propositions was number 33: "To burn heretics is contrary to the will of the Spirit."

A few years earlier in 1511, Desiderius Erasmus, staying with Thomas More in More's house, the Old Barge in Bucklersbury, had written *Moriae Encomium, In Praise of Folly,* deliberately playing on More's name to praise him as "a man for all seasons" and to celebrate Folly at the same time. Erasmus imagined someone asking "What injunction is there in Sacred Scripture commanding that heretics be extinguished by fire rather than confuted by argument?" The question in his book was answered by "a sour old fellow, whose haughtiness marked him a theologian." This fool argues for the fire by misconstruing Paul to the Corinthians and citing a passage in the Old Testament on witches. Erasmus says no more to ridicule the scriptural basis for religious persecution and to underline this obvious truth: nowhere in the New Testament is there a command to kill or coerce the heretic. Persecution for Erasmus is folly, ironically praised and contrasted with the truly praiseworthy Christian folly of following Christ.

As the storms of the Reformation destroyed the peace of the Church, Erasmus in 1534 published his *De sarcienda Ecclesiae concordia—Repairing the Harmony of the Church.* Speaking with great moderation of the contemporary controversies, he once again mocked those who "impotently shout, 'Heresy! Heresy! To the fire! To the fire,' interpreting what is ambiguous to the worse" and creating sympathy for those they denounced. Harmony was at the heart of Christianity. Harmony—Gratian's musical metaphor for the play of the canons—could not be restored by violence.

Erasmus must stand as one of those "great minds," recognized by John Paul II, as "truly free and full of God," who were in some way able to withdraw from the climate of intolerance. Two of his greatest contemporaries, Thomas More and Bartolomé de Las Casas, did not abandon the idea that heresy should be suppressed by force. Erasmus' lone voice was lost in the storm. The folly of force in the service of Christ was the law and order of the day.

Ideas do have consequences. Let erroneous ideas freely circulate, and you will have erroneous actions. One bad idea will propagate another bad idea. Who says A must say B. Once committed to allowing freedom of conscience and freedom of expression, you cannot draw the line to quash a question or prevent a publication. Therefore, error has no rights. If you have the power, you should smash or squash the error before it multiplies, or infects, or triumphs. It took the Catholic Church over fifteen hundred years of experience to acknowledge that this kind of reasoning in morals is folly far different from the folly of following Christ; that abstractions such as error do not reflect the rights of human beings; that the use of force to control ideas or govern thought violates the very conditions on which any advance in truth depends. Such acknowledgment by the Church came on December 7, 1965.

The Requirements of the Human Person

The teaching of St. Augustine, of St. Thomas Aquinas, of Lucius III, of Leo X, of Leo XII, of Gregory XVI, of Pius IX, of Leo XIII, and of the magisterium for fifteen hundred years was to be definitively rejected by a general council of the Church. The Second Vatican Council taught that freedom to believe was a sacred human right; that this freedom was founded on the requirements of the human person; that this freedom was at the same time conveyed by Christian revelation; and that the kind of respect that must be shown for human freedom of belief had been taught from the beginning by Jesus and his apostles, who sought not to coerce any human will but to persuade it. No distinction was now drawn between the religious freedom of infidels, in theory always respected and sometimes in fact abridged, and the religious freedom of heretics, once trampled on in theory and in practice. Now each human being was seen as the possessor of a precious right to believe and to practice in accordance with his or her belief. Religious liberty was acknowledged as the requirement of human nature and of revelation. The state's interference with conscience was denounced.

The experience of ideological tyranny under the recent totalitarian regimes had educated European episcopates in the requirements of spiritual liberty. Ideological tyranny continued to exist in the Soviet Union and Eastern Europe, turning the bishops of the countries oppressed by Communism into champions of freedom. The bishops from Africa and the Middle East were already apprehensive of what Islamic fundamentalism would demand. With the realism of a generation that had survived the two world wars, almost everyone, bishops included, saw the absurdity of claiming religious freedom for their own religion and for no one else's.

Within the Church, the most influential of contemporary Catholic philosophers, Jacques Maritain, maintained that the human person, oriented to God, could not be subjected to the state in responding to God. Theological opponents and political enemies had been attacking Maritain since the 1940s as another Lamennais. As early as 1945 a warning had been sounded in a work ominously entitled *De Lamennais à Maritain*. And *"la grande attaque"* had been mounted against Maritain by ecclesiastics in Rome only four years before Vatican II. But Maritain, a layman, could not be silenced by ecclesiastical edict; and he had, besides, wonderful friends, most notably Giovanni Battista Montini, the future Paul VI. Maritain could not be trashed.

Above all, there were the example and influence of the United States. Where else had Christianity thrived so well as in this nation where freedom of religion and the separation of Church and State were enshrined in the constitution of the country? For the bishops of the United States, freedom of religion was their issue. A bloc, powerful in their resources, the bishops had an articulate advisor and draftsman in John Courtney Murray, a leading American Jesuit, silenced in the years preceding the council, then shoehorned into its advisors by Cardinal Francis Spellman, archbishop of New York. The lustre of the American experience was not lost upon the Fathers of Vatican II.

The minority in opposition strenuously maintained that the teaching of the magisterium was being abandoned; they cited express texts and hitherto unchallenged papal statements. On the eve of the council, Alfredo Ottaviani had attacked "the very recent Catholic liberalism," which he identified with Maritain, Murray, and the Dominican Yves Congar. Their method in disposing of past authority was illegitimate. A Catholic could not say that part of an encyclical was "valid only for its time and circumstances." What the magisterium taught was always valid. These liberals supported freedom of worship and were guilty of indifferentism. They defended freedom of speech, an absurd doctrine. They defended freedom of thought, "an erring and unlawful state of mind." Under the false veil of justice they hid "the virus of atheism." Ottaviani quoted a speech made by Mussolini on March 18, 1931: "religious unity is one of the great strengths of a people." On the floor of the council and behind the scenes Ottaviani worked hard to prevent adoption of the new doctrine. Could heretics be permitted "freedom of propaganda?"

Ernesto Ruffini, cardinal-archbishop of Palermo, speaking to the council, actually quoted Gregory XVI and Pius IX on "the folly" of freedom of conscience. It was, as St. Augustine had said, "freedom to go to hell." Marcel Lefebvre, superior of the Congregation of the Holy Spirit (the Spiritaines) and titular archbishop of Phrygia, said sarcastically that what the Declaration on Religious Liberty proposed was "a new law," rejected many times by the Church. Leo XIII had "solemnly condemned it" as contrary "to Sacred Scripture and Tradition." Lefebvre asked where the concept of religious liberty came from:

> Is this concept new or has it already been affirmed for many centuries? The reporter [of the conciliar text] at p. 43 responds to this question. He writes: 'By a long evolution—historically positive, moral—we have reached this concept, which did not begin to have force before the eighteenth century.' By saying as much he has undermined by his own declaration the whole argument of the Declaration. Where did this concept begin to have force—in the Church's tradition or outside the Church? Evidently it began among the so-called philosophers of the eighteenth century: Hobbes, Locke, Rousseau, Voltaire, who in the name of the dignity of human reason tried to destroy the Church, provoking the killing of numberless bishops, priests, nuns, and believers.
>
> Catholic liberals with Lamennais attempted in mid-nineteenth century to accommodate this concept with the teaching of the Church; they were condemned by Pius IX.

Lefebvre concluded: "The Church of Christ alone has a true right to religious liberty."

The minority, with strong connections within the curia, was able to stave off action by the council until its fourth and final session. The majority, first aided by John XXIII and then by his successor, Paul VI, brought the document to a vote. The final tally was No, 70; Yes, 2,308. On December 7, 1965, 101 years after *Quanta cura*, Paul VI promulgated *Dignitatis humanae personae* as the teaching of the Church. Among those subscribing their names to the final text were Ernesto Ruffini and Alfredo Ottaviani. Marcel Lefebvre did not sign. No doctrine had undergone a greater change at the council than that on slavery; but that change went unnoticed even by this Spiritaine devoted to the evangelization of Africa. Contending that the Church had "married the Revolution," he went into schism.

Lefebvre had an inexact understanding of history. The doctrine of freedom had been proclaimed by Lactantius. The first defenders of religious freedom for dissident Christians were devout Christians, asserting it in the name of Christianity—the ex-Dominican Sebastian Franck; the ex-priest Menno Simon; the Congregationalist minister Roger Williams; and then most persuasively for educated Englishmen and Americans, the devout Protestant layman John Locke. These writers of the sixteenth and seventeenth century were reinforced by others—Baurch Spinoza, writing as an unorthodox Jew; the French encyclopedists, often deists; the religious sceptics such as Tom Paine. The American constitution was shaped in an intellectual climate in which religious intolerance was on the defensive. The chief shaper of the nation's freedom of religion was James Madison, himself a Christian, who defended freedom for everyone and wrote that to rely on governmental support is "a contradiction to the Christian Religion itself, for every page of it disavows a dependence on the powers of the world."

John Courtney Murray, whose teaching on religious freedom was now vindicated, commented as the council ended its third session, "Development of doctrine is *the* issue underlying all the issues at the council." The promulgation of *Dignitatis personae* was a triumph of development. It showed that development could mean the flat rejection of propositions once taught by the ordinary magisterium. Ottaviani, Ruffini, and Lefebvre did not make up the doctrine for which they fought. They were giving voice to what they thought was immutable. Not just the teaching of three nineteenth-century popes was rejected. The repudiated doctrine was the teaching of theologians, bishops, and popes going back to St. Augustine in the fourth century. Remarkably, the reasons for the change lay as much outside the Church as in the Church's internal development of the Church's own commitment to the freedom of the act of faith.

The old message of intolerance, massively delivered over fifteen hundred years, might itself have been understood as a development of doctrine that was irreversible. How could it be swept away by one pope and council? Vatican II itself did not attempt to grapple with this question. *Dignitatis humanae personae* did not mention the teaching of the past. It based itself on the freedom to believe traditionally accorded to the unbaptized. It did acknowledge that sometimes even this freedom had been violated and blandly ascribed the violations to "the vicissitudes of history," as if historical circumstances were human actors. Only thirty-three years after the council did John Paul II supplement this deficiency by acknowledging that some members of the Church had used force to convert the unbaptized.

Admitting individual mistakes and identifying individual perpetrators was not the same as explaining how the Church could teach one thing in the past, another thing today. "If what is being taught is true," wrote Lefebvre in protest, "what the Church has taught is false." Lefebvre loyally reflected the learning of the seminaries that an about-face was impossible. The dilemma seemed inescapable: Admit it, you were wrong then, or you are wrong now. The dilemma made the council uncomfortable. Vatican II made the change and left it to be explained.

Another question lurked, also unasked. If fifteen hundred years of doctrine could be cancelled by one council and pope, why could the new teaching not be trumped in turn? The question could only be successfully answered by believers who saw the consonance of the new teaching with Christ's commandments of love. For them, there was as little chance of reversing *Dignitatis humanae personae* as there was of an oak tree turning into an acorn or a flowering mustard plant reverting to a seed.

Reticence to reject the past by explicit reference to the rejected doctrine was, no doubt, the price paid for the unity finally achieved. *Dignitatis humanae personae* was, consequently, not an explicit demonstration of how a course of development could be changed by a deeper course of development reversing the first. Nonetheless, the conclusion from the council's action that everyone could draw was that not everything everywhere taught by the Church on serious questions of moral conduct was forever. Political development of the world toward democratic government; philosophical development in understanding the human person and the human person's search for truth; the negative experience of terrible totalitarian regimes; the positive experience of religious freedom under the American constitution—these developments and experiences had made intolerable the doctrinal development of intolerance and made the defenders of the old orthodoxy on this subject appear to be creatures from a cave where sunlight had never penetrated. What Murray had been silenced in the 1950s for questioning, what Ottaviani in 1960 had taught as the doctrine of the Church, was now gone beyond recall. What had been folly for the pope in 1832 now earned the praise of pope and council in 1965. Were there other major moral teachings even then in the process of transformation?

CONJOINED BY GOD, DISJOINED BY GOD

If the Unbeliever Separates

On August 19, 1959, Angelo Roncalli, Pope John XXIII, had occasion to pronounce upon the marriage of a woman named Lo Ma to a man named Phan. The couple had been married in China sometime before 1941. Neither was a baptized Christian. Phan had left Lo Ma in China and had emigrated to Indonesia. In 1944, during the Japanese occupation, when fathers feared their daughters would be violated, the father of Dorothy, a twenty-one-year-old Catholic, gave her in marriage to Phan; the marriage was civilly recognized in 1946. Phan's union with Lo Ma remained as an obstacle to a religious marriage. By the rules of the Catholic Church, Dorothy's union with Phan was both adulterous and bigamous. She, nonetheless, had five children with Phan and wanted to remain with him. He had no desire to become a Catholic, so the Pauline privilege had no application. On Dorothy's petition, submitted by the archbishop of Djakarta, Pope John XXIII declared Phan and Lo Ma's marriage to be dissolved.

Djakarta, August 19, 1959 is, from one perspective, an act of kindness performed by a pope who was exceptionally kind, the simple solution of a family problem, the restoration to the sacraments of a woman pained by the sins she had become entangled in. From a different perspective, the case looks like magic, a species of legal legerdemain without roots in human experience, at best a lawyer's device that only lawyers would think well of.

Paul's Pronouncement

To put *Djakarta, August 19, 1959* in its proper context, we must go back to Corinth nineteen hundred years earlier. Before the canon of the New Testament was formed, Paul wrote the Corinthians whom he had converted, answering their questions. To the married, he gives not as his teaching but as the Lord's a prohibition of divorce and of remarriage following divorce (1 Cor 7:11). He continues:

> To the rest, I—not the Lord—say,
> If any brother has an unbelieving wife, and she
> agrees to live with him, let him not dismiss her,
> And if any woman has an unbelieving husband, and he
> agrees to live with her, let her not dismiss the husband;
> For the unbelieving husband is sanctified in the
> believing woman,
> And the unbelieving woman is sanctified in
> the brother.
> Otherwise your children are unclean,
> but now they are holy.
> But if the unbelieving man separates, let him separate.
> Neither a brother nor a sister is enslaved
> in these matters,
> but God has called us in peace.
> For how do you know, woman, if you will
> save your husband,
> and how do you know, man, if you will
> save your wife? (1 Cor 7:12–16).

This text, Erasmus dared assert, is *omnium difficillimus,* "the most difficult of all."

Consciously speaking for himself, not Christ, Paul admits the possibility of ending the marital tie between a believer and an unbeliever. The marital bond tying the believer after the departure of the unbeliever is, in Paul's eyes, a species of slavery. This slavery ends, therefore the marriage ends. In a culture where mixed marriages could be the result of a conversion, Paul puts a gloss on what he has heard as the teaching of Jesus. Paul does not explicitly say that the abandoned convert may remarry. That his own teaching has an impact on the marital rights of the unconverted spouse does not occur to him. In the same letter to the Corinthians, he asks, "What have I to do in judging outsiders?" (1 Cor 5:12).

The teaching of Jesus was open to other interpretations, affected no doubt by the cultures in which they were formulated. Lawrence Stone's work, *Road to Divorce,* shows how England between 1534 and 1960 moved from a society in which the legal termination of marriage was relatively unusual to a society in which one in three marriages is terminated by divorce. Stone argues that no single cause—"legal or economic and social, or cultural and moral, or intellectual"— accounts for the change, and adds, "History is messier than that." It is a caution worth recalling as one takes up the history of Paul's text as I propose now to do. The text does not explain the development; but without the text, the development must have been different. The development is still *in fieri.* It has problems. It has not ended. What it foreshadows can only be a matter of speculation. At the heart of the development is the nature of marriage. I propose here to review the history, the current practice, and certain of the problems.

Isaac's Interpretation

About A.D. 380, the first Latin commentator on Paul's epistles—an author surmised to be Isaac, a Roman lawyer and like Paul a convert—argued that Paul permitted the convert to marry again.

Isaac wrote:

> "If the unbeliever separates, let him separate." He guards the intention of religion by commanding that Christians not leave their marriages. But if the unbeliever separates in hatred of God, the believer will not be guilty of the dissolved marriage; for the cause of God is greater than the cause of the marriage. "A brother or sister is not bound to slavery in such matters"—that is, the reverence of marriage is not owed to him who hates the Author of marriage. For a marriage which is without devotion to God is not confirmed, and because of this it is not a sin in him who is dismissed on account of God if he will join himself to another. Contempt of the Creator, therefore, dissolves the law of marriage as to the one who is abandoned, so that he may not be accused when coupled to another.

The clarity of the conclusion-the marriage is dissolved, remarriage is not sinful—is distinctive. Explained in this way, the power of the abandoned convert to dissolve his or her first marriage appears as a radical power of divorce vested in the convert by apostolic authority. Isaac supplied a key concept, "confirmed" (*ratum*), that he appeared to deny to at least some marriages of unbelievers, and he supplied a reason trumping indissolubility. He did not pause at the paradox he produced: the evil act of an unbeliever had the extraordinary effect of ending a marriage that God had made indissoluble. Focused on the freedom obtained by the convert, Isaac saw only the advantage achieved by the abandoned Christian.

None of those later acknowledged as Fathers of the Church had gone so far or was to go so far. Augustine, who, in all probability knew of this opinion, did not mention it in expounding 1 Corinthians 7. There was, moreover, an unacknowledged legal problem. Roman law did not recognize the convert's right to remarry. Isaac appeared to be claiming that that right could be unilaterally exercised without regard to secular legislation. No case has been discovered where the issue was discussed. No law in the subsequent Roman legislation on marriage and divorce, extensive as it is, addressed the case; Justinian, conspicuous in his theological knowledge, did not acknowledge it in collecting old law or in the promulgation of new law on the subject of divorce. The inference could be drawn that the privilege was superfluous: the preconversion marriages of a convert were disregarded, treated in practice as dissolved.

Isaac himself did not have recognition retroactively conferred upon him as a Father of the Church. The supporter in 390 of a losing candidate for bishop of Rome, he continued in a bitter struggle with the winner, Damasus. His name became unmentionable and was detached from his pathbreaking work, the first Latin commentary on Paul's epistles. The text was attributed to St. Ambrose or to St. Gregory the Great or to St. Hilary or to St. Augustine. Under one or another of these attributions, Isaac's passage on the convert's right to remarriage came cloaked with great authority when the study of canon law began in twelfth-century Bologna.

Isaac Incorporated

Gratian, whose *Harmony of Unharmonious Canons* was to form part of the corpus of the canon law, accepted Isaac's formulation: "Contempt of the Creator dissolves the law of marriage as to the one who has been left." Gratian also appropriated Isaac's key concept "*ratum*" and answering the question, "Is there marriage between unbelievers?" generalized:

> That saying of Augustine, "That marriage is not confirmed which is without God" does not deny that there is marriage between unbelievers. For one marriage is lawful and not confirmed, another is lawful and confirmed. Lawful marriage is that contracted by legal institution or the customs of a province. Between unbelievers this is not confirmed because their marriage

is not firm and inviolable. When a bill of divorce is given, it is lawful for them to separate from each other and to couple with others by the law of the forum, not by the law of heaven which they do not follow.

Attributing to St. Augustine the crucial judgment on the status of the marriage of unbelievers—"that marriage is not confirmed [*ratum*]"—Gratian easily accommodated Isaac's interpretation of St. Paul, assigning the interpretation to Pope Gregory I and concluding, "it is not necessary to follow the one who separates and, while she is alive, it is lawful to marry another." But if both were converted, there was "confirmed marriage between them, which can be in no way dissolved." In this fashion, in what was to become the textbook of canon law for the next eight hundred years, the convert's right to dissolve was set out. In 1157, the same rule, attributed to St. Ambrose, was adopted by Peter Lombard at Paris in his *Sentences,* which became the teaching text for medieval theology.

In 1199, Innocent III replied to a question posed by Uguccio, the leading canonist of Bologna. Innocent's octogenarian predecessor, Giacinto Bobone, Celestine III, had expanded Isaac's reasoning to permit dissolution of a marriage between two Christians if one of them apostatized. That was greater contempt of the Creator, according to Celestine, than what was exhibited by the departure of an unconverted spouse. Celestine's ruling unsettled Bologna. Uguccio asked Innocent, the new pope, if it held. No, Innocent replied, the marriage of believers was confirmed and so could not be dissolved even by apostasy. Gratian's conclusion held only as to the unbaptized. At the same time Innocent expanded the grounds for relieving the convert; it was not only the unbeliever's separation but his blasphemy or his drawing the convert to mortal sin that left the convert free to remarry. Innocent III's letter entered the authoritative collection of Gregory IX as the decretal *Quanto te* in the title *De divortiis.* Divorce in the modern sense was not the topic of this section of the law. But the convert's rights did amount to true divorce, approved by the Church.

In the next generation, a curial cardinal, Hostiensis, addressed the question of how the convert's right to remarry was to be determined. The convert's bishop was to have a hearing, determine that the unbelieving spouse had indeed separated in contempt of the Creator, and then enter a decree of divorce dissolving the first marriage. The English theologian, Richard of Middleton, and the Parisian theologian, Guillaume of Auxerre, read Gratian literally: it was the contempt of the Creator that dissolved the marriage; no more was needed. But the prevailing view, sponsored by other theologians, was different. It was the convert's second marriage as a Christian that dissolved the first marriage contracted in unbelief. As Thomas Aquinas put it, "the more firm" dissolved "the less firm."

Despite the doctrine that marriage is naturally indissoluble, the exception was unchallenged by the major theologians.

In an age when the Church had undertaken the regulation of marriage but many dioceses lacked courts, it did not seem strange that the dissolution of a true and lawful marriage could take place without a judicial act. Nor did it seem strange to either the canonists or theologians that the marital rights of an unbeliever could be terminated by a Church in which he did not believe. Because the Pauline text spoke of the unbeliever leaving, it appears to have been assumed that the unbeliever had abandoned his or her marital rights and would never want to reclaim them. How the unbeliever's blasphemy or drawing to mortal sin amounted to the forfeiture of the unbeliever's marriage and how these acts were to be proved was not determined by the decretals. It came to be required that formal interrogations, called interpellations, be submitted to the unbeliever to ascertain his or her state of mind. But so little were some theologians sensitive to the rights of the unbelieving spouse that Thomas Aquinas, as a young theologian, maintained that, after the convert had dissolved his marriage and remarried, the unbeliever could not remarry but was "in punishment" barred from a second marriage.

The theologians' analysis put forward a highly original theory of divorce. The second marriage of a convert dissolved the first marriage to which he or she was a party. As the second marriage was effected by the convert and the convert's new spouse, the existence of the first marriage depended on the will of the convert and the will of one person in no way connected with the first marriage. These two private persons were viewed as having power to terminate a union that otherwise no law and no authority could touch.

The simplicity of the divorce mirrored the simplicity of marriage itself. As marriage in the eyes of the Western Church was effected by the exchange of consent between a man and a woman (no priest was essential), so divorce was effected by the act of two private persons. A more democratic, less bureaucratic, less clerical solution could not be imagined. In the course of time the Church would seek to regularize the process, to make sure that the interpellations were made. But the radical power to break the old bond was vested in the new couple. Those who had been joined by God in the first marriage were separated by the consent given one another by the second couple. Was that not man separating what God had made one? The theologians did not pursue the question. Implicitly, it would seem, it was assumed that the authorization of the Apostle Paul was a divine warrant empowering each abandoned convert and his or her new spouse to do more than man could do, to end an intolerable slavery to a bond supposedly unbreakable but discovered to be less firm than the bond now newly formed.

What became known as the Pauline privilege was in place. From the teaching of St. Paul to the teaching of St. Thomas Aquinas, twelve hundred years had elapsed. The most intense development had been from Gratian, about 1139, to Innocent III in 1199, the creative age of canon law. The development dramatically demonstrated the freedom of canonists, theologians, and popes to shape the demands of marriage. Faced with the words of Christ, "What God has joined together, let no man separate," the creative lawmakers had subordinated this text to the occasional needs of the occasional convert (Jewish, Moslem, pagan). Two human beings, one of them not a party to the first marriage, could dissolve it. For another three centuries no startling changes occurred. The possibility of still greater development remained. The *Djakarta* case was yet undreamed of.

If Necessity Urges

Under the stimulus of European expansion to the Americas and the missionary activity accompanying it, the Pauline privilege entered a new phase. Converts, especially Indian chiefs, tended to have more than one wife. According to the decretals, they were validly married, and according to commentators on the decretals, they were married to the first wife they had taken. That posed a problem upon conversion if the chief had developed a fondness for a later wife or had abandoned the first. Conscientious missionaries would tell him he must return to his original spouse. Even the notorious liberal on divorce, Cardinal Cajetan, took this position. The missionaries groaned at the difficulty they faced.

In 1535, Alessandro Farnese, Paul III, in response to the same initiative of the bishops of Mexico that led to *Sublimis Deus* in favor of the liberty of the Indians, proposed a solution for their marriage problems. His bull, *Altitudo divini consilii*, was strong in invoking the wisdom of the Almighty, weak in its conclusion: If an Indian could not remember who his first spouse was, the Indian was free, upon conversion, to choose among his wives the wife he would now marry. The bull merely helped chiefs with poor memories. It was a boy sent to do a man's errand, and it did not do it. *Altitudo* was a desperate expedient, significant as a symptom of the problem.

Thirty years later, after renewed cries of discouragement from the missions, Michele Ghislieri, Pius V, made a bolder effort to relieve priests and bishops "tormented with the gravest scruples" when they received an Indian and one of his several wives as converts. "Because it would be very harsh to separate these Indians from the wives with whom they received baptism, especially because it would be very difficult to find the first spouse," the bull *Romani pontificis* read, "We, by apostolic authority, declare that marriage lawfully exists [between the Indian and the spouse he received baptism with]."

Romani pontificis did not explain how the pope had power to declare the marriages of the Indian converts and their chosen wives to be lawful. The title of the decree recalled the title of Nicholas V's bull in the fifteenth century that asserted the power of the pope to dispose of the lands and persons of the infidels. It could be inferred that Pius V was exercising an analogous authority here to promote the faith. Alternatively, the decree could be read as an extension of the Pauline privilege: the converted Indian was being dispensed from the obligation of ascertaining the willingness of his first spouse to convert and was given freedom to remarry as though the condition set by St. Paul had been met. Or maybe the decree only applied if it was "morally impossible" to find the convert's first wife. The theology behind the decree was impenetrable.

A dozen years later, Ugo Buoncompagni, Gregory XIII, made a still bolder move, acting at the request of Claudio Aquaviva, general of the Jesuits, who had voiced the concern of Jesuit missionaries. The specific situations addressed were those of slaves removed from their lawful spouses to "most remote regions." If one of these pagan slaves wanted to convert, there was no way of telling if his distant spouse would have refused to convert or shown contempt of the Creator or even had already become a convert. Yet it was important that converts be free to marry "lest they not persist in the faith." In a bull grandly beginning *Populis et nationibus* the pope therefore dispensed converts in the regions covered by the decree—Angola, Ethiopia, Brazil, and "other parts of the Indies"—so that they could marry "during the lifetime of an unbelieving spouse" without having knowledge of that spouse's unwillingness to convert. The geographical area covered was broad. The reason given was also very broad. Marriages among unbelievers, Gregory wrote, "are indeed true marriages, but yet are not to be judged so confirmed that they cannot be dissolved, if necessity urges." "Necessity" was apparently to be judged by the pope; but the pope delegated the power to dispense in these cases of slaves and their spouses to Jesuit confessors and to the bishops and parish priests in the affected areas.

Even if it were discovered later that the absent unbelieving spouse had become a convert by the time of the dissolution of the marriage, the dissolution held. The marriage undergoing dissolution was then between two Christians. In such a case, the pope exercised a prerogative papally assumed in the fifteenth century, the power to dissolve the unconsummated marriage of two Christians; the dissolved marriage could not have been consummated post-conversion as the spouses were continents apart. Such, at least, was the theology implicit in the bull.

Two apparently unusual papal powers were, therefore, being exercised. Delegation of the powers made their likely use close to common. *Populis et nationibus,* issued in 1581, made it easy to accept slaves as converts with new spouses. Tomás Sanchez, the leading moralist on marriage of the next generation, interpreted the action dissolving the convert's first marriage as possible "by virtue of the privilege of Christ, who granted it in favor of the faith." Benevolent in intention, the bull was based on a cruel reality of the slave trade, its separation of spouses, without so much as a comment on this practice.

What had Gregory XIII done? Had he created for converts a regime of divorce to be granted by parish priests? Had he asserted a power over nonsacramental marriages greater than the power of the Church over sacramental marriages? How far did necessity go in justifying divorce and authorizing use of the awesome power to dissolve unions that according to theology were indissoluble? These questions were not explicitly asked, and whatever answers were implicit in the bull were not explicated.

The Roman Curia was remarkably circumspect about the powers exercised in *Altitudo, Romani pontificis,* and *Populis et nationibus.* The decrees were not made part of the general law of the Church. The texts of the decrees were hard to get hold of. In 1750, Alfonso de'Ligouri did not even know the names of the edicts, although references to them could be found in theologians like Sanchez. In practice, rulings from Rome in the eighteenth and nineteenth century restricted divorce and remarriage to the case of the convert whose unbelieving spouse refused to live with him or her.

This reversion to the narrow rule of Innocent III began to change in 1891 when Pietro Gasparri published his treatise *De matrimonio* and, under the heading "Full Divorce—That is, as to the Bond," reproduced the three papal decrees of the sixteenth century and took up the position of Sanchez: the popes had power in favor of the faith to do what they had done in those decrees. In time Gasparri became a leader in the making of the new Code of Canon Law, issued in 1917. In Canon 1125 of the new code the three old decrees were "extended to other regions in the same circumstances." If "the same circumstances" were taken literally, the documents had almost no application. If the decrees were applied by analogy, a great deal was opened up. *Romani pontificis* was eventually interpreted by leading American canonists to apply to those they termed "successive polygamists," that is, to unbaptized persons who had married, divorced, and married again. They, too, had the right on conversion to choose which of their spouses they would now marry. The publication of the texts as appendices to the Code inaugurated the rapid development of the marriage law of the Church as the Church responded to the divorce culture of the twentieth century.

Out of Deeds Comes Law

In 1924, in a case from Helena, Montana, Gerard G. Marsh, unbaptized, had married Frances E. Groom, an Anglican. They divorced a year later. Marsh sought to marry Lulu LaHood, a Catholic. Achille Ratti, Pius XI, dissolved the Marsh-Groom marriage "in favor of the faith" of LaHood. Similar papal dissolutions of marriage followed. In 1934, the Holy Office issued regulations entitled "Norms for the Dissolution of Marriage in Favor of the Faith by the Supreme Authority of the Sovereign Pontiff." The Norms required the petitioner's local bishop to report "if any danger of scandal, wonderment, or calumnious interpretation is to be feared among Catholics and non-Catholics, as though in practice the Church favored the use of divorce." In the same cautious spirit the Norms were circulated in secret to the bishops of the world. Their general availability was not to be announced.

The logic of the Norms was that the pope had power, in favor of the faith, to dissolve any nonsacramental marriage whose existence impeded the spiritual life of a believer. In 1947, in a case from Monterey-Fresno, Eugenio Pacelli, Pius XII, dissolved a marriage which had been entered by the Catholic party with a dispensation, so that the marriage had taken place before a Catholic priest in a Catholic church. As an unbeliever was a party, it was nonetheless nonsacramental and its dissolution was papally authorized after it was broken by civil divorce, with the unbaptized party now baptized and desiring to marry another Catholic. Such dissolutions had never before been done. Theological criticism of the practice was rejected by Franz Hürth, the leading Jesuit moralist in Rome. The criticism was due, he wrote, "to an exaggerated indissolubility of marriage."

Is indissolubility a quality that can be exaggerated? Is not a tie either dissoluble or indissoluble, just as one either is dead or alive, a virgin or not one? Marriage, according to the magisterium, is intrinsically indissoluble. But now it appeared that what was intrinsically indissoluble might be dissoluble extrinsically, that is, by the application of superior power from outside the union.

Identified by Hürth as the Petrine privilege in distinction to the old Pauline privilege, the papal power was used by John XXIII. In *Djakarta, August 19, 1959,* set out in chapter 24, the pope dissolved the marriage of Phan and Lo Ma in favor of the faith of Dorothy. The petition for dissolution emphasized that Dorothy's five children by Phan had been brought up as Catholics; that, on their account, it would be "very difficult and, as it were, morally impossible, to break up common life with Phan"; and that Dorothy found it "very hard" not to receive the sacraments. Not emphasized but mentioned was that in 1947 Phan had been called back to China by his mother's illness and had resumed life with Lo Ma, fathering a daughter by her. When his mother died, he returned to Dorothy and "broke off marital relations" with Lo Ma but did send her money for their daughter's schooling. No mention was made of any divorce from Lo Ma, nor was mention made of any attempt to involve her in the process. The natural indissolubility of marriage was, in the most ample way possible, subordinated to the reception of the sacraments and the elimination of sin on the part of the Catholic party to Phan's second marriage.

This development of sixty-eight years from Gasparri's book in 1891 to *Djakarta, August 19, 1959,* can be understood at one level as reflecting the experience of canonists in the Roman curia, like the missionaries in the New World, becoming acquainted with the multitude of marriage cases created by unbending application of the old rules. The men in the curia, benevolently responding to urgent necessities, had come up with a solution in which the key was placed in the curia. The result was that a lawful, valid, consummated but nonsacramental marriage, celebrated with proper dispensation before a Catholic priest, could be set aside to eliminate a sin on the part of a Catholic not a party to the dissolved marriage. The changes can be seen, more broadly, as reflecting the experience of Catholics increasingly marrying the unbaptized in a culture where civil divorce was widespread.

John XXIII and Paul VI dissolved thousands of nonsacramental marriages. The customary charge was two hundred dollars, a sum small in any single case, large when multiplied. In 1970, Rome suddenly suspended the practice, while Paul VI was still the pope. The suspension coincided with the Church's battle against introduction into Italy of a divorce law and the Church's efforts to repeal it. Conversion of the person whose marriage was being dissolved was again required as if only the Pauline privilege worked. The pope's power was debated in a committee the pope set up. In 1973, the old practice resumed. The rules governing it were modestly revised and reissued, although "privately" and still not officially made public.

In 1980, a commission created to revise the 1917 Code of Canon Law published the proposed new text. The commission had begun its work in 1963; from 1973 to 1980 it had revised the original draft, consulting all the bishops, the bishops' conferences, the Roman congregations, and the competent university faculties. Now in 1980, the draft took its "final step" as it was submitted once more to the fathers of the commission. Proposed canon 1104 declared that a marriage in which at least one party was unbaptized "can be dissolved by the Roman Pontiff in favor of the faith." Canons 1659 through 1662 sketched the procedure "for the instruction of the process." Two years later, in January 1983, the new code was promulgated. The five canons were gone.

Hot on this disappearance, an explanation appeared in an article published by Umberto Betti, O.F.M. Betti had been one of a small, select group of theologians chosen by John Paul II to meet with the pope and methodically review every canon proposed in the penultimate draft. According to Betti, the objection had been raised in this group that the papal power exercised in privilege of the faith cases appeared to rest on an unsupported theological foundation, namely, that as Vicar of Christ, the pope was like Christ himself man-God, able to "derogate from the laws of nature, among them the indissolubility of naturally lawful marriage." Betti put the case for the power in a preposterous way, while touching on a central difficulty. But apparently as nothing better was put forward, the pope's special committee had decided that the canons be dropped to permit "deepening" of the consideration of the vicarial power and to put into an ecumenical context the pope's "extra-ecclesial power."

Publishing his account almost simultaneously with the appearance of the new code, Betti was plainly pleased with what had happened. The central canon on dissolution in favor of the faith had "disappeared without a trace." But Betti, in making the most of his victory, overlooked three new canons that survived. Canon 1150 said simply that "the privilege of the faith enjoys the favor of the law," a kind of privileging of a privilege now unmentioned. And canons 1148 and 1149 preserved the teaching of *Romani pontificis* of Pius V and of *Populis et nationibus* of Gregory XIII, without mentioning the privilege of the faith in so many words. Canon 1148 addressed the case of an unbaptized man who "has simultaneously several unbaptized wives." He converted. "It would be hard for him" to remain with the first wife. He "can retain one of them, dismissing the others." The same held for an unbaptized woman with several unbaptized husbands. The requirement of simultaneity of spouses eliminated the earlier benign interpretation of *Romani pontificis* that the spouses could be successive. Canon 1149 dealt with an unbaptized person unable to restore cohabitation with an unbaptized spouse "by reason of captivity or persecution." After reception into the Church, the baptized spouse "can contract another marriage." Canon 1150 rounded out these provisions with a single sentence: "In a doubtful matter the privilege of the faith enjoys the favor of the law."

These canons made no reference to any action by the pope. They made available to any convert in the situations described the right to terminate his or her marriage after a determination, in the case of a simultaneous plurality of spouses, that it would be hard to treat the first one as the lawful one or, in the case of certain enforced separations, a determination that cohabitation was not possible. The only reference to a privilege being exercised was in the very general language of canon 1150. Without stating that the old marriages were dissolved or were invalid, these canons boldly authorized the convert to enter a new marriage. Indeed canon 1148 made explicit the expectation or requirement—which alternative was not entirely clear—that the convert enter a new marriage with the chosen spouse according to canon law with a dispensation from disparity of religion. The canons preserved the essence of *Romani pontificis* and *Populis et nationibus* and preserved their silence on the underlying theology. On their face, canons 1148 and 1149 permitted divorce in the several situations they described. The theological rationale remained to be enunciated.

The retention of canons 1148 and 1149 while jettisoning the central canon on the power to divorce defies logic. It does not defy explanation for those familiar with the workings of other legal systems. A legal system is not a logical system. It is a system for balancing values—balancing them as the body balances blood and oxygen, cholesterol and oxidants. This kind of balance does not work by syllogisms but, in the case of a corporate organism, by prudent choices as to how much of one element the organism can take without impairing another element. In the case of divorce, the makers of the law judged that some divorce could be recognized in the 1983 code itself, more divorce would be reserved to the pope, and the name "divorce" would never be used. A balance was struck. A balance of this kind is not eternal. It is open to revision.

As the Code of 1917 had been superceded, nothing in canon law clearly authorized the papal practice of dissolving particular marriages in favor of the faith. Canonists naturally asked if the privilege would no longer be granted. In September 1983, the Congregation for the Doctrine of the Faith assured the apostolic delegate to the United States that the Norms of 1973 were still in force. As all public law supporting them had disappeared, their validity appeared to rest on the simple assertion that the pope would follow them.

In 1980, a survey of dioceses in the United States showed that, in the previous year, they had accepted 1,320 privilege of the faith cases. A similar survey, ten years later, showed the number fallen to 612; ten years after that, in 1999, the number was 353. The most striking feature of the survey was the variation among dioceses. In 1979, Chicago led with 87 cases followed by Los Angeles with 86 and Louisville with 56. In the later surveys, Los Angeles led the list with 57 and 43 for 1989 and 1999 respectively. Chicago, Detroit, and Indianapolis were among the leaders. New York reported 6, 0, and 12. Zero was often the report of some dioceses. Clearly the attitude of diocesan officials and dissemination of information about the privilege affected its use. The figures reported did not reflect the number of dissolutions actually effected in Rome; but the dioceses would not have taken the cases if Rome were not receptive.

The same randomness observed in the United States was also true of other countries and continents. In 2002, 649 petitions were received in Rome, 363 of them from the United States, followed by 58 from Germany and 47 from the United Kingdom; from all of Africa there was only 1. The Congregation for the Doctrine of the Faith, reporting these statistics, noted that it was a year after the papal approval of new norms and that the congregation had sent out in various languages some material "to facilitate the preparation of the cases in the diocesan phase." Many dioceses could not have been interested.

The excuse for quasi-secrecy—produced nearly seventy years after the Norms of 1934 were issued—was that the media would have distorted the information. Of course the media would have said that the Church was running a divorce mill. It would have been an exaggeration, no doubt unfairly exploited. But the truth—that the pope was granting divorces—would have been at the core of the story available anyway to anyone who cared to look or to ask. The anomalous concealment was partial and symptomatic of theological difficulties.

In 2001, John Paul II had issued a revised set of rules to govern the privilege. The pope still supplied no public law authorizing its use. Gasparri in 1891 had written of "full divorce—that is, as to the bond." Later usage spoke of "dissolution," as if "divorce" was a word to be avoided. No difference between dissolution and divorce in fact existed, except as to the authority ending an existing marriage.

The form used by the Congregation for the Doctrine of the Faith (the CDF) in the present pontificate is as follows (translated from the Latin):

Of the Dissolution of a Marriage
in Favor of the Faith

[Reference is made to the baptism or lack of it by one or both of the parties and to the fact that "a process to obtain dissolution" was begun in a particular diocese. The CDF is asked:] "Is the Most Holy to be offered advice to dissolve, in favor of the faith, the above-referenced marriage, so that the petitioner can lawfully and validly enter a new marriage before the Church?" The answer follows as a decree: "Yes." There follows the record of the pope's own assent in these words:

> Our Most Holy Lord John Paul II, by divine providence pope, on the report given of all of the above, benevolently deigned to give approval in favor of the grace according to the above-reported Decree.

The formula conveying the papal decision is ambiguous. Is the pope dissolving the marriage or is he authorizing the petitioner to proceed to a second marriage? His approval is *pro gratia*, "on behalf of the grace" or, as translated above, "in favor of the grace." But does approval on behalf of or in favor of it mean that the pope accomplishes the dissolution? The CDF affirmatively advises the pope "to dissolve" the marriage; presumably, he acts on this advice.

Gasparri understood the privilege of the faith cases to involve two steps. The first was the papal dispensation permitting a second marriage to take place. The second step was the second marriage. Only the second marriage actually dissolved the bond of the first. The operation of the Pauline privilege was the model. But the Pauline privilege was an imperfect analogy. In that case, in Thomas Aquinas's memorable words, "the more firm" dissolved "the less firm," that is, a sacramental marriage replaced a nonsacramental one. Cases of privilege of the faith could involve one nonsacramental marriage replacing another, as happened in *Djakarta, August 19, 1959*. So the old explanation would not work. The conviction has become firm among canonists that it is the pope's act that breaks the first bond.

However the privilege was understood, John Paul II, who is untiring in his insistence on the indissolubility of marriage, appears as a principal in its dissolution. John Henry Newman would describe such a development as "a difficulty."

Out of Difficulties Comes Development

The *Catechism of the Catholic Church,* approved by John Paul II in 1992, denounced divorce as "a grave offense against the natural law." In four paragraphs devoted to the offense, the catechism did not mention divorce by exercise of the Pauline privilege or by exercise of the privilege of the faith; nor were these two privileges mentioned in the index or in any other part of the book. In this way, what John Paul II presented as "a sure norm for teaching the faith" concealed the practice and taught nothing of the doctrine justifying it.

The secrecy with which the norms governing the process were published and republished, the suspension of the process from 1970 to 1973, the elimination of explicit reference to the process in the new code of 1983, the silence of the catechism of 1992, all reflected the uncertainties of a doctrine whose destined development was uncertain. What was missing was an explanation commanding agreement as to the theological basis for the practice. Every theory offered was subject to objection.

The most basic difficulty was posed by Scripture. "In the beginning," Jesus said, marriage was not dissoluble. Presented in the Gospels as a teaching to the Jews, the text affirmed indissolubility. "What God has joined together, let no man separate," Jesus said (Mk 10:6–9; Mt 19:4–6). Could his command be circumvented or reinterpreted?

By nature, the Church had long taught, marriage is indissoluble. So Innocent III, writing the bishop of Tiberias, had interpreted the words of Jesus and ruled that the marriages of unbelievers in the crusader Kingdom of Jerusalem were valid. Incorporated into canon law as the decretal *Gaudemus,* this ruling had governed the missionaries in the Americas, Africa, and Asia and had caused the crises of conscience leading to the extraordinary solutions of Pius V and Gregory XIII. Not only were the marriages of unbelievers valid, but Innocent expressly declared, "the sacrament of marriage exists among believers and unbelievers, as the Apostle shows"; the pope went on to quote 1 Corinthians 7:13.

The theologians embraced natural indissolubility and sought to find a reason for it. The most appealing argument was advanced by Thomas Aquinas in *The Truth of the Catholic Faith or Summa Against the Gentiles.* Love made it fitting that marriage be "entirely indissoluble." As Thomas put it:

> The greater a friendship is, the firmer and more lasting should it be. Between husband and wife there appears to be the greatest friendship for they are united not only in the act of carnal coupling—which even among beasts makes a certain sweet partnership—but for the fellowship of all of domestic life. Hence, in sign of this fellowship, as Genesis 2 says, a man puts away both his father and his mother for the sake of his wife.

Genesis 2:24 had said "they shall be one flesh." In Thomas's argument it was not only the physical unity of the flesh in intercourse which established indissolubility. Indissolubility was indicated by the psychological unity reached in a friendship which was maximal. *Maxima amicitia* is Thomas's phrase. Friendship—Thomas's term for the love of another being because of that being's similarity to oneself, as distinguished from concupiscence or the love of another because of a deficiency in oneself—stressed the equality of the spouses and the uniqueness of marital love. Without demonstrating that natural law required indissolubility, Thomas declared it fitting that marriage be indissoluble. This conclusion was stated as to all marriages. It has remained a Catholic teaching. As Shakespeare put it in Sonnet 116:

> Love is not love
> Which alters when it alteration finds.

Vatican II, speaking of all marriages, declared that "the mutual gift" of the spouses urged "their indissoluble unity." Marriage, John Paul II instructed the Roman Rota in 2001, was "the sacrament of something that was part of the very economy of creation; the conjugal covenant was instituted by the Creator." Indissolubility, the pope told the Roman Rota in 2002, was not a law extrinsic to marriage, not something extra imposed upon the marital union. Divine design made it this way by nature. Human nature, as fashioned by God, made indissolubility an "essential property of marriage." For that reason, the pope instructed the advocates of the Rota, for lawyers to seek to destroy a marriage by divorce, as distinguished from seeking the civil benefits of a divorce, was to act for "an end contrary to justice."

Indissoluble by their nature and by the nature of human beings, in some sense a symbolic sign, formed by God at their inception, subject to the express command of Christ not to set asunder, the marriages of the unbaptized seemed to be unlikely candidates for dissolution by a pope. Observation suggests that many marriages involving an unbaptized person or two unbaptized persons are marked by fidelity and fruitfulness, caring and constancy, mutual tenderness and deep love, in degree no different from the marriages of the baptized. The category "less firm" is a legal conclusion. The down-putting phrase simply reasserts the canonical practice that treats these marriages as dissoluble if dissolution will be of benefit to the faith of a beliver. Yet in the very allocution to the Rota in which the pope speaks of the injustice of seeking to end a marriage, John Paul II referred in passing to the dissolution of sacramental, unconsummated marriages and to cases involving the privilege of the faith. On what basis did the pope act?

The approach favored by several authorities boldly asserted that, when the pope acted to dissolve a nonsacramental marriage, he acted as more than a human being, so that "man" was not dissolving the affected marriage. The foundation of this position went back to Lotario de'Segni, Innocent III, the most self-confident of popes. According to his understanding of his own office, he was "less than God" but "more than man." Defending the power of the pope to transfer a bishop from his see, Innocent wrote:

> Sacred Scripture has taught us that "those whom God has joined together, man may not separate." But conjugal joining is of two kinds: one according to the flesh, which is called carnal, the other according to the spirit, which is not unfittingly called spiritual. . . . Carnal joining effects this, that they are two in one flesh, according to what the Truth said, "They, therefore, are not two but one flesh." Spiritual joining effects this, that they are two in one spirit, according to the saying of the Apostle, "Who adheres to God is one spirit with him." To both carnal and spiritual joining applies what was set out above, "What God has joined, let man not separate"; so

it is not lawful for a man to divide those coupled lawfully in marriage nor to separate those joined canonically in spiritual marriage, as are a bishop and his church.

It could seem from this that the Supreme Pontiff could not divide a spiritual marriage, that of a bishop and his church; but according to custom, which is the best interpreter of the laws, and according to the sacred canons, it may be held that by resignation, deposition, and translation, which are reserved to the Apostolic See alone, the Supreme Pontiff has plenary power over these affairs. That will cause no scruple of doubt in those who understand it properly; it happens not by human but by divine authority, and in this matter is carried out by the Supreme Pontiff, who is called not the vicar of mere man but truly the Vicar of the true God. Although we are successors of the prince of the apostles, we are not the vicar of any apostle or man, but we are the Vicar of Jesus Christ himself. Wherefore, whom God had bound by a spiritual union, no man, because not the vicar of man, but God, because the Vicar of God, separates, when we on occasion remove bishops from their sees by their resignation, deposition, or translation.

Under the imperious impetus of Innocent III the papacy saw what its role could be. The curial canonists throve on metaphor. It was irrelevant that neither a bishop or his see had existed when the Lord spoke of marriage. The lawyers saw the appropriateness of applying his words in the church context. The application created a legal difficulty. But legal metaphor could come to the rescue. The pope was no man when he was God's substitute! The point was made again by Innocent III in *Quanto personam,* a letter to the bishop of Metz. The pope's dissolution of a bishop's marriage to his see was "not by human but rather by divine authority."

As one reads these exuberant epistles, both issued in 1198 by a pope only a few months in office, one wonders if the power asserted to divorce a diocese from its head was being sharpened to use on troubled human marriages. A slightly later ruling by Innocent III, *Inter corporalia,* did teach the same doctrine and emphatically made this point: "Between bodily matters and spiritual matters we have recognized there to be one difference, that bodily matters are more easily destroyed than built, spiritual matters more easily built than destroyed." If this were the case, in teaching that the pope could destroy the spiritual marriage of bishop and see, was he not effectively claiming the power to dissolve any human marriage? Whatever the pope had in mind, he did not follow through on it.

When in 1234 the definitive collection of decretals was assembled under Gregory IX, *Inter corporalia* and *Quanto personam* entered the collection; they were placed not in *De divortiis* but among rules regulating the administration of dioceses.

Innocent's premise, that the pope had a unique status as the vicar of God or of Jesus Christ (he used God and Christ interchangeably in the formula), represented a mutation in theology. Earlier authorities had spoken of bishops or even priests as vicars of God or of Christ. Henry de Bracton, a good twelfth-century lawyer familiar with canon law, had written of the king of England as "the vicar of God." For Innocent, as his emphatic "truly the Vicar of the True God" made clear, the pope's position was different: it was unique. The doctrine underlay *Unam sanctam* issued in 1303 by Benedetto Gaetani, Boniface VIII. The words of Christ, "Feed my sheep" (Jn 21:17), were construed by the pope to mean that all human beings were committed to Peter. Boniface VIII concluded: "Therefore we declare, announce, and define that it is necessary to salvation that every human creature be subject to the Roman Pontiff." Possession of this unlimited jurisdiction was assumed by Nicholas V, Calixtus III, and Alexander VI as they disposed of the lands of unbelievers in Africa or the Americas.

Pronouncements of this kind by Innocent III, who accepted England as a papal fief, or by the popes whose grants to Portugal and Spain were prized by their rulers, have an archaic ring. Do popes today believe that every human creature is subject to their jurisdiction? As recently as 1960, on the eve of the Second Vatican Council, Alfredo Ottaviani, cardinal and prefect of the Holy Office, set out the following in the fourth edition of his treatise on public ecclesiastical law:

> The vicarial power is exercised not as proper to the Church over her own subjects but by the Church as acting in place of Christ over his subjects; for by the vicarial power the Roman Pontiff can do what he cannot otherwise reach by force of naked spiritual primacy over the Church and by force of the commands of the Church.

Ottaviani illustrated the use of the vicarial power by the pope dissolving a non-sacramental marriage. He explained the extraordinary extent of the vicarial power by stating, "As to all creatures Christ has commanded the Church to do what is necessary to save them." The exercise of this power, Ottaviani maintained, "touches the rights and the duties of the unbaptized." How could that be? Ottaviani's answer was that marriage was "a sacred matter" and its regulation therefore fell to Christ's vicar.

The extensive concept of papal power is, therefore, not a dead relict of the Middle Ages. It has been present in the minds of modern members of the Roman curia and appears in works written in Roman seminaries. A handbook on favor of the faith cases in North American dioceses adopts the same position: "the pope in using vicarious authority is not acting in his own name as head of the Church and is not exercising jurisdiction over ecclesiastical matter, but over divine matter." I was surprised but should not have been, given this literature, to hear an American canonist compare exercise of the Petrine power to a priest's consecration of bread and wine as the Eucharist, a miraculous transformation effected by extraordinary authority.

A further question is raised by the invocation of vicarial power. The theory gives the pope power to act as God, but abruptly limits that power when it comes to the consummated marriages of the baptized. These marriages, John Paul II has said, may be dissolved by no human power nor by the vicarial power. He repeats what he notes is common teaching "and is to be held as definitively defined doctrine." But when he gives a reason for the line drawn what he says is, "The opposite affirmation would imply the thesis that there does not exist any absolutely indissoluble marriage." The present practice implies that most of the marriages of the world are not indissoluble; this implication does not impede the practice.

The practice, championed by some of those professionally familiar with its use, appears to be wholly benign. Its exercise achieves what Erasmus had analogously urged in 1516, commenting on St. Paul to the Corinthians. Impressed by the number, especially in England, who were "stuck" in unhappy unions, Erasmus had argued for the pope's power to end distressed Christian marriages. The pope already did it, he observed, for marriages that were *ratum non consummatum*, confirmed but not consummated. How, he asked, did the act of intercourse make an already valid sacramental marriage utterly unbreakable? The line the popes had drawn to limit their power could properly be eliminated for one purpose: to help many to salvation.

Erasmus's argument was lost in the turmoil of the Reformation and the negative Catholic reaction to Luther's and Calvin's defense of divorce. But the rationale put forward by Erasmus was the rationale put forward for the privilege of the faith. Helping many to salvation, the privilege legitimized marriages, led to the Catholic upbringing of children, solved difficulties for Catholics seeking to marry unbaptized persons. So beneficent a power was hard to criticize. Almost as hard to criticize in curial circles was an explanation celebrating the unique role of the pope. Outside those circles, among Catholics when they heard of the privilege, there was wonder if not incredulity. As to unbelievers, who among them supposed or would admit that a pope could affect his or her marital rights?

No pope today would undertake to dispose of Antarctica or of extraterrestrial space in the way Nicholas V disposed of West Africa. The reason is obvious. No one would obey him. Is there any more reason to think that a papal rescript dissolving the union of two unbelievers would be given effect if it affected their property, the custody of their children, or their visitation rights? The system worked smoothly because no tangible consequences followed for the couple on whose marriage the pope acted.

The absence of any measurable effect on the couple whose marriage was dissolved by the pope underscored another problem with the exercise of papal jurisdiction. However broadly that jurisdiction was envisaged, what was offered was, at best, a theory of why papal jurisdiction could exist. The theory did not bring the affected couple before the pope. To do that, notice and process would be necessary. The Norms issued in 2001 do take pains to specify, "Let each spouse be heard." The hearing is to be in the local diocese as its bishop prepares the case to be sent to Rome. The defender of the bond is assigned the duty of objecting if there are reasons against the papal dissolution, but the mere validity of the marriage is not reason in itself. The civil decree of divorce or nullity is to be among the papers sent to Rome. As there is no way either the local bishop or the pope could compel the attendance of the unbaptized party whose marriage is undergoing scrutiny, the Norms tacitly assume that evidence of the civil decree is sufficient if the unbaptized party does not participate in the process. In theory, the marriage of two persons is now being dissolved. Yet the presence of both persons is not treated as indispensable.

In 1962, a bishop inquired if the papal rescript granting the privilege had to be communicated to the respondent if the respondent had "refused to cooperate or testified reluctantly" or if it could "be prudently foreseen that such a notification might beget odium towards the Church or serious difficulties for the petitioner." The Holy Office answered: "It is understood that the favor is to be communicated according to the prudent judgment of the Ordinary." Pursuant to this response, a person's marriage could be terminated by the pope and, if the local bishop so determined, he or she would never know it. In the same vein, there is no indication in *Djakarta, August 19, 1959* that Lo Ma was to be told that her marriage with Phan was over.

A somewhat distinct basis for the power has been proposed by canonists who have not been persuaded by the vicarial theory. The Church, they say, is a perfect society-perfect not in the sense of being without flaws, but in the sense of being complete. The Norms of 2001 reflect this view in their title, *Potestas*

Ecclesiae—"The Power of the Church." As a perfect or complete society, the Church must possess the means—"the plenitude of power"—to accomplish its end. Its chief end is the salvation of souls. When a marriage is dissolved, it is dissolved to make a present or potential Catholic spouse free to receive the sacraments. A privilege that, practically speaking, is so necessary must be among the powers that the Church possesses. The writers defending this analysis have added that, since the power pertains to salvation only, it cannot be brought to bear on temporal goods—a rejection of the old use of the vicarial power to distribute the property, countries, and persons of unbelievers.

Three objections can be offered to this explanation. First, only a tiny number of the broken marriages of the unbaptized are actually subjected to papal dissolution; so the power cannot be very necessary. Second, marriage is not a merely spiritual matter; it is the union of two persons. To say that the privilege of the faith affects a merely spiritual domain is to make a more modest claim than the assertion of the vicarial power over property and territory. The privilege, however, appears to bear on more than a spiritual realm; it bears on beating hearts within human bodies. Third, the objections already noted as to vicarial jurisdiction have not been resolved. That the Church is a complete society does not appear to bring with it a warrant to judge those outside the society. The case once made by Las Casas against Vitoria and all defenders of papal jurisdiction over infidels has never been refuted. Moreover, the needs of the Church are not a substitute for bringing before a tribunal the couple whose marital rights are at stake. Jurisdiction of the persons affected may still be lacking. Divorce affects the rights of both parties. How can the pope grant it without hearing the parties? According to the canon law itself, a judgment of nullity of marriage "suffers from the defect of irremediable nullity" if "it was rendered between parties at least one of whom did not have standing in the trial" or if "the right of defense was denied to one or the other party." If that is the law of annulments, why is it not the law as to papal dissolutions of marriage? Any non-Catholic, notified by a diocesan tribunal that his marriage may be dissolved by a papal rescript, might conclude that the matter was not within the papal jurisdiction and that accordingly he had no need to expend time and energy and money in defending the marriage. It is not evident that his voluntary absence from the process confers jurisdiction on the pope to dissolve his marriage.

To use round numbers, the population of the world is over six billion, of whom approximately one billion are baptized Catholics and another billion are baptized Christians in other churches. The theorists of the privilege of the faith say that the Catholic Church has jurisdiction over the marriages of the five-sixths of the world who acknowledge no allegiance to the Catholic Church. To these non-Catholics it would appear preposterous that their marriages could be judged valid or invalid or could even be entirely dissolved by a person they do not recognize as having any connection with them. The proposition that such jurisdiction exists would be dismissed by the non-Catholic world as madness or a joke. Anglicans, Orthodox, Protestants would likely find papal jurisdiction over their marriages to be as objectionable as would Buddhists, Hindus, Jews, and Moslems, not to mention the agnostics, atheists, undeclareds, and unsures that populate the more sophisticated sections of the world. In an age of Christian ecumenism, an implicit imperialism might be most offensive to non-Catholic Christians. A decent respect for the opinion of mankind requires the defenders of the privilege to take this probable reaction into account.

Suppose the privilege of the faith is examined not in terms of jurisdiction, but in terms of what is accomplished. Functionally considered, dissolution of marriage in favor of the faith is a determination that an earlier nonsacramental marriage by the Catholic or the intended spouse of the Catholic does not stand in the way of the Catholic now receiving the sacraments. Functionally considered, the papal exercise of power is the exercise of power over a Catholic's admission to the sacraments. It appears to be the exercise of a power within the competence of the head of the Church. Functionally considered, the power is not the exercise of jurisdiction over a universe some of whose members may never have heard of the pope and none of whose members acknowledge his authority to determine the existence of their marriages.

The trouble with this approach is that it sidesteps the status of the old marriage. If that marriage is not dissolved, the person marrying the Catholic is a bigamist, and the Catholic is a party to the bigamy. Unless the old union is terminated, the new is not justified, or polygamy is possible. It is highly unlikely that polygamy is being permitted in this way.

Whenever divorce is part of a social system, divorce operates to end a marriage by force of the law. No government treats marriage as dissoluble by a married person who does not attend to the requirements set by law. In other words, there is no distinction in the world at large between intrinsic and extrinsic indissolubility. All marriages are regularly treated as intrinsically indissoluble. To concede, as the canonists do, that natural marriage is extrinsically dissoluble is to concede that divorce is doable. The question is what law can do it.

Suppose, then, that one concluded that the old marriage has been terminated by a divorce granted by civil authority. The objection that polygamy is being permitted disappears. The objection based on a lack of hearing for the couple also disappears. The civil court has decided the parties' rights. The power of the pope has not been extended over people uncaring or unknowing of its existence. The marriage of the unbelievers, intrinsically indissoluble, has been extrinsically ended.

To this analysis it will be objected that, as marriage is a sacred matter, the civil authority is powerless to end it; only the Church has competence. But this answer seems to reflect the unwillingness of the Church to give up authority over a matter where, for some centuries in Western Europe, the Church was the sole authority. This authority has been pushed aside by a regime of civil marriage and civil divorce. Many people are married before judges, city clerks, or registrars. If these people are regarded as joined by God, why are they not regarded as separated by God when civic officials divorce them? Defenders of the death penalty, faced with the argument that only God can dispose of human life, have argued that the state in conducting an execution is God's agent. If the state can be conceived of as exercising divine power here—and the conception is nourished by St. Paul's view of the sword of the state as God's minister (Rom 13:4)—is it not possible to think of the state as God's minister in unmaking marriage?

It will be said that marriage is only made by divine institution, not dissolved by it. But this response merely restates the Church's claim to a monopoly over marital dissolution. The history of the Church in the first millennium does not support that claim even as to Christians, let alone unbelievers. Today, the diocesan tribunal processing a petition for exercise of the privilege of the faith certifies that there is no hope of the couple's reconciliation, basing its judgment in part on the decree of divorce. Plainly, the Church does not favor the use of civil divorce. But, given the present procedure incorporating reference to the decree of divorce, for the Church to recognize that civil authority has already terminated the marriage would not be a very big step in practice. To acknowledge the effect of the civil divorce would be a very big step in doctrine, at one stroke giving up the claimed exercise of a special power and recognizing the competence of secular governments to grant divorce.

Acceptance of the efficacy of civil divorce would not explain a case like *Djakarta, August 19, 1959* as far as its reported facts go; nor would it explain canons 1148 and 1149, which on their face make no requirement of civil divorce. Therefore, recourse cannot be had to civil divorce alone to explain the extent of the exercise of the privilege. At the same time the likelihood of civil divorce being possible in the *Djakarta* case and in the cases envisaged by canons 1148 and 1149 would explain why the privilege of the faith did not seem anomalous in such situations.

Erasmus observed that when a bishop declares a marriage to be invalid, he acts to disjoin a couple once believed to be joined by God. The decree of nullity, he suggested, can be seen as a disjoining by God of what God did not join. Reference to God in these contexts is not to visible divine action but to what is viewed with religious reverence as done in accordance with the will of God. A formal canonical declaration of nullity is treated in this way by Catholics; so is "full divorce—that is, as to the bond," when the divorce is effected by papal rescript or by exercise of the Pauline privilege.

According to the theologians, marriage is made by the exchange of consent between man and woman; a priest or other official is a mere witness to the exchange. God's part in forming the union is through the action of the couple. Also, according to the theologians, in the Pauline case the second marriage of a convert dissolves the first marriage; so that God's part consists in the action of the second couple that brings about the dissolution. If God acts invisibly in forming marriages and dissolving them in the Pauline case, it may be asked why God's action should be restricted to the papal process in the case of the privilege of the faith.

The great majority of married persons in the world have no connection with the Catholic Church. They consider themselves married because they have complied with the teachings of their religion or the laws of their state, or both; they do not necessarily believe that they have been joined by God. The Church, nonetheless, presumes that the many various conjugal unions are effected by God. May we not suppose that such marriages, once entered, are joinings by God that can be disjoined by the civil means ordinarily available? Are such disjoinings as much by God's power as were the original joinings?

Obviously the magisterium has not answered these questions affirmatively, but the need for development of the underlying doctrine has been acknowledged. In 1995, Umberto Betti, who in 1983 had celebrated the disappearance of the canons on the privilege of the faith, commented again on their disappearance. As Betti now enlarged on his earlier report, on September 17, 1982, he had argued before John Paul II that the practice of dissolving the marriages of the unbaptized was "destitute of a secure theological foundation" and that "the extraecclesial power" of the pope "to derogate from the natural law of indissolubility of marriage" was still "entirely to be demonstrated." The pope responded that he had confidence in the judgment of Paul VI approving the Norms of 1973 but that "such a grave question ought to be explored more deeply." Betti records no further discussion. The five canons were withdrawn from the Code of Canon Law promulgated in 1983. Betti did not explain how canons 1148, 1149, and 1150 had survived or why he and the pope did not notice that they contained the essence of the power said to be devoid of theological foundation.

Janusz Kowal, a Polish Jesuit teaching at the Gregorian University, has noted that when, nearly twenty years later, John Paul II approved the new norms governing privilege of the faith cases, it appeared that "he had reached the same certainty" as that of his predecessors who had dissolved marriages of the unbaptized since 1924. The deepening of the doctrine that had occurred, Kowal intimated, was the move from the pope's vicarial power to the purely spiritual plenitude of power of the Church. Kowal also suggested that there was movement towards "an always more unitary explanation of the different forms of exercise of such power, including the Pauline privilege." The term "Petrine privilege"—apparently an attractive parallel to "Pauline privilege"—had never been used in official documents and now disappeared from use. Consolidation of the powers as "the power of the Church" shifted the focus from power personal to the pope, but did not explain how the Church had jurisdiction over nonmembers of the Church or over persons not brought before a tribunal of the Church.

Canons 1148 and 1149 of the 1983 Code make general the ability of a convert to disregard a marriage contracted before baptism in three specified situations—where it would be hard to live with the first of a plurality of spouses; where "captivity" blocks cohabitation; where "persecution" blocks cohabitation. If the Church has power to legislate this broadly as to the validity of a convert's new marriage, why could the Church not recognize that separations effected by civil divorce can be as much an obstacle to cohabitation as prison or persecution? Why is the polygamist or polyandrist who converts in a better position than one with several spouses serially married?

As the development of doctrine now stands for Catholics, all the marriages of the world, save those between two baptized persons, are in theory dissolvable by the Church in a process culminating in action reserved to the pope. Adultery can be avoided by a papal grace. A bigamist can make the sin disappear by securing the disappearance of a previous marriage. A papal rescript does the work. The development from the words of Jesus in Mark and Matthew has been great. The development would not have occurred in a culture where civil divorce did not exist.

Is this development beyond change? It is embodied in the practice of the popes for the last eighty years. It had its first employment in the sixteenth century. It had its first explanation in the fourth century in Isaac's interpretation of the passage in Paul. It has its foundation in the assertion of authority by the Apostle. It is unlikely to be abandoned. Not completely reconciling the practice of papal divorce with the doctrine of indissolubility, John Paul II has continued the practice, in the apparent trust that doctrine will mature. The development must be awaited.

"A brother or a sister is not enslaved in these matters," Paul wrote at the start of the development. To hold a believer bound by a marriage that he or she could dissolve was to deprive the believer of a rightful liberty. For all believers who do not have knowledge of the privilege of the faith or access to it as a solution, is it not a form of enslavement to hold them bound in a broken marriage that could be dissolved? For all those whose different beliefs make them treat the civil dissolution of marriage as final, is it not to enslave them to assert that only the Church has power over their marriages?

To restate the difficulties from which development will come, it is the present teaching of the Church that

1. All marriages are naturally indissoluble.
2. Only the Church has power to end a marriage.
3. Polygamy is contrary to the secondary precepts of the natural law; the Church does not accept polygamy.
4. Under certain circumstances, a convert to Christianity can dissolve his or her existing marriage to an unbaptized person by marrying another person.
5. Under certain circumstances, the pope can dissolve, in favor of the faith of a Catholic, an existing marriage in which one party is unbaptized and to which the Catholic need not be a party.
6. Under certain circumstances, currently specified in canon law, the marriages of unbaptized persons are dissolved by law when one party to the marriage converts and marries again.

The exception proves the rule, that is, the exception tests the rule. Sometimes the larger principle hides in the exception. Favor of the faith has created an exception to the indissolubility of marriage, making it dissoluble under specified circumstances. Adequate explanation of the privilege and its mode of exercise has not been made. The doctrine has developed without resolving the tension between natural indissolubility and the power to divorce.

THE TEST OF THE TEACHING

How Development Can Be Dated, Cannot Be Denied, and Should Neither Be Exaggerated Nor Ignored

The death of Jesus occurred in Palestine under the Roman rule of Pontius Pilate. The event provides an approximate date for the doctrines ascribed to Jesus—when they were enunciated, when they were collected, when they were edited—so that the kernel of Christian morals must be placed in the first century of the Christian era, with roots in the Hebrew Bible and the Mediterranean world that can also be approximately dated. Subsequently, Christian morals were articulated by the authorities later recognized as the Fathers, men living within the Roman Empire at particular dates. Moral rules were occasionally formulated by councils or by popes. Beginning in the twelfth century in Western Europe, an immense corpus of learning attentive to morals came out of the new universities and was the work of theologians and canon lawyers. Interacting with the learning—feeling it, leavening it, applying it—were the lives of millions of persons who professed the faith.

Continuing into the present millennium with the papal publication of rules governing the dissolution of marriages by the pope, the enunciation of Christian morals has been a historical enterprise, each state of it bearing a date. What bears a date will become dated, that is, appropriate to its date and not completely appropriate to a new date. To discard the dated and to preserve the permanently vital is the work of development.

The famous formula of Vincent of Lérins is "that we may hold to be believed what has been believed everywhere, ever, by everyone." Vincent added: "But perhaps someone asks, 'Will there, then, be no progress in the Church of Christ?'" He answers this anonymous questioner, "There will be, plainly and fully. For who is so envious of men and so exiled from God as to try to forbid it?" To disarm the questioner, he adds, "Yet that is not to be change but truly progress in the faith." He goes on to give the biological metaphor later used by Newman: it will be the way the identity of the person is preserved as a child becomes an adult. The same always and, still, growth. Growth without change. Reconciliation is no easier and no harder than when Vincent wrote.

Development is a form of change. Change is unsettling and for that reason resisted or denied. Change is especially unsettling because change in area X may be used to justify or to imply a change in area Y; and the resister is sure that area Y can never change. The proper course, however, is neither to deny or resist changes that have demonstrably taken place, but to challenge their bearing on the doctrine the resister sees as solid and unshakeable. If the resister is right, the justification or implication from area X will not affect his citadel. Yes, but the development will be put forward as an analogy; and morals, like their cousin, law, proceed by analogies. That can't be helped. The resister to change will have to discount the analogy, show the differences in the essential features of X and Y, and the strength of his position on Y in its own right. He has some reason to dislike being forced to deal with the development that constitutes the analogy; he has no reason to deny the development.

If development is easy to exaggerate by partisans of change, it is even easier to ignore. Millions of Catholics are unaware of the particular changes that have taken place in moral teaching. The change on usury happened long ago and may be dismissed as merely a change in economic conditions with no sense of the fierce theological battles that accomplished the change. Religious liberty and the abolition of slavery were effected by secular laws. The laws were accepted as good laws before the formal magisterium altered. Vatican II on these subjects did not affect the conduct of any believer. The development under way on divorce is unknown except by specialists. Ignorance of the changes made or in progress assures a contented assumption that all morals are beyond alteration. But to close one's eyes or to be merely uninformed as to what has happened and is happening produces a false security. Ignorance is a baseless bulwark of belief.

The deepest resistance to change may arise at the vital core of the resister. Life certainties are being disturbed. The resister has staked his or her salvation on the truth of certain religious propositions and on the impossibility of error in any one of them. It is unbearable that any of these propositions should fall into doubt, desuetude, or repudiation. Analogy again is agonizing. If this one goes, why not that one? The resister's rock will become a mound of broken boulders. Better to shut one's eyes, better to cling to the old fortifications, than let anything be displaced. The impulse comes from the heart. The human heart hungers for certainty about the human person's destiny after death. Danger lies in any religious truth being open to development. Development may dissolve doctrine at its core. Change has to be fought lest the whole edifice of belief crumble.

We can recognize this existential dread. All of us share it. Recognition and sharing do not release us from confronting change when change has occurred. But the greatest obstacle to acknowledging that change has occurred is what appears as a concomitant of the acknowledgment: the admission of error. Could the Church actually have been wrong on a moral question? *Absit!* many an old theologian would have cried. The disinclination to recognize the possibility ignores the infallibility with which the Church is endowed. The infallibility is true of teaching within strictly defined limits. Those limits must be respected. More importantly, the implication of infallibility must be drawn. If the Church is infallible only under certain specified conditions, the Church is fallible the rest of the time. The doctrine of infallibility is an invitation neither to dogmatism nor skepticism, but to the admission of mistakes where the rest of the time they may have been made.

It may be said that the Church will lose moral authority by acknowledging error in its moral teaching. Who will trust a guide that admits mistakes? Fear of this question often dogs authority. It may be answered by three analogies, none of the situations exactly the same as that of the Church, but close enough to be helpful. Do parents lose or gain authority with their children when they admit to a mistake in guiding them? For modern children, the parents' candor enhances respect for their parents' wisdom and loving care. Does a judicial system gain or lose authority by admitting errors? In the United States an elaborate system of appeals has been set up to correct errors by courts, with state courts sometimes subjected to additional correction by federal courts; it is assumed that error may occur. The Supreme Court itself often reverses its views on the constitution, finding its earlier reading of the text erroneous. Yet nowhere, it may be guessed, is the prestige of a judicial system higher than in the United States. Finally, the modern scientific enterprise is built on the assumption that any conclusion is open to challenge and correction; answers are always tentative, hypothetical, subject to refutation or revision. Yet scientific knowledge is probably the most highly prized secular knowledge that the present world possesses. Admitting error, the Church would not fare worse than parents, judges, or scientists, except perhaps among those who have conceived of the magisterium as a perfect machine perfectly enunciating moral truth in all ways at all times in all places.

How We Are Innocent Despite the Development of Our Descendants

The difficulty in writing about development in morals is to understand and not to judge those whose moral standards have been surpassed. Can anyone today contemplate the slave trader and slaveholder without a shudder of disgust? Can anyone empathize with the bigot putting a torch to the stake where the condemned heretic will be incinerated? Abstractly, we may concede that the slaveowner and the persecutor thought that they acted justly. In our bones we experience repugnance and even righteous rage.

To counteract these impulses, impossible to eradicate entirely, I offer three analogies. They are not perfect—what analogy is? But looking at ourselves as our descendants may look at us may ease the severity of our judgments of our ancestors and diminish the prejudice we bring to their case.

Imagine an intelligent, inquisitive friend, inclined to contrarian positions and unwilling to accept many cliches. He ruminates on evils associated with the automobile industry. "Autos, buses, trucks, they pollute the country," he exclaims. "Do you realize how much air pollution is attributable to the automobile? It's estimated at 60 million short tons of pollutants in our country. Even worse, autos cripple and kill—over 6 million accidents annually; over 3 million persons injured; over 40,000 persons killed within the fifty states. Automobiles kill more people than the Atlantic slave trade did. You may say that drivers don't deliberately kill; but we, as the group engaged in the common enterprise of driving, know in advance each year that, as a result of our collective activity, there will be 40,000 more corpses."

At this point you may begin to think of all the advantages automobiles bring and to murmur that our economy, indeed our whole society, could not exist without them. So why is your friend trying to convince you that you cooperate in a system of killing? You dismiss his observations as intellectual banter. You would be appalled if the bishops of the United States announced that driving was a sin, and if confessors began asking, "Have you driven a car? How many times?" The sin of automobile driving is not only unknown, it is scarcely conceivable.

A second analogy: You have a charming friend who is a vegetarian. You are impressed by the strictness with which she keeps from eating meat. You explore the basis of her conduct. "It was health, to begin with," she assures you. "You do have a duty to preserve your body. Meat's not exactly good for you. Then I began to think about the way meat is produced—the way chickens and cattle are bred for slaughter. I found it repugnant to benefit from the process. Then I read a philosopher who argued that animals have rights. Jane Goodall, after a lifetime of studying chimpanzees, maintains that they not only have feelings but spiritual moments. Harvard Law School's Larry Tribe has suggested that at least chimpanzees are protected from enslavement by the Thirteenth Amendment: the amendment doesn't speak of human slavery but bars 'slavery' generally. Animals do have sensations and perceptions, and some do exercise some sort of practical judgment. I began to see my species gave me no reason to dine on theirs. I came to believe, as Matthew Scully puts it, 'that animal welfare is not just a moral problem to be solved in statutes, but a moral opportunity to fill out our own lives with acts of compassion.' You find cannibalism nauseating. I feel the same way about eating my fellow sentient creatures."

Impressed as you may have been by such a candid declaration of conscience, you would still be more than surprised if the pope should issue an encyclical entitled *Iura animalium*, stating without ambiguity that it was intrinsically evil for any human animal to eat any other animal.

After these two exercises of imagining the improbable, suppose you encounter Charles Colson or someone like him who has worked in prison reform. He informs you of what life is like in many prisons he has visited—the repeated humiliation of body searches, the occasional bursts of brutality, the constant specter of sexual assault, and, above all, the absence of any hope. In addition to such conditions that can vary—there are model penitentiaries as well as bad ones—he notes that prisons are inefficient in changing conduct. The recidivism rate in the United States is close to 50 percent three years after release; in California it's 70 percent, eighteen months after release. At least a portion of the recidivists have been made more likely to commit crime by their time in prison, for prisons, in general, are destructive of persons. Finally, he notes that the prison system, in the vast majority of cases, punishes the innocent along with the guilty. To your "How?" he answers, "By inflicting deprivation on the prisoners' families, taking away a husband or a wife, a father or a mother, a son or a daughter and causing great emotional distress and much financial hardship to those entirely innocent of the crime for which the prisoner is incarcerated. We wonder at China in the Sung era, which deliberately imposed shame on the entire family of one judged guilty of serious crime or for some crimes punished the wife along with the culprit who was her husband. We don't shame the family, we merely destroy its normal life. How can we say we do not punish the innocent?"

Avoiding this question as not within your responsibilities, you would doubtless be taken aback if a general council of the Church listed among the great evils of the age "the system of incarcerating persons to the great detriment of family life"; and your surprise would turn to shock if moral theologians then began to say that no conscientious person could vote for legislators who imposed incarceration as a punishment for crime.

I put these analogies forward not as an advocate of the abolition of automobiles or of a ban on carnivorous dining or of the end of the prison system, although I think the arguments just considered are not frivolous and might, in some future age, carry the day, especially if new technical and scientific developments made automobiles, meat, and prison obsolete. It is worth considering for a moment that no conventional form of transportation, of eating, or of restraining criminals is immutable and that our present forms are open to serious criticism. But I advance these analogies with another purpose: to suggest the magnitude of the moral mutation that occurred when another common societal arrangement—one far older than transportation by automobile or punishment by prison—was declared to constitute an offense against God. I mean the institution of human slavery. That to have a man or a boy, a woman or a girl as a slave was evil was once not a moral rule anywhere in Christendom. As we have seen, the sin of slaveholding was an unknown sin. However unlikely, however unthinkable, the declaration that automobile driving, or meat eating, or incarcerating criminals is sinful, none of such mutations would equal the discovery, after centuries of Christianity, that it is wrong to own a human being.

A heavenly choir may be imagined made up of former slaves such as Bathilde, Felicity, Patrick, Useful, and Vitale and of slaveholders such as Popes Gregory the Great, Pius V, and Pius VII and Saints Alfonso de'Ligouri and Pedro Claver and missionaries of the Dominican and Jesuit orders and nuns of the Augustinian and Carmelite communities. What pope could retroactively disqualify from this assembly those who had owned human beings? Who could now find guilty of gross sin those who so earnestly had sought to glorify God?

Historians have existed who have thought it their duty to pronounce moral judgments on the deceased. Lord Acton is a famous example of this school. Can such judgments be fair, and what do they mean? They are not fair because elementary justice demands that he who is to be judged should have a hearing: the dead are powerless to defend themselves. The historian who assembles the evidence to judge those no longer alive, however fairly he presents what he finds, is both a prosecutor and a judge; there is no spokesperson for the defense. The historian brings to the task his own perspective and preferences.

As to what the historian's judgment means, it affects his subject's life, liberty, and fortune neither in this world nor in any world to come. It bears only on the subject's reputation, which now is wholly detached from the subject himself. Without jurisdiction and without the power to execute judgment, the historian expresses his own values and evaluates his subject in terms of them, often determining no more than that his subject did not have the standards of the present. Is that a judgment or a foregone conclusion? It may make a historian swell with pride to be able to set down Thomas More as a persecutor or Abraham Lincoln as a lawyer who acted for a slaveowner. Beyond the self-satisfaction of the self-appointed judge, what do we learn except that moral standards have changed?

No figure of the past will meet the standards of the present. Can moral judgment be based on the unavoidable difference? To draw examples from American history, Washington, Jefferson, and Madison owned slaves because they lived in Virginia in the eighteenth century. May we judge them as having engaged in intrinsically evil behavior? Brandeis, Holmes, and Hughes, three titans of the Supreme Court, upheld racial segregation in the schools in 1926. Thirty years later their position would have been racist. Shall we condemn them morally as racist in the Washington of 1926? St. Augustine and St. Thomas Aquinas were defenders of the lawfulness of human slavery and of the rightness of religious persecution. Are we in a position to judge them as teachers of unjust doctrine? It is evident, I believe, that if each generation is free to measure its predecessors morally, using the criteria now accepted, no one will escape condemnation. We must be judged by the moral criteria we know.

Judgment of the status of past moral doctrine presents a different question. We are all convinced that enslaving human beings is bad. How shall we characterize the once universal teaching that you acquire a slave baby lawfully by owning the baby's mother? We are almost all convinced that a moderate profit on a loan is acceptable. How shall we characterize the teaching that taking such a profit offended divine and natural law? The Second Vatican Council in its enumeration of evils such as slavery listed, after "tortures inflicted on the body or on the mind," this sin: "efforts to coerce rational minds (*animi*) themselves." In *Veritatis splendor* such thought control joined John Paul II's enumeration of intrinsically evil acts. In this light, ecclesiastical efforts of the past to compel heretics to recant appear to be stamped as always and everywhere offensive to God. Not judging as morally bad the persons who once upheld such coercion, can we regard the doctrines themselves as other than erroneous? Just as the humors of the body, the ubiquity of phlogiston, and the orbiting of the sun around the earth were once put forward in good faith but have been discarded as errors, so certain moral doctrines are now seen as wrong. Pragmatically, they may have worked for the good, as the usury rule arguably worked. Practically, they may have been all that human beings of an earlier period could accept. But to say they were correct in their time and erroneous now does not seem possible. They have been superceded because experience has demonstrated their error. We can explain how they came to be taught, we can set them in the intellectual context in which they were engendered, we may even find excuses for their being adopted, but can we see them now as other than mistakes?

The same is true of some other assertions of ecclesial authority. It was maintained by Pope Stephen II that Constantine had donated Rome, all the provinces of Italy, and the Western Hemisphere to the papacy. The donation was used as the basis for papal resistance to the Lombards in 754 and thereafter as the basis for papal claims to jurisdiction in Italy. As noted earlier, it was expansively read to include in the gift all the islands of the world. The document of donation was pronounced a forgery by Lorenzo Valla and, independently, by Cardinal Nicholas of Cusa. The politically advantageous and blatantly fraudulent document was probably produced by Stephen II's chancery. Today no one would dream of maintaining its authenticity, although for seven centuries or more it was put forward as the basis of the temporal power of the popes. A ghost of the old claim surfaced in the Syllabus of Errors containing the following proposition condemned by Pius IX: "Removal of the civil power enjoyed by the Apostolic See would be particularly conducive to the freedom and happiness of the Church."

The Church, Vatican II teaches, is "holy and always in need of purification"—a paradox parallel to being unchanging and able to change. John Paul II made the paradox more understandable by distinguishing the Church from its members. It is the members who "all those times in history departed from the spirit of Christ." The pope spoke of repentance for "errors," among them holding "that an authentic witness to the truth could include suppressing the opinion of others." How many of his predecessors had so held and so taught, he did not say. But it was by acknowledging such sin and error that the Church should prepare and purify itself for the third millennium. As he repeated as the millennium approached, "Although many acted here in good faith, it was certainly not evangelical to think that the truth should be imposed by force." He added immediately that there had been "a lack of discernment by many Christians in situations where basic human rights were violated." Almost, not quite, the papal record on slavery was put forward as a proper subject for penance.

But the Church only speaks and acts and lives through its people. When one recognized as a Father of the Church cited the example of force used on Paul as authority for force in the service of truth, later generations heard not the voice of St. Augustine but the voice of the Church. When one recognized as a Doctor of the Church taught that a heretic could not be forgiven more than twice, theologians heard not St. Thomas Aquinas, but the Church. When a series of popes presided over the Universal and Roman Inquisition and turned relapsed heretics over to executioners employed by the Papal States, it was believed that the Church was acting and teaching by its deeds. It is difficult to draw a line between the authorities of the Church and the Church. It is unnecessary to draw a line if it is acknowledged that the Church is not always infallible.

Just as in physical science, experiment and discovery compel the abandonment of a once-prized theory, just as in theology the temporal power of the pope over Rome, Italy, the Western Hemisphere, and all the islands is no longer defended, so in morals, experience and new perceptions compel the abandonment of past positions. Abandoned, they are seen to have been mistakes. In the words of that leading theologian of the twentieth century, Karl Rahner, S.J., speaking generally of Catholic theology, "many doctrines which were once universally held have proved to be problematic or erroneous." The Church, in effect, although not always in words, acknowledges that it erred and moves on to the new doctrine. Doing so, it confronts change, acknowledges change, and affirms its own life as a living and growing body.

How Precedent Deters but Does Not Defeat Development

The Church is not a dictatorship in which a word from the top determines what must be done or believed; the parts of the Church's body interact organically. The Church is not a university in which originality of thought is prized; a premium is attached to what was originally given, what is described as "the deposit of faith," a metaphor focused on what has been bestowed rather than on what is grown. Some have spoken of the Church as an army; the expression "Christian solider" was even adopted by Erasmus. But an army does not propose moral precepts. To do so requires the criticism of experience in the light of fundamental principles; a command and obey structure does not foster such criticism. Like a judicial system, the Church honors precedent and slowly alters it in application. But the Church as a whole does not decide cases, it proclaims the Gospel. No institutional analogue is adequate for the delicate and demanding work of those who articulate the developing moral doctrine of the Church, preserving what was given and taking experience into account.

As the history of usury demonstrates, much of the teaching of morals has been by papal pronouncements of law; and, as that history also demonstrates, the reception of a law by the Christian people is essential to its vitality. The process is not one of ratification but of giving reality to the law in the consciences of the faithful. If the faithful do not comprehend the reason of the law and how it comports with their obligation in conscience to God, the law will lapse as it did in the case of the sixteenth-century commands on usury. *Cessante ratione, cessat ipsa lex,* "When the reason for the law ceases, the law itself ceases." The old canonical maxim applies when consciences, bound to obey God, cannot grasp the law's rationale. Capacity to receive does not extend to receiving what is contrary to conscience.

Prominent in the work of articulating doctrine have been the popes. Speaking as the head of the institution and cabined by its procedures and precedents, each pope has had individual experiences that mark his attitude and inflection. Both Gregory I and Gregory XVI were monks, but how different it was to be the confident inheritor of imperial Rome and to be the harassed caretaker of ways battered by the French Revolution and Napoleon!

Institutionally, the popes have been dependent on the appropriation of experience by those retrospectively identified as the Fathers and by the later canonists and moral theologians. Taken as a body, these men (until recent times they were all men) were self-consciously truth-seekers and, perhaps for that reason, not always free from self-righteousness. Ascetically disciplined, usually bound by vows of chastity, poverty, and obedience, they were not venal, not ambitious, not self-seekers. They did not have the freedom of the French philosophers or the conveniences of an American academic. The best of them had work they found serious and important. They brought to it energy, intelligence, and devotion as they worked in channels constructed by their predecessors.

A contrast is sometimes drawn between canonists and theologians. The canonists were trained in the law of the Church and of the Roman Empire. As lawyers, they were used to distinguishing cases and proposing practical solutions. In the Roman curia they were close to the pope and conscious of his legal prerogatives. The contrast can be overdone. The canonists were not ignorant of theology nor insensitive to its requirements; the theologians had to know the law. But Gratian differs from Peter Lombard, Hostiensis from Aquinas, Gasparri from Häring. Training and experience made the difference.

Experience, especially experience enlarged by empathy, adds to the force of a teaching. No theologian has been so persuasive on sexual morals as Augustine. Because he wrote the most famous of autobiographies suggesting his sexual experience, he spoke as an expert. Thomas Aquinas, notably reticent as to all things concerning himself, plainly defers to Augustine as the one who knows about sexual matters; Thomas has to persuade by the force of intellectual analysis and, sometimes, by the depth of his empathetic appropriation of another's experience. A modern instance is provided by Bernard Häring, to whom much is owed in reviving moral theology. His work has gained credibility by his *Embattled Witness,* a memoir setting out his life in the German army on the Russian front and his escape from the Communists after the war by serving a Polish congregation: the reader sees Häring's consciousness and range of sympathy expand.

The ordinary moral theologian makes available to his readers little of his life. The typical theologian, prior to 1960, was male, celibate, and ordained. He probably had not had the sexual odyssey of an Augustine or the military odyssey of a Häring, and he would not likely have had the intellect of an Aquinas. He would have in adolescence entered on study for the priesthood, and more likely than not would have been the member of a religious order, which had chosen him to study moral theology. As a priest he would, until recent times, have been subject to ecclesiastical censorship of what he wrote. If a member of an order, he would not only have had a censor from the order but he would have been concerned to protect the reputation of his brethren, particularly from critics from another religious order. "They watch each other like hawks," a Dominican philosopher once remarked to me.

Limited by their training and by censorship, often with limited experience of the world, the moral theologians generally entered on the exposition of moral theology by following in the steps of their predecessors. In this way a tradition was constructed. Some subjects, usury for example, were exhaustively treated. Other topics, bribery for example, received relatively little treatment. To a considerable extent, precedent, not the significance of the topic, determined the extent of the treatment. Experience was captured in the precedent, but the range of experience considered was narrowed.

That precedent has played a large part in the presentation of Catholic moral teaching is evident. To the ordinary force that precedent has in any institution respectful of its past, there has been the added weight of authority—authority that in a few cases might be clothed with the infallibility granted the Church but generally cases possessed of no more than an arguable definitiveness. In addition to the teaching of general councils and popes explicitly announcing, defining, and defending a doctrine as authoritative, teaching is understood to be conveyed in the Catholic Church by "the ordinary magisterium." That teaching is to be regarded as infallible when it is "explicitly set out as to be definitively held." The ordinary magisterium is the teaching of the bishops in communion with each other and Rome, acting not as a collective body but with moral unanimity putting forward Catholic doctrine. Evidence of the ordinary magisterium consists in the treatises of theologians and the catechisms approved by bishops as well as in answers and rulings issued by the Holy See. By its very nature this teaching does not have the compact formulation of a conciliar or papal pronouncement, nor the stamp of authority that is easily identified when attached to a conciliar or papal pronouncement. What the ordinary magisterium is conveying is not to be determined by mere nose-counting of the teachers. Rather, it is what is commonly taught without denial, what is peacefully in possession, what is supported by the citation of unchallenged authorities; but to enjoy the status of infallibility, it must also be "explicitly set out as definitively to be held."

It will be seen on reflection that there are problems with establishing the ordinary magisterium exercising infallible authority. How is it to be distinguished from custom that is not doctrine? When a teaching is uncontroverted, is it explicitly set out as definitively to be held? What appeared to be the ordinary magisterium, from the first century to the twentieth, taught that it was not sinful for a Christian to own slaves. How, say, in A.D. 400, or 800, or 1400, or even A.D. 1800, would any person instructed in this way have been bound to find it sinful? Today the teaching on slavery is different. Similarly, as late as 1960, it was reasonably maintained that the ordinary magisterium taught that it was the duty of Catholic states to suppress heresy. The change that occurred in 1965 suggests that the discernment of what is binding in the ordinary magisterium is not always easy. Rahner has observed: "mere de facto universality of Church doctrine related to the faith is not enough."

Fallibility in moral teaching is illustrated by the role that chance or mischance has played in it. Here are three illustrations: (1) the Latin mistranslation of Luke 6:35 on lending, a mistranslation that became a basis for papal teaching, as shown in chapter 18, "Unnatural Reproduction"; (2) the misattribution of Isaac's commentary on Corinthians to various Fathers, a misattribution that enabled the commentary to be accepted as establishing the Pauline privilege, as shown in chapter 24, "If the Unbeliever Separates"; (3) the misreading of Paul to Philemon so that its message became à la Bossuet a particularly strong endorsement of the propriety of property in persons rather than a passionate plea for the freedom of Useful as interpreted in Chapter 5, "God's Slaves." A person of a particular sort of piety could believe that each of these chance turns was providentially planned. Such a piety would read every accident as divinely designed; mistakes and serendipities alike would glow under such a gloss. As Stephan Kuttner once remarked to me, "Three examples usually suffice to make a point." The accidental play of human events has contributed, sometimes to the bad, sometimes to the good articulation of moral teaching.

The difficulty of distinguishing what is irreformable from what is transient has been enhanced by an approach to authority reflected in a teaching of the Second Vatican Council that deliberately embraces fallible teaching:

> The faithful ought to concur in and adhere to, with religious deference of mind, the judgment of their own bishop uttered in the name of Christ about faith and morals. This religious deference of will and intellect is particularly to be given to the authentic teaching of the Roman Pontiff even when he does not speak ex cathedra. . . .

If a theologian takes this teaching at the letter, accepting and adhering to the possibly mistaken teaching proposed, how could he or she ever investigate a doctrine and engage in the probing and testing necessary for the development of morals?

The Congregation for the Doctrine of the Faith, under the prefectship of Cardinal Joseph Ratzinger, has acknowledged that the conciliar text does not require literal obedience. In a significant "instruction" in 1990 addressed to "the churchly vocation of the theologian," the CDF began with an acknowledgment of the overriding demand of truth and observed precisely: "Investigation of the truth is inbred in human nature; ignorance holds it in a state of slavery." Jesus Christ liberates human beings from this state. "According to Christian faith, knowledge and life, truth and existence are intrinsically joined." Called to explore and to expound the truth, a theologian may encounter "difficulties" in what is proposed by the magisterium. Avoiding the media, he will bring the difficulties to the attention of the competent authority, stimulating the magisterium to "a deeper presentation of the doctrine." Yet "difficulties may remain," and the theologian may conclude that for him "the arguments to the contrary appear to prevail. Therefore, he thinks that he cannot offer the assent of his intellect to it": his duty or office then is "to await a deeper investigation of the question." The CDF's Instruction does not seem to contemplate open debate. Transparency does not appear to be highly prized. Nonetheless, two capital points are acknowledged. First, the theologian's assent is not required. Second, truth is the overriding value. The limitations are prudential.

History is edifying; that is, history builds faith. It must be examined to understand what faith requires. Imagine a triptych in a church showing Gregory I in the center with Gregory XIII on his right and Gregory XVI on his left. The central panel itself contains three scenes: St. Gregory bestowing freedom on Thomas and Montana is its core panel. Flanking the core are panels showing St. Gregory examining the British boys in the Roman slave market and

St. Gregory conveying the church slave John to the bishop of Porto. The large panel on Gregory the Great's right shows the sixteenth-century Gregory granting priests the faculty to divorce African converts from their distant pagan spouses; the left large panel shows the nineteenth-century Gregory graciously receiving Palmerston's letter against the trade: the evangelized British now instruct the pope. The triptych would be superficially disconcerting. With visual compactness it would capture the course of changes demonstrating the development of moral teaching.

St. Paul told slaves to obey their masters. St. Augustine accepted the institution of slavery as a consequence of sin. St. Gregory the Great purchased slaves. St. Thomas Aquinas defended slavery as a useful addition to natural law. St. Pedro Claver commissioned the purchase of slaves. St. Alfonso de'Ligouri owned a personal slave. The example and teaching of the saints show that slavery was not always and everywhere considered to be evil, as it is now taught to be by John Paul II.

It is most likely that it is the weight accorded precedent, infallible and fallible, that accounts for the uneven development of moral doctrine by those officially charged with its articulation. The usury rule was substantially modified by the theologians themselves in the face of conservative opposition. Revision on divorce was undertaken first by university theologians, then by canonists led by Pietro Gasparri. The teaching on religious freedom was belatedly changed in 1965 after a strenuous theological struggle. The development of doctrine on slavery took place almost entirely outside of the domain of the moral theologians. They knew the great commandments. Precedent told them that the great commandments did not prohibit slavery. Quakers, Methodists, evangelical Anglicans, the government of Great Britain, and the American Civil War transformed modern consciousness so that by 1965 when Vatican II condemned slavery its evil was not an issue. The moral theologians, hemmed in by precedent, were among the last to acknowledge the new norm.

An earlier change in morals was effected by the laity without input from the teaching of the universal Church. No Father of the Church, no general council, no pope proclaimed the Roman law of the enslavement of prisoners to be at an end as far as Christian prisoners of war were concerned. Antoninus of Florence and Bartolus testify to the modern custom cancelling Roman law without citing any authority requiring it. It appears to have been a conclusion reached by Christian belligerents warring with each other.

The shift may make one ask, If they thought they shouldn't enslave each other, how could they think it right to kill each other? The answer is, People are not always consistent. In the same way, it could be asked, If it was not right to enslave Christians in war, why was it right to hold as slaves those who became Christians by baptism after they were enslaved? The answer is the same: the inconsistency of human beings. Stumbling and inconsistent, the laity still achieved a mitigation that the magisterium failed to attempt. The requirements of love were at least half-grasped by those in combat. That each person is the image of God; that each person is destined to live with God; that each person is a brother or a sister; that each person is to be loved as another self—all these teachings appear to exclude utterly the reduction of others to slaves or the destruction of others by putting them to death. Obviously it is one thing to repeat the teachings, another to internalize and act upon them.

In each of the instances of development what can easily be determined is the official position at a given time. Far less easy to determine are the views and practices of the Christian faithful. In the case of usury, it is clear that Christian bankers and businessmen thought the usury rule too rigorous. In the case of divorce, the present rule excludes many Catholics from communion. In the case of religious liberty, public opinion, including the opinion of Catholics, was far in advance of the 1965 Declaration of Religious Freedom. By 1965, in no civilized country was slavery considered to be a defensible institution.

Benefitted by precedent because precedent provided framework, direction, continuity, but handicapped by precedent because it discouraged initiative and openness to experience, moral doctrine has developed.

That Form and Formula Fail
to Foil Development

Conditions and practices have at times anticipated the development of moral doctrine within the Church and given rise to the development. An economy based on commercial credit preceded the revision of the rules on usury. The rise of democratic, liberal societies, most notably the United States, preceded Vatican II's Declaration on Religious Liberty. The very general practice of civil divorce preceded the current practice of divorce by papal rescript. The abolition of slavery almost everywhere was in advance of Vatican II's categorical condemnation of slavery.

It has proved difficult to set out moral positions with entire consistency. For example, the prohibition of profit on a loan coexisted with acceptance of profit on annuities, a form of credit differentiated from lending only by a legal line. Coercion to make an unbeliever accept the faith was rejected in principle; but coercion to make a heretic profess the faith was accepted. It was seen to be against a divine commandment to dissolve the marriage of two baptized persons, even if years ago they had ceased to believe; it was seen as exercise of a divine prerogative to dissolve the marriage of two unbaptized persons who did not acknowledge in any way the power of the Church. That each person is the image of God, to be loved as one loves oneself, was proclaimed as central to Christianity. Yet it was considered neither unChristian nor unnatural to categorize other persons as commodities to be sold. Development, it may be ventured, has occurred as these inconsistencies were worked out in the case of usury, religious liberty, and slavery; and development is occurring now in relation to divorce. At times, the true principle has been hidden in the exception.

One implication that may be drawn from these observations is that moral theologians are often catching up with what is already established, that, at least in the cases looked at here, they did not lead the way. A somewhat different implication could also be drawn, that experience and empathy are necessary before a practice can be definitively known as good or bad. Spectacularly, in the case of slavery, the moral theologians did not incorporate the experience of the slaves into their teaching. Remarkably, in the case of usury the theologians came to listen to the bankers and businessmen. Belatedly, in the case of religious freedom the teachers of moral doctrine took into account political experience. Timidly, the canonists have listened to the stories of modern marriage. The great formulas of moral theology have needed to be fed by the most extensive empathy.

The intrinsic is not a talisman in morals. What was perceived as intrinsically evil in making money out of money was dissolved by introducing titles that extrinsically justified profit. What was perceived as intrinsically evil in divorce was removed by the invocation of extrinsic authority. Contrariwise, slavery was extrinsically justified by property titles but came to be seen as intrinsically offensive to human dignity. What was once seen as self-evidently or intrinsically absurd, that error should have rights, was bypassed once it was seen that rights belong to persons; it is now, in the words of John Paul II, "intrinsically evil" to "coerce rational minds."

What is true of the intrinsic bears as well on the proposition that negative commandments are unalterable. Adultery is always wrong. Usury is always wrong. The reason is that, by definition, each of these terms denotes a wrongful act. The commandments "You shall not commit adultery" and "You shall not take usury" are always binding, not because each prohibition is cast as a negative but because the object of the prohibition is by definition evil. The commandment "You shall not kill" is not universally valid, despite being a universal negative, because killing may be done in self-defense, or in defense of others, or in war, without being necessarily sinful. Those who think a universal negative must always hold are, therefore, mistaken. If there are exceptions to be made to this conclusion, they are so rare that they do not disprove the general truth that the form of a prohibition does not prevent development.

Contra naturam is a category of sin with powerful resonance. To be against nature is to be, with peculiar perversity, against the order of creation designed by the Creator. It is the category deployed by Thomas Aquinas and by many other theologians to denominate sexual sins such as sodomy. The categorization is the condemnation. Sins against nature are greater than adultery, seduction, or rape, even though the latter injure others and the former seems to injure no other person. Why should this be so? Thomas answers: "Just as the ordering of right reason proceeds from man, so the order of nature is from God Himself: wherefore in sins contrary to nature, whereby the very order of nature is violated, an injury is done to God, the ordainer of nature."

Usury, a preoccupation of many scholastic moralists, was handled in a parallel way. That money is a human invention was ignored. The sin was seen as making the naturally sterile bear fruit. It was, as it were, the mirror opposite of sodomy, where what nature intended to be employed reproductively was made sterile. In usury, money bore offspring. Dante makes the treatment of the two sins alike in hell: they deny "the goodness of nature."

> e però lo minor giron suggella
> del segno suo e Soddoma e Caorsa
> *Inferno* XI, 49–50.

Sodom, the biblical site for one sin, and Cahors, a French town reputed to hold usurers, are paired.

Slavery, too, is against nature. We are born free. So said Roman law, classifying the conditions of man. So said Gregory the Great expounding the virtues of liberating a slave. So said Thomas Aquinas speaking of nature's first intention. But this institution, according to which persons are turned into property, was not condemned by its category. Thomas could not accept its contrariness. It becomes for him not an affront to humanity but a useful addition to what nature has prescribed. Dante is unaware of slaveholding as a sin. *Contra naturam* does not decide. The heavy category is lightly discarded when property in humans is at issue.

No formula is firm enough to forestall bending or an end run. "What God has joined together, let no man separate." The teaching appears to be comprehensive and exceptionless. Many have thought it so. But before it had even entered a written gospel, Paul had made an exception to it on the ground that

God had called Christians not to slavery but to peace. It took legal ingenuity to explain how the exception and its subsequent expansion could coexist with the apparently ample command now proved to be permeable.

Neither "intrinsic" nor "unnatural" are always decisive. The nature of the general subject of a prohibition is equally unable to dam development. There are those who say, when they hear about the development for the usury rule, "That was an economic rule that changed with economic circumstances. If a rule involves human nature, it cannot change in this fashion." That economic circumstances played a part in producing the usury rule is undeniable; the development of the rule was due not only to those circumstances but to changes in the analyses made by theologians and to their acceptance of the experience of other human beings. The rise and fall of the usury rule is not merely an epiphenomenon of economics, but a reassessment based in part on experience.

Religious freedom is dependent to a considerable extent on the development of political institutions. But the recognition of the right of everyone to religious freedom transcends any particular political framework. It corresponds to an insight into human aspirations and capabilities, confirmed by experience. It flows from judgments on the nature and destiny of human beings.

Marriage is an institution shaped by social expectations and customs touching it, the roles assigned by a society to men and women, and the treatment and education of children. Despite the many external forces affecting marriage, it in itself involves an intimate exchange, sexual and psychological, emotional and intellectual, between human beings. No institution is more rooted in human nature than marriage, no institution more capable of bearing the burden of love. If the rules on the dissolution of marriage develop, as in fact they have developed, human nature, as well as the nature of marriage, is responded to and affected.

The judgment that to hold another in slavery is an evil act is a judgment as to the requirements of human nature. No changed economic conditions, no shift in political institutions, no social shift in gender roles accounts for the perception that the relation of master and slave is destructive of human dignity. A new understanding of old human nature nourished by empathy is at the heart of the profound change.

These four examples demonstrate that the development of moral doctrine can and does occur by human experience leading to better understanding of human nature. That the subject of development is deeply rooted in human nature does not prevent development. The moral teaching of the Church is presented as the requirement of revelation and the demand of natural law. In the case of usury, for example, the New Testament basis for the strict rule prohibiting profit on a loan was based on a mistaken text; the prohibition was teased out of an analysis of the nature of a loan of fungibles. When the basis in the New Testament was found wanting, reassessment of the requirements of justice in lending led to a very substantial reformulation of the teaching. Analogously, rethinking of the teaching of the New Testament, accompanied by reconsideration of what human nature requires as to the freedom of each person and the freedom of belief, led to very substantial changes on slavery and religious persecution as experience demonstrated their evil. The acceptance of divorce for the unbaptized discloses both a new reading of natural law and a developing interpretation of the New Testament.

That Development Cannot Exceed Capacity

Development does occur in the understanding of the demands of Christian revelation. No new revelation is made. The revelation itself does not change. Yet change occurs. How does it occur? As Vatican II answers this question, by deepening the understanding of the revelation.

Deepening occurs in three ways. First, by prayer, by meditation, by giving full attention to the revelation. The process, as Newman maintains, is one of purification. The stream is muddier and more turbulent in its early stages than it is as the water moves from shallows, the banks widen, the current quickens, and the sediment is washed away. Or, to drop the metaphor, empathy with those seen as brothers and sisters leads to the rejection of practices formerly considered to be compatible with Christianity such as the enslavement of human beings and persecution for the sake of religion. The teaching of Paul to the Philippians applies. Love must "abound" in order to "test what is vital" (Phil 1:9–10). Love accomplishes this task by abounding "in knowledge and in insight of every kind," that is, by empathetic identification with the other.

Secondly, development occurs by empirical investigation. Such investigation occurs not only in the laboratory but in the observation of human practices.

In this way the human experience of slavery and of religious persecution, of the use of credit, and of marriage as an institution has affected what is perceived as natural law in relation to these subjects. As the understanding of the nature of such practices has changed, so has the reading of revelation in regard to them.

Deepening, finally, occurs by the development, intellectual, moral, emotional, and social, of human beings. How do we know such development occurs? We know it empirically. The practices of enslavement and of persecution that appeared appropriate to our ancestors are to us absurd, unjust, outrageous beyond comprehension. For us it is madness to maintain that one may own another or have a duty to suppress another's thought. Our judgment comes not merely from reflection on revelation but from an enhanced capacity to comprehend what the pursuit of truth and the pursuit of happiness by human beings depend upon. Is that to assert boldly that human nature has changed for the better in the last two thousand years? Obviously we still can comprehend the motivations and decisions of those who acted in the first century. The change is not radical. But as we cannot accept slavery and religious persecution as these practices were once accepted, there has been a change in us.

Omne quod recipitur in aliquo recipitur in eo per modum recipientis, "All that is received in someone is received in him through the medium of the receiver." The old scholastic maxim is fundamental. It is true not only of earthen containers and of digital computers. It is true of human beings. A clod confronted by a genius will not comprehend what he is being told. A brute instructed by an angel will miss most of her nuances. I do not suggest that the Christian revelation was given to clods or brutes but that the capacity of those receiving it was limited by their education, their social conventions, their language, their own experience of life. Whatever revelation was given could not, at least in its enunciation, application, and development, exceed the capacities of those who received it.

Suppose a college of master moralists working within the boundaries of the Catholic tradition. Let us limit the membership to twelve, each one responsible for articulating some major moral insight. Let us set aside the inspired writers of sacred scripture, who enjoy a special status theologically. In terms of the themes of this book, I would propose these authors in these categories:

The Development of Moral Doctrine

St. Augustine, for providing the rule of faith (see chapter 33).
Vincent of Lérins, for providing the criteria of universality.
John Henry Newman, for championing development in general.

Religious Freedom

Desiderius Erasmus, for scoffing at the stupidity of intolerance.
Jacques Maritain, for showing how the human person transcends the state.
John Courtney Murray, for leading the Church to become the champion of freedom.

Marriage

Isaac, for formulating the Pauline privilege.
Thomas Aquinas, for empathetically putting the case for the natural fittingness of lifelong marital commitment.
Tomás Sanchez, for extending the privilege of the faith.

Slavery

Gregory of Nyssa, for attacking the arrogance of the owners of humans.
Bartolomé de Las Casas, for finally questioning all titles to Indians or Blacks.
Jean Bodin, for attacking the rationalizations of Roman law.

That leaves no room for the moralists who made the usury rule or for those who transformed it. The other topics are more central. Our moralists include one cardinal (Newman), three bishops (Augustine, Gregory, and Las Casas), one monk (Vincent), two Dominicans (Thomas Aquinas and Las Casas), one Augustinian canon regular (Erasmus), two Jesuits (Sanchez and Murray), two lawyers (Isaac and Bodin), and one philosopher (Maritain). Three were adult converts (Isaac, Newman, Maritain). Their nationalities are African, American, British, Dutch, French, Greek, Italian, and Spanish. The diversity of their origins and careers is instructive. No unique formula exists to produce a master.

Each of these authors in his field of competence could be acknowledged as one of those "great minds" saluted by John Paul II as "truly free and full of God." Yet none of them were capable of rising above their circumstances in all areas of moral doctrine. Augustine justified the physical coercion of fellow Christians and Thomas Aquinas justified their physical extinction if they relapsed. Both also justified slavery. Gregory, Las Casas, and Bodin criticized slavery but did not put an ax to its roots. Erasmus had no criticism of the European slaving of his day. Las Casas had no criticism of the Inquisition. Isaac and Sanchez shone only on marriage. Maritain showed a strange nostalgia for the obsolete rules on usury. Murray ignored the problem of papal jurisdiction over the marriages of those outside the fold. Vincent and Newman saw that development occurred in the teaching of the faith, but said nothing as to the teaching of morals. In sum, faced with practices that challenged the Gospel, none of these great minds had the capacity to address all the moral problems besetting Christian life in the world. The college of master moralists is an honorific fantasy and an emblem of the limited capacity of human minds to perceive moral requirements.

That Development Runs by
No Rule Except the Rule of Faith

The *A, B, L, E* of Development

A is for analogy, always a powerful tool of argument in law and morals. For example, the general privilege of the faith developed by analogy with the Pauline privilege. The analogy was emphasized by calling the development Petrine. Peter matched Paul. But analogies always limp. They omit or add features not in the original. The so-called Petrine privilege brought in the pope as an extra weight.

B is for balance. Justice is represented with scales, but balance in this context does not refer to measuring poundage. It refers to the vital balance of organic functions necessary to sustain life in a living organism. Like it or not, balance limits logic in any legal or moral system. Like it or not—and today none of us like it—balance once limited the rights of baptized slaves in the Christian community. The whole Christian message was not to be encapsulated in a demand for emancipation. The organism was thought to need more growth to accommodate such a social upheaval.

L is for logic, the working out of the implications of a premise. Who says A must say B, but may not be allowed to get further in the alphabet if the vital balance of the organism is affected. Those who trust in logic alone to win an argument for development in a particular area do not recognize how balance will curtail the force of their reasoning.

E is for experience, without which moral insights are not examined. Experience here is understood broadly to include empathy, identification with the experience of the other. It took nearly seventeen hundred years of experience to convince all theologians that persecution does not promote faith. Logic and empathy got Roger Williams, Baruch Spinoza, John Locke, and James Madison there ahead of Las Casas, Lugo, and Ligouri. Precedent hampered, not helped. In the end, the American experience was decisive.

Analogy, Balance, Logic, Experience—development is able to occur by means of these devices. They are the tools of teaching. They are not the content nor the rule determining development.

The Rule

Paul to the Philippians sets what can be a program:

> That your love abound more and more
> In knowledge and in insight of every kind
> So that you test what is vital
>
> (Phil 1:9–10)

It is Paul's expectation that increase in love is increase in knowledge and insight (*aisthesei*). The increase comes from identification with the other, who is not alien but another self. In Thomistic terms when you increase your love of God you learn as the friend of God to love his friends. As John Dunne likes to put it, "The love is from God and of God and towards God." This love is not merely an internal act of the will, but the act of the whole person, made concrete in response to other human persons. Realized in this way, love cannot abide human enslavement or the coercion of belief. Of love's lastingness, marriage is the symbol, although a question remains as to whether any couple should be made to signify such permanence, against its will and it must be acknowledged that the popes have subordinated the symbol to the salvation of souls, although only to permit love to flourish in a new conjugal union.

Development may be in the direction of greater liberality or greater strictness in morals. No irresistible momentum moves to tighten or to relax the rules. The usury rule first became tighter, articulated in terms of the requirements of justice, then lighter, a basic admonition not to exploit one's needy neighbor. The teaching on religious liberty first denied it and imposed a duty on rulers to suppress it. This duty to suppress has been supplanted by an injunction to governments not to violate it. One governmental obligation replaced another governmental obligation. For individuals, there was enhanced recognition of the freedom of their consciences from all coercion, physical or psychological, and a corollary obligation placed on others not to coerce.

The development of the rules regarding marriage have run in two different directions. For over one thousand years divorce and remarriage were permitted by the governing civil law and no general legislation of the Church prohibited them in every case. Eventually, the Catholic Church took the position that a consummated marriage between two baptized persons was dissolved only by the death of one of the spouses. Neither the Churches in Eastern Christendom nor the Churches born at the Reformation share this position; but the Catholic position has developed so strongly that any relaxation of it would be difficult. At the same time the Catholic position has evolved to the point that, in principle, two-thirds of the marriages of the world—all the marriages where at least one party is unbaptized—are subject to divorce by the pope or his delegates or by application of relevant canons.

The course of moral doctrine, like that of great river, appears to follow no rule. Plunging over heights, striking boulders, creeping in almost motionless channels, it defies prediction, can scarcely be the subject of science. Newman provided a checklist of the characteristics of true development, among them the requirement of not contradicting a previous teaching. But in the development of morals, the honorable possession of one kind of property becomes a hideous affront to humanity; the pursuit of profit by lending moves from disreputable exploitation to wholesome commerce; the suppression of heresy stops being the ruler's duty and becomes a violation of human rights; and marriage that only God can dissolve is dissolved by a rescript from the pope or the second marriage of a convert.

A checklist is a mechanic's tool, useful for a quick overview; it is not to be slavishly followed. The testing of what is vital implies that what is vital will survive; what is ephemeral will be discarded. The test cannot be, Does Rule X contradict Rule Y? The rules governing particular actions have changed too often and too much to settle a dispute by recital of their conflict. Set too narrowly the test of contradiction of past teaching, and you end with Marcel Lefebvre accepting without noticing it the profound change on slavery but incapable of accepting a change in the teaching on religious liberty. Newman's checklist is not the rule of faith. Qualifications, extensions, rejections create substantial difficulties. As Newman famously acknowledged, "Ten thousand difficulties do not make one doubt." Neither do they make the rule of faith. That rule depends upon the teaching of the Lord Jesus.

Asked by his interlocutors to name the greatest commandment, Jesus would not be fenced into a single commandment by the question. He said that it is to "love the Lord your God with your whole heart, your whole soul, your whole mind, and your whole strength" (Mt 22:37). On these two commandments "hang the law and the prophets" (Mt 22:40). The specific commandments can be kept only as implementations of these two. The rule of faith, according to Augustine, follows: "If it seems to anyone that he has understood the divine scriptures, or any part of them, in such a way that by that understanding he does not build up that double love of God and of neighbor, he has not yet understood them."

Development proceeds directed by this rule. The love of God generates, reinforces, and seals the love of neighbor. What is required is found in the community's experience as it tests what is vital. On the surface, contradictions appear. At the deepest level, the course is clear.

ABBREVIATIONS

AAS   *Acta Apostolicae Sedis, Commentarium officiale* (Rome, 1909–).

AS   *Acta sanctorum,* ed. Jean Bolland, S.J., and others (Brussels, 1863–).

ASS   *Acta Sanctae Sedis in compendium opportune redacta et illustrata* (Rome, 1865–1908).

Bradley   Keith Bradley, *Slavery and Society at Rome* (Cambridge: Cambridge University Press, 1994).

CC   *Corpus christianorum: Series latina* (Turnholti, Belgium: Brepols, 1953–).

CCC   *Catechism of the Catholic Church* (Vatican City: Libreria Editrice Vaticana, 1992).

CIC   *Corpus iuris canonici,* ed. Emil Friedberg (Leipzig, 1879–1881).

CIC (1917)   *Codex iuris canonici* (Rome: Vatican Polyglot Press, 1920).

CIC (1983)   *Codex iuris canonici* (Vatican City: Libreria Editrice Vaticana, 1989).

CLD   *The Canon Law Digest: Officially Published Documents Affecting the Code of Canon Law,* ed. T. Lincoln Bouscaren, S.J., and James I. O'Connor, S.J. (Milwaukee: Bruce Publishing, 1934–1986). Volume XII, ed. Arthur J. Espelage, O.F.M. (Washington, D.C.: Canon Law Society of America, 2002).

Collectanea *Collectanea S. Congregationis de Propaganda Fide seu Decreta Instructiones Rescripta pro Apostolicis Missionibus* (Rome: Vatican Polyglot Press, 1907).

CSEL   *Corpus scriptorum ecclesiasticorum latinorum* (Vienna, 1866–).

Davis, 1966 David Brion Davis, *The Problem of Slavery in Western Culture* (Ithaca: Cornell University Press, 1966).

Davis, 1975 David Brion Davis, *The Problem of Slavery in the Age of Revolution* (Ithaca: Cornell University Press, 1975).

Davis, 2001   David Brion Davis, *In the Image of God: Religion, Moral Values, and Our Heritage of Slavery* (New Haven: Yale University Press, 2001).

Denzinger, 1955   Heinrich Denzinger, *Enchiridion Symbolorum Definitionum Et Declarationum De Rebus Fidei Et Morum,* ed. Karl Rahner, S.J. (Friburg in Br.: Herder, 30th ed., 1955).

Denzinger, 1965   35th edition of above, ed. Adolf Schonmetzer, S.J.

DHGE   *Dictionnaire d'histoire et de géographie ecclesiastiques,* ed. R. Aubert (Paris: Letouzey et ané, 1960–).

Digest   *Digesta, Corpus iuris civilis,* ed. Theodor Mommsen and Paul Krueger (16th ed., Berlin, 1954).

DTC   *Dictionnaire de théologie catholique* (Paris, 1903–1950).

Frend   W. H. C. Frend, *The Rise of Christianity* (Philadelphia: Fortress Press, 1984).

GCS   *Die griechischen christlichen Schriftsteller der ersten drei Jahrhunderte* (Leipzig, 1897–).

Garnsey   Peter Garnsey, *Ideas of Slavery from Aristotle to Augustine* (New York: Cambridge University Press, 1996).

Glancy   Jennifer Glancy, *Slavery in Early Christianity* (Oxford: Oxford University Press, 2002).

Herrmann-Otto   Elisabeth Herrmann-Otto, *Ex Ancilla Natus: Untersuchungen zu den "Hausgeborenen" Sklaven und Sklavinnen im Westen Römischen Kaiserreiches* (Stuttgart: Franz Steiner, 1994).

Hopkins   Keith Hopkins, *Conquerors and Slaves: Sociological Studies in Roman History* (Cambridge: Cambridge University Press, 1978).

Las Casas   Bartolomé de Las Casas, *Obras completas,* ed. Paulino Castañeda Delgado, Angel Losada, and others. (Madrid: Alianza Editorial, 1988–1995).

LTK   *Lexikon für Theologie und Kirche,* ed. Michael Buchberger (Freiburg im Breisgau, 2nd ed., 1957).

Maccarone   Michele Maccarone, *Vicarius Christi: Storia Del Titolo Papale* (Rome: The Lateran University, 1952).

Mansi   G. D. Mansi, ed., *Sacrorum conciliorum nova et amplissima collectio* (Florence, 1759–1767; Venice, 1769–1798).

MBR   *Magnum Bullarium Romanum a beato Leone Magno usque S.D.N. Benedictum XIII* (Luxemburg, 1727).

McGreevy   John T. McGreevy, *Catholicism and American Freedom: A History* (New York: W. W. Norton and Company, 2003).

NCE	*New Catholic Encyclopedia* (New York: McGraw Hill, 1966).
Periodica	*Periodica de re morali canonica liturgica* (1911–1982); *Periodica de re canonica* (1982–).
PG	*Patrologiae cursus completus . . . Series graeca,* ed. J. P. Migne (Paris, 1857–1866).
PL	*Patrologiae cursus completus . . . Series latina,* ed. J. P. Migne (Paris, 1844–1865).
Raccolta	*Raccolta di Concordati su materia ecclesiastiche tra la Santa Sede e le Autorità civili,* ed. Angelo Mercati (Rome: Vatican Polyglot Press, 1954).
Sacramentum Mundi	*Sacramentum Mundi: An Encyclopedia of Theology,* ed. Karl Rahner, S.J., and others (New York: Herder and Herder, 1969).
Vat. II	*Acta Synodalia Sacrosancti concilii Oecumenici Vaticani Secundi* (Vatican City: Vatican Polyglot Press, 1970).
Verlinden	Charles Verlinden, *L'Esclavage dans L'Europe Médiévale* (Bruges: De Tempel, 1955) (vol. 1): (Ghent: University of Ghent, 1977) (vol. 2).

ONE.   Father Newman Startles

Newman's originality: Owen Chadwick, *From Bossuet to Newman: The Idea of Doctrinal Development* (Cambridge: Cambridge University Press, 1987), 149–160. Newman's place: his *Essay on the Development of Christian Doctrine* is "the almost inevitable starting point for an investigation of development of doctrine." Jaroslav Pelikan, *Development of Christian Doctrine: Some Historical Prologomena* (New Haven: Yale University Press, 1969), 3. Newman does not use only the biological analogy; his analogies for doctrinal development are various, opening the way to misunderstanding, argument, and development of the idea of development. Cf. Aidan Nichols, O.P., *From Newman to Congar: The Idea of Doctrinal Development from the Victorians to the Second Vatican Council* (Edinburgh: T & T Clark, 1990), 58; Nicholas Lash, "Literature and Theory: Did Newman have a 'theory' of development?" in James D. Bastable, ed., *Newman and Gladstone Centennial Essays* (Dublin: Veritas Publications, 1978), 161–173.

"That which is intrinsically and per se evil": Newman to Allies, Nov. 8, 1863, John Henry Newman, *Letters and Diaries*, ed. Charles Stephen Dessain (London: Thomas Nelson and Sons, 1976), vol. 20, 554–556. Allies's letter described: 554. Newman's reference to St. Paul was to Paul's letter to Philemon, returning the slave Onesimus to his owner. Fifteen years later, Newman wrote in the same vein to William Robert Brownlow, an Anglican canon of Plymouth, who had lectured on the evils of slavery in the Roman Empire. How could St. Paul and St. John Chrysostom have accepted the institution if it was really "a first class evil?" Newman to Brownlow, 1878, quoted by Brownlow in his *Lectures on Slavery and Serfdom in Europe* (1892; reprint, Negro Universities Press, 1969), xvii.

Less tactfully than Newman, the *Pilot,* the paper of the Boston diocese, in 1851 attacked the abolitionists who claimed that "slavery is, in itself, intrinsically evil. This is nonsense, and it is so patent that we have never seen even a respectable attempt to prove it." See quotation in McGreevy, 53.

"Reason attests there are objects": John Paul II, *Veritatis splendor,* sec. 80.1, *AAS,* vol. 85, p. 1197 (1993); "the norms which prohibit": ibid., sec. 82.1, p. 1199; "the universality and immutability": sec. 90.1, p. 1205; "the negative commandments": sec. 52, p. 1175.

TWO.   Concubines, *Castrati,* Concordats—
Is There Teaching There?

"Therefore when anyone takes up the name of Abbot": *Regula S. Benedicti*; chap. 2, *Commentaire sur la Régle de Saint Benoit,* ed. Paul Delatte (Sablé-sur-Sarthe: Abbaye de Saint-Pierre de Solesmes, 1913), 46.

"Without the way": Thomas à Kempis, *De Imitatione Christi* (London: Kegan Paul, Trench, Trübner, 1892), Book 3, chap. 56; "your excellent examples": Book 3, chap. 18; "the lively examples": Book 1, chap. 18.

"It is not only a matter here of hearing and accepting": *Veritatis splendor,* sec. 19.1, *AAS* 85, 1149; "His actions and his commandments": sec. 20.1, *AAS* 85, 1149. The new Code of Canon Law, issued in 1983, acknowledged the place of example in teaching. The instruction of Christians is to be such "that the faith of the faithful, through doctrinal instruction and the experience of Christian life, becomes living, manifest and productive." The canon is addressed to those responsible for teaching. It gives equal weight to verbal teaching and the experience of those being taught, experience necessarily in interaction with their teachers as well as with the wider Christian community. The examples encountered are essential to the catechism. See *CIC* (1983) canon 773.

"sing the divine praises": Alfonso de'Ligouri, *Theologia moralis,* ed. Léonard Gaudé (Rome, 1905), Book III, n.274, holding that the more probable opinion is that such castration is unlawful mutilation, but that the opinion allowing it is also probable; exclusion of *castrati* from Sistine Chapel: *Cathlicisme: Hier-Aujourd'hui-Demain,* ed. G. Jacquemet (Paris: Letouzey et Ané, 1948) 606.

"The Church condemns and always prosecutes": Alessandro of Alessandria, *Tractatus de usuris,* A. M. Hamelin, O.F.M., ed., *Un traité de morale économique au XIV Siècle* (Louvain: Édit. Nauwelaerts, 1962), 181; the contrary conclusion of St. Antoninus: infra, chap. 19; acceptance by Cajetan: Tommaso de Vio (Cajetan), *De cambiis,* chaps. 4 and 8 in Cajetan, *Scripta philosophica: opuscula oeconomica-socialia,* ed. P. Zammit, O.P. (Rome, 1934).

Ruffini's argument: Ernesto Ruffini, *Oratio,* Sept. 23, 1965, *Vat. II,* 3:2:356. Concordats made since 1915 included those with Lithuania (1922); with Poland (1925); with Romania (1927); with Italy (1929); with Austria (1933); with Germany (1933); with Portugal (1940); with Spain (1953); and with the Dominican Republic (1954). See *Raccolta,* vol. II. In each case, the Church was privileged in one or more ways. For example, in Lithuania, priests sentenced to prison by the civil authority were to undergo this punishment in a monastery (Art. XIX, *Raccolta,* p. 7); the Dominican Republic pledged itself to build the cathedral church and the offices and residence of the archbishop (Art. VII, *Raccolta,* 298); Spain recognized the Catholic, Apostolic, Roman Religion as "the sole religion of the Spanish nation" (Art. I, *Raccolta,* 272).

Gregory II on divorce: Gregory II to Boniface, November 21, 726, *Monumenta Germaniae Historia, Epistolae Merovingici Et Karolini Aevi* (Berlin, 1892), 3, 276; Celestine III on divorce: *Decretales,* 4, 7, 19, *CIC II.*

THREE.   Morals without Experience and Empathy
Are like Sundaes without Ice Cream or Sauce

"Either ethical precepts are independent": E. O. Wilson, *Consilience: The Unity of Knowledge* (New York: Knopf, 1998), 260.

"The past experience revived": T. S. Eliot, "The Dry Salvages," sec. II, *Four Quartets* (London: Faber & Faber, 1944).

FOUR.   God's Slaveowners

The curse of Canaan as prefigurement of Canaanite slavery: Robert Alter, *Genesis* (New York: Norton, 1998), 41. How the curse of Canaan as biblically presented became the curse of Ham and of black descendants attributed to Ham is a tangled tale, investigated and set out with erudition by David M. Goldenberg, *The Curse of Ham: Race and Slavery in Early Judaism, Christianity and Islam* (Princeton: Princeton University Press, 2003). The name Ham itself is of unknown origin and has in Hebrew no connotation of blackness (p. 149). The difficulty of explaining why Ham was not cursed but his son was led Philo to maintain that Ham was "virtually cursed" (p. 150). In time, the expansive reading that the curse fell on Ham was adopted both by rabbinic writers and by Christians including Ambrose, Ambrosiaster, John Chrysostom, and Vincent of Lérins. This reading made the curse applicable not only to Canaan but to Ham's other sons (pp. 159–160). Rabbinic commentators, possibly as early as the second century of the common era, saw a similarity between the name Ham and words based on the Hebrew roots for "dark" and for "heat." By the fourth century, Ham was identified in the Palestinian Talmud as black

(p. 156). As the three sons of Noah were presented by Genesis 9:19 as the source of the world's population after the Flood, it was convenient to make this identification as a way of accounting for the Blacks from Africa familiar to the Hebrews. The identification was strengthened by Genesis 10:6 naming the first son of Ham as Kush. In other parts of the Hebrew Bible, Kush was sometimes, although not always, treated as the equivalent of Nubia/Ethiopia (p. 25): the Black, Ham, could be seen as the father of the whole race of Blacks. Black slaves could be seen as Kushites, exemplifying the working of the curse of Ham's descendants (p. 166). By the time of the controversy over slavery in the United States, defenders of the status quo confidently asserted it to be in accordance with the divine plan announced in the doom pronounced by Noah (p. 176).

Strained as the argument seems today and thin as it must appear to anyone not seeking anthropology in the Bible, the staying power of this extraordinary exegesis points to its attractiveness to the beneficiaries of Black enslavement.

Esau and the Edomite slaves: Alter, *Genesis,* 127.

The booty from the Midianites as fantasy: "little that is factual," Martin Noth, *Numbers: A Commentary* (Philadelphia: The Westminster Press, 1968), 229. "I received the tribute": *Ancient Near East: Supplementary Texts Relating to the Old Testament,* ed. James B. Pritchard (Princeton: Princeton University Press, 3rd ed., 1969), 275.

Slaves at Solomon's smelter: Nelson Glueck, "The Third Season of Excavation at Tell El-Kheleifeh," *Bulletin of the American School of Oriental Research* 79 (1940), 5; Isaac Mendelsohn, *Slavery in the Ancient Near East* (New York: Oxford University Press, 1988), 95.

"the souls of men": this mode of somewhat ironically reminding the readers of the Apocalypse that slaves were human beings continued to be used in medieval Europe: see, e.g., Verlinden, 2, 776.

Roman Italy as slave society: Bradley, 12–13; slaves individually owned: ibid., 10–12. See also Glancy, 42–45; Hopkins, 169–173; Joseph Vogt, *Ancient Slavery and the Ideal of Man,* trans. Thomas Wiedemann (Cambridge: Harvard University Press, 1975), 142; Dale B. Martin, "Slavery and the Ancient Jewish Family" in *The Jewish Family in Antiquity,* ed. Shaye J. D. Cohen (Scholars' Press, 1988), 113–129. Rural occupations of slaves: *Digest* 33.7. Slaves, slaveowners, and freedmen make up the early Christian communities: Wayne A. Meeks, *The First Urban Christians* (New Haven: Yale University Press, 2nd ed., 2003), 21 and 63–64. In the first official report by a Roman governor on the Christians, he notes that to obtain information about the sect he has tortured two slave girls who "minister" for them. Pliny to the Emperor Trajan, *Letters,* ed. and trans. Betty Radice (Cambridge: Harvard University Press, 1969) book 10, letter 96, vol. 2, p. 288.

libido dominandi, the lust to dominate: see, e.g., Augustine, *De civitate Dei,* ed. Bernard Dombart and Alphonsus Kalb (Leipzig, 1877), I, 30, 29–33: "the lust to dominate had inhered in a purer form in the whole Roman populace" and, when it had conquered a few powerful men, imposed on the rest "the yoke of slavery."

Slavery for debt: see E. C. Urbach, "The Laws Regarding Slavery as a Source for Social History of the Period of the Second Temple, the Messiah and the Talmud," *Papers of the Institute of Jewish Studies, London,* ed. J. G. Weiss (Jerusalem: Magnes Press, 1964), vol. 1, 93–94; auction of naked captives: Glancy, 86.

Sales of slaves in market: Bradley, 51–54, citing *Digest* 21.1.38.2; transportation to unknown places: ibid., 46–47; naming by owner: Leonhard Schumacher, *Sklaverei in der Antike: Alltag und Schicksal der Unfreien* (Munich: C. H. Beck, 2001), 268.

Not many slave families: W. V. Harris, "Demography, Geography and the Sources of Roman Slaves," *Journal of Roman Studies* 89 (1999), 68.

Number of slaves and numbers supplied from different sources: Harris at 62, challenging Walter Scheidel, "Quantifying the Sources of Slaves in the Early Roman Empire," *Journal of Roman Studies* 87 (1997), 158; see also Bradley, 39; number taken at Tiberias: ibid., 45. A close survey of legal and literary texts concludes that reproduction by slave women, although not systematically organized, played a significant part in the continuation of slavery in the Roman Empire: Herrmann-Otto, 411. *Vernae:* on use of the term in the Roman Empire: ibid., 1071.

Frequency of emancipation: Hopkins, 115–116. Hopkins notes that Felix, the procurator before whom Paul was tried, was an ex-slave. The Roman proverb: 119–120.

talking tools: Marcus Terentius Varro, *Rerum rusticarum,* with an English translation by William Davis Hooper (Cambridge: Harvard University Press, 1954), I, 17, 1. Humane management: ibid., I, 17, 5–7.

"Servant" as English translation of Hebrew and Greek for "slave": *The Oxford English Dictionary,* prepared by J. A. Simpson and E. S. C. Weiner, (2nd ed., Oxford: Clarendon Press, 1989), vol. 15, p. 27. "Slave" may have been a rarer word than "servant" although *sclaue* is already in use in thirteenth-century England and is, later, once employed by Chaucer, as Troilus declares he will serve Pandarus:

> Right as thi sclaue, which so thow wendes
> For ever more, unto my lyves ende.

Troilus and Criseyde, II, 391–392, *The Riverside Chaucer,* ed. Larry D. Benson (Boston: Houghton Mifflin Company, 1987), 519.

"Slave" had no connotation of blackness in fourteenth-century England when Wyclif translated the Bible into English and chose "servant" as the equivalent of the Latin *servus*. He was followed by William Tyndal, Myles Coverdale, and the Geneva Bible.

By the sixteenth century, "slave" was easily used by Shakespeare to describe Caliban, a native of the island now ruled by Prospero and treated as a degraded monster, e.g., *The Tempest* I, 2, 322–377, *The Complete Works of Shakespeare,* ed. David Berrington (New York: Longmans, 1997), 1535. Caliban is seen as a "black cloud," ibid. II, 2, 20, p. 1542. Arguably, at least, "slave" carried a racial connotation. The translators of the King James Bible may have chosen to avoid this problem by retaining "servant" as the standard translation. "Servant" as "slave" in the American South: see the *Oxford English Dictionary,* 15, 27. Proper translation of terms meaning slave: *The Anchor Bible,* ed. David Noel Freedman (New York: Doubleday, 1992), 6, 62, Vogt, *Ancient Slavery,* 142 (on *doulos*) and 147 (on *doule*).

Softening of servitude to service is not confined to English. In a modern French translation, the majority of times the biblical words for slave are translated "*serviteur*" (e.g., Dt 5:21; Lk 7:9), and for slave girl "*servante*" (e.g., Ex 20:10; Ps 116:16; Lk 1:38). Occasionally, however, *esclave* is used (e.g., Lev 25:46; 1 Cor 7:22; Apoc 18:13). See *La Sainte Bible traduite en français sous la direction de L'École Biblique de Jérusalem* (Paris: Les Éditions Du Cerf, 1956).

"No slave can serve two masters," Lk 16:13. In Mark "No man can serve two masters."

FIVE.   God's Slaves

On the relation of the laws protecting Hebrew slaves to the stories in Genesis of Jacob's service to Laban and in Exodus of Israel's slavery in Egypt, see Calum Carmichael, "Three Laws on the Release of Slaves, (Ex 21, 2–11; Dtn 15, 12–18; Lev 25, 39–46)," *Zeitschrift Für Die Alttestamentliche Wissenschaft,* 112, 509–525 (2000). Carmichael also points to other inconsistencies between the law on Hebrew slaves in Ex 21:2–11 and Dt 15:12–18 and accounts for them as responses to earlier narratives of Hebrew slavery. Scepticism as to enforcement of the laws: Mendelsohn, *Slavery in the Ancient Near East,* 90, citing the sages of the Talmud for the scepticism.

A difficult text is the following:

> You shall not surrender to his master a slave who has taken refuge with you. Let him stay with you anywhere he chooses in any one of your settlements, wherever suits him best; you shall not force him. (Dt 23:15–16).

If read as applying to slaves of the Israelites themselves, these verses offer limitless sanctuary to runaways and subvert the slave-based society. Read in context after sanitary rules "when you are encamped against an enemy" (Dt 23:9–14), the verses suggest that the compilers of the legislation addressed the case of a runaway from the enemy—he was not to be returned, he was to be allowed "to stay with you" and to choose "among your settlements." These settlements are distinct from those that are not Israel's. To the same effect see Ronald Knox at the verse cited in *The Holy Bible* (New York: Sheed & Ward, 1954). Calum Carmichael offers an alternative suggestion that the text is not a statute, but the expression of an ideal inspired by the story of Jacob's flight from service to Laban and his subsequent reception as a brother by Esau (Gen 32:4–Gen 33:17). See Calum Carmichael, *Law and Narrative in the Bible* (Ithaca: Cornell University Press, 1985), 237–240.

"Eyeless in Gaza": John Milton, *Samson Agonistes*, l.40, *The Works of John Milton* (New York: Columbia University Press, 1931), vol. 1, pt. 2, p. 338.

Footwashing as a slave's task: Carl W. Weber, *Sklaverei im Altertum* (Düsseldorf: Econ Verlag, 1981); see also Abigail in 1 Sam 24:41.

Slave girl of the Lord: see Joseph Vogt, "Ecce Ancilla Domini: The Social Aspects of the Portrayal of the Virgin Mary in Antiquity," in Vogt, *Ancient Slavery*, 146–169.

Sexual service of masters: "the more slave girls the more lewdness," Hillel, *mishnah, Aboth* 2.1, *Abodah Zaron, Hebrew-English Translation of the Babylonia Talmud*, ed. I. Epstein (London: Soncino Press, 1988). See also Glancy, 23. Nearly 400 years later, Jerome takes a master's use of a female slave as a comparative for bad sexual conduct by a husband with a wife. See Jerome to Oceanus, *PL* 22, 693.

Christianity as revenge of the slaves: Friedrich Nietzsche, *On the Genealogy of Morals*, trans. Walter Kaufmann and R. J. Hollingdale (New York: Vintage Books, 1967), 34 and 144; "the weak" who are willing to forgive: 47.

Slave as dishonored being: Orlando Patterson, *Slavery and Social Death* (Cambridge: Harvard University Press, 1982), 12–13.

The ideal slave of God could be viewed as providing the model for the monk in the Rule of St. Benedict. The monk is far from a nothing. He is a person dedicated to God, for whom the abbot has the responsibility of a father. From a secular point of view the monk has given up autonomy. Chapter 1 states: "The Abbot is believed to hold the place of Christ." He is, the rule continues, a shepherd in charge of sheep. He is to punish the disobedient by beating. Chapter 5, "On obedience," provides that the monks' obedience is to be instant, "not living according to their own choice, nor obeying their own desires and pleasures, but walking by another's judgment and command." What is ordered to be done is to be done "without the heart murmuring" and "without hesitation, delay, lukewarmness, grumbling or objection. For the obedience given to Superiors is given to God since He Himself has said, 'He who hears you hears Me.'" Chapter 7, "On humility," enumerates twelve degrees of humility, of which the fourth is "perseverance in obedience, even when meeting injustice."

Parables reinscribing the structure: see Glancy, 120, 175.

Paul in Ephesians: Until near the end of the eighteenth century no one doubted that Paul had written Ephesians. Since then, there has been challenge and doubt. I agree with those who have concluded that the doubt is not justified. See Markus Barth, *The Anchor Bible: Ephesians* (Garden City: Doubleday, 1974), 49; Joseph A. Grassi, "The Letter to the Ephesians" in *The Jerome Bible Commentary*, ed. Raymond Brown et al., (Englewood Cliffs: Prentice Hall, 1968), 342. The arguments from differences in style, adduced against Pauline authorship, would prove that Shakespeare could not have written both *King Lear* and *The Tempest*.

There are also passages on masters and slaves in the Pastoral Epistles, where the modern weight of authority has been against Pauline authorship, but where Luke Timothy Johnson has come to its defense. See Johnson, *The First and Second Letters to Timothy: A New Translation with Introduction and Commentary*, 14. *The Anchor Bible*, vol. 35A (New York: Doubleday, 2001). In 1 Tim 6:1–2, Christian slaves are told to respect all their masters and not to disrespect Christian masters "because they are brothers"—a sign that religious brotherhood might be thought to relax the rules of bondage. In Titus 2:9 it is said: "Slaves are to be under the control of their masters in all respects, giving them satisfaction, not talking back to them or stealing from them, but exhibiting complete good faith, so as to adorn the teaching of God our saviour in every way." It is notable that these letters show more concern for slaves' poor behavior than for that of their masters.

A good historian comments: "Paul's message was not directed to the outcasts and misfits of society—the inhabitants of the highways and byways—or even primarily to slaves. In this respect the difference between him and his Lord was fundamental." Frend, 105. The comment is curious. The Lord never addressed slaves. Paul included them in one or more letters.

the leader to lead by lowering himself: Dale B. Martin, *Slavery as Salvation* (New Haven: Yale University Press, 1990), 117–126.

Paul's return of Onesimus: David Daube has argued that Paul believes that by baptism Onesimus is a new person and therefore no longer the slave of Philemon, see Daube, *New Testament Judaism: Collected Works of David Daube*, ed. Calum Carmichael (Berkeley: The Robbins Collection, 2000), vol. 2, 553–556. I don't find the argument persuasive: not only does Paul return Onesimus as though the latter could be ordered to return and was owed to his master, but the position that baptized slaves were free would have been a major challenge to Roman law, and it is not compatible with Paul's explicit recommendation in 1 Corinthians 7:20: "Let each one remain in that calling the Lord appointed for him and in which he was when God called him." No suggestion here that the convert, a new man or woman, is free to act without reference to his or her former state.

Philemon would have to be a clod: "What rock would these words not soften? What wild beast would they not tame and lead to act most humanely?" John Chrysostom, "Homily

III on the Epistle to Philemon," *PG* 62, 715. For the speculation as to Useful's later career: see Joseph A. Fitzmeyer, S.J., *The Letter to Philemon: A New Translation and Commentary*, 14–15, in *The Anchor Bible*, vol. 34C (New York: Doubleday, 2000).

My reading is in accord with Helmut Koester, *History and Literature of Early Christianity* (Philadelphia: The Fortress Press, 1984), II, 135. As Daniel Boyarin has observed, how Philemon is read depends on choices in the larger corpus of Paul. If read in the light of Galatians 3:29, it is "a deft effort to pressure Philemon to free Onesimus." Boyarin, *A Radical Jew: Paul and the Politics of Identity* (Berkeley: University of California Press, 1999), 5.

In *Philemon's Problem: The Daily Dilemma of the Christian* (Chicago: Adult Catechetical Teaching Aids, 1973), pp. 5–6, James Tunstead Burtchaell, C.S.C., has pinpointed Philemon's choice—obey Paul and find all his slaves desiring baptism and freedom as a corollary, or disobey and be thought a disobedient ingrate by Paul and fellow Christians. It's hard to see why he would have preserved the letter if he disobeyed. He could have freed Useful as an exception and kept his other slaves.

SIX.   The Pope's Slaves

"On a certain day when merchants had recently arrived": Bede, *Historia ecclesiastica gentis anglorum*, ed. Charles Plummer (Oxford: at the Clarendon Press, 1896), Book 2, chap. 1, pp. 79–80. On the status of the story as Northumbrian legend: J. M. Wallace Hadrill, Bede's *Ecclesiastical History of the English People* (Oxford: Clarendon Press, 1988), 51.

A variant of this legend, with two different puns, was told by Las Casas in his presentation in 1550 of a defense of the Indians: "Why did he [Oviedo] not imitate Saint Gregory, who on noticing certain Angles who had been reduced to slavery asked the name of the province from which they had been taken and was told that it was called Deira. 'It is indeed rightly called Deira,' the holy man said, 'for they are led from anger [*de ira*] to Christ's mercy.' He asked what the name of their king was and was told that he was called Adelle. 'Rightly so,' Gregory said, 'for he will sing alleluia to the Lord.'" Bartolomé de Las Casas, *In Defense of the Indians*, trans. Stafford Poole, C.M., (DeKalb: Northern Illinois University Press, 1974), 347.

"Correct all these matters": Gregory to Peter, March 16, 591, St. Gregory the Great, *Registrum epistularum libri VIII–XIV,* ed. Dag Norberg, *CC,* vol. 140A, Appendix, p. 1093; canon of Chalcedon: Mansi, 7, 159.

boys "to advance in servitude": Gregory to Candidus, September 595, Register VI, 10, *Registrum,* 140, 378–79; "to buy Barbaracini slaves": Gregory to Vitalis, Feb.–April, 599, Register IX, 124, *Registrum,* 140A, 675; "Moreover, a certain man": Gregory to Narses,

June, 597, Register VII, 27, *Registrum*, 140, 485; "Moved by the grace": Gregory to Felix, January, 599, Register IX, 99, *Registrum*, 140A, 611–612; "boys whom he has bought": Gregory to Romanus, defender of Sicily, October, 599, Register X, 1; *Registrum*, 140A, 825; "bought equally": Gregory to Fortunatus, February, 599. Register IX, 105, *Registrum* 140A, 657; purchase and circumcision of Christians forbidden: *Theodosiani libri*, 16.9.1, ed. T. Momsen (Berlin, 1905), I:2, 895.

In another case, a woman was dismissed by her husband on the ground that she was a slave. She made her way to Rome and established to the pope's satisfaction that "there was no stain of slavery in her." Gregory, therefore, directed Fortunatus, the local bishop, to compel her husband to take her back. Gregory to Fortunatus, 597, Register VI, 1. The implication, at least, of the pope's ruling is that the woman's suit would have failed if she were found to be a slave.

"It is clear that nature": Gregory, *Regula pastoralis* 2.16, *PL* 77, 34. Gregory's grandfather, Felix III: Henry Chadwick, *The Church in Ancient Society: From Galilee to Gregory the Great* (Oxford: The Clarendon Press, 2000), 658; "from the beginning nature": Gregory to Montana and Thomas, September 595, Register VI, 12, *Registrum*, 140, 180.

Servus servorum: Charles Plummer, Notes, Bede, *Historia*, II, 38. Augustine had observed that slaves who were permitted to have property could have slaves, and that one of the latter was "a slave of a slave." See François Dolbeau, "Nouveaux sermons de saint Augustin pour la conversion des paiens et des donatistes." *Revue der Études Augustiniennes*, 37 (1998), 275. Perhaps more pertinently in the background is Paul's claim "I have enslaved myself to all" (1 Cor 9:19), and even farther back, Abigail's posture before David (1 Sam 24:41).

Christians showing off slaves: Clement of Alexandria, *Pedagogus, PG* 8, 649.

"an institution of the *ius gentium* . . .": *Digest* 1.5.4.

"This sentence is penal": Augustine, *De civitate Dei* 19.15; origin in Noah's curse: ibid., 19.19. Slavery among third-century Christians: Frend, 419–420; among fourth-century Christians: ibid., 570.

treatment of slaves: Tertullian, *De resurrectione carnis*, chap. 57, *PL* 1, 879; "might order him": Augustine, Sermon 112, chap. 9, *PL* 38, 889.

Gregory of Nyssa on the pride of slaveowners:

What is such a gross example of arrogance . . . as for a human being to think himself master of his own kind? . . . You condemn man to slavery when his nature is free and possesses free will, and you make law in competition with God, overturning his law for humankind. . . . You have forgotten the limits of your authority and that your rule is confined to control over things without reason. . . . Why do you go beyond what is subject to you . . . counting your own kind on a level with four-footed things and even things without feet? . . . Irrational beasts are the only slaves of humankind. . . . But by dividing the human species in two with "slavery" and "ownership" you have caused it to be enslaved to itself and to be the owner of itself.

"I bought slaves and slave girls." For what price? What did you find in existence worth as much as this human nature? What price did you put on rationality? How many obols do you reckon the equivalent of the image of God?

He who knew the nature of humankind rightly said that the whole world was not worth giving in exchange for a human soul. . . . Has a scrap of paper and the counting out of obols deceived you into thinking yourself the master of the image of God? [Gregory, "The Fourth Homily," *Homilies on Ecclesiastes: An English Version with Supporting Studies*, ed. Stuart George Hall (Berlin–New York: Walter de Gruyter, 1993), 73–74. See also Richard Klein, "Gibt es eine slavenethik bei Gregor von Nyssa? in *Gregory of Nyssa: Homilies on the Beatitudes*, ed. Hubertus R. Drobner and Albert Viciano (Leiden: Brill, 2000), 593–604.

Preaching on Ecclesiastes, understood by him to be the work of Solomon, Gregory has as text the pseudonymous author's declaration: "I possessed slaves and slave girls, and I had a great household of slaves" (Eccl 2:7), a declaration that is a prelude to developing Solomon's theme that wisdom is superior to riches. Gregory as homilist goes well beyond the text to see Solomon as accusing himself of pride. The argument, it seems to a modern reader, is irresistible, and the conclusion inescapable: you, dear sinner in my congregation, must free your slaves. The conclusion is never reached. The preacher goes on to denounce usury in lending money, drinking too much, and cultivating a delicate palette. Sins are being scorched. There is not a whisper of abolitionism. The institution was too entrenched to be shaken, or even stirred, by such fine rhetoric. We don't know if Gregory of Nyssa himself owned slaves. We do know that his brother, Basil the Great, cited the biblical stories of Canaan and Esau to show the appropriateness of slavery (Garnsey, 45). And Gregory of Nazianzus, the third of this trio of sainted Cappadocian theologians, owned slaves he bequeathed to a female relative and to the church of Nazianzus (Garnsey, 32–33). Gregory of Nyssa, the bishop of a small diocese, had neither the power nor the authority nor, it would appear, the desire to destroy a system that pervaded society.

No concientious objectors to slaveowning: far from it. Athenagoras observed to Marcus Aurelius that "we [Christians] have slaves; some, many; others, a few." *Embassy for Christians*, c. 35, *PG 1*, 968–969.

SEVEN.   Human Slaves as God's Slaves

Calixtus on marriage of a slave: *Elenclos* 9.12.25, *GCS* 26.250. On the author, see R. Gögler, "Hippolytus," *LTK,* 3:378–379.

The difficulty of determining the extent and effect of Calixtus's ruling: it is recorded as a reproach by his enemy, so one cannot say that marriage was routinely available for Christian slaves. The code of laws issued under Theodosius II, a Christian emperor, determined that slaves were juridically incapable of marriage (*Codex Theodosianus* 12.1.6). In the *Digest,* published in 533, enslavement ends a marriage; the slave no longer is juridically capable of expressing the marital affection essential to a marriage: *Digest* 49.15.12.4. No Roman law protected a slave union from violation by adultery. Yet Justinian legislated as a Christian ruler, giving what is "useful to our subjects" so that "we may preserve their souls": *Codex Iustiniani* 1.5.18.

"so many thousands of men," Patrick, *Confessio,* in *The Book of Letters of St. Patrick the Bishop,* ed. D. R. Howlett (Dublin: Four Courts Press, 1994), 52. Slavery continued in Christian Ireland. Irish penitentials assigned penance to an owner having intercourse with his slave girl and provided for her liberation if she bore his child: e.g., Finnian, *Penitential* (circa 520), n.39 and 40 in John T. McNeill and Helen M. Gamer, *Medieval Handbooks of Penance* (New York: Columbia University Press, 1991), 98; Cummean, *Penitential* (circa 650), n.26 and 27 in ibid., 105. In the Christian era, a slave girl was still referred to as a form of currency. One female slave was equated to a dozen fowls or a dozen shekels: *The Irish Canons* (circa 675), in ibid. 119. The life of a bishop had the value of seven slave girls, the wounding of a bishop the value of five: *The Canons of an Irish Synod,* n.1 and 5, ibid., 124.

"she was, by divine providence, kidnapped": Anon., *Vita Sanctae Balthildis, Scriptores Rerum Merovingicarum* (Hannover, 1888), 2, 483; see the editorial introduction to her life, p. 475, for her bad press and the date of her regency; for her antislavery measures: *Vita,* 494. Her biographer does not describe how she was seized or at what moment she regained her freedom. Modern historians add little to the ancient *Vita.* See L. Van der Essen, "Bathilde," *DHGE,* 6, 1321–1322. Her feast day is January 30. *AS,* January, III, 347.

Canon 17 of the Council of Clichy in 626 had followed Roman law decreeing that a Christian could not be the slave of a non-Christian. See Carlo De Clerq, *La législation religeuse franque de Clovis à Charlemagne* (Louvain, 1936), 65. But there is no legislation by the Church in the period covered by De Clerq that forbids enslavement of a Christian by a Christian.

Blandina: Eusebuis, *Historia ecclesiastica* (Greek, with English translation by Kirsopp Lake), (New York: G. P. Putnam), 5.1–56, setting out the letter from Lyons and Vienne. At 5.1–67 he notes Marcus Aurelius's order reinforcing the persecution. The commemorative letter is also printed in *AS,* June, vol. 1, which reports the church in Blandina's honor.

Aquila and Vitale: Ambrose, *De exhortatione virginitatis,* chap. 1, *PL* 16, 337–338; see also *AS,* November 3, vol. 2, 585.

The martyrdom of Felicity and Perpetua: *AS,* March 7, vol. I, 630–632; "perpetual felicity": Augustine quoted in ibid., 631.

EIGHT.   A Girl Named Zita and Other Commodities

Bernardo de Ranemis, Notarial Act, November 6, 1469: Verlinden, vol. 2, pp. 611–612, n.269.

the buyer's right to judge for the soul and body of the slave: see, e.g., Iris Origo, "The Domestic Enemy: The Eastern Slaves in Tuscany in the Fourteenth and Fifteenth Centuries," *Speculum* 30, 334 (July 1955). Like the occasional reference to slaves as souls (*animae*), the clause in a sale setting up the purchaser to judge on behalf of "soul and body" of the slave reveals a consciousness of dealing with a human being. At the same time the clause conveys to the purchaser a right that intrudes into the conscience of the slave. Another example of this clause at Zara, October 5, 1367: Verlinden, 2, 726 (sale of a father and his daughter, aged fourteen).

Zita: It was not unusual for slaves to be designated not by their original names but by baptismal names; see, e.g., notarial act of August 1, 1427, in Verlinden, 2, 369–371. Zita is a Christian name, in all probability bestowed at baptism. As the name is that of an Italian saint, it was likely given to her after her arrival in Italy. The saint herself was a girl from a village near Lucca who, at the age of twelve, was driven by poverty to go to the city and, in the words of her contemporary biographer, "give herself" to work for a Lucchese family. She served them faithfully, obediently, chastely, and cheerfully until her death at the age of sixty (*AS,* April 27, vol. 3, 500–515). Her reputation as a saint, at first confined to Lucca, had grown so that Dante disdainfully identified a councilman of Lucca as "one of Saint Zita's elders" (*Inferno* 21:38). What saint's name would have seemed more appropriate for a slave? What name, if reflected on, more sharply conveyed the implication that a person who was the image of God was being bartered?

Geographic origins of slaves sold at Venice: Verlinden, 2, 554–667; the whiteness of Circassian girls: e.g., ibid., 2, 303 (Naples); Blacks, ibid., 2, 657–660.

Sclavus and *sclava:* Verlinden, 1, 211–218; 2, 128–130; purchase in 1192 by Venetians: ibid., 2, 551–552.

The role of Venice: ibid., 2, 550–666; "a center of distribution": ibid., 2, 663; Venetians at Tana: ibid., 2, 924–947.

"bargaining to sell his daughter": Dante Alighieri, *Purgatorio* 20, 80–81, *The Divine Comedy*, ed. Charles S. Singleton (Princeton: Princeton University Press, 1973), 218; identification of the transaction: ibid., commentary at 486.

Florence as a market: Origo, "The Domestic Enemy," 324–328; decree of the Priors: Verlinden, 2, 360; variety of owners: Origo, 321, 348; *le schiavette amorose:* ibid., 321; Lorenzetti frescoes, ibid., 325; the spread of slavery in Tuscany, ibid., 325; register, gender, and age: Verlinden, 2, 362; report to Cosimo: Origo, 337; complaint to Datini: Verlinden, 2, 368–369; Datini to his agent: Origo, 339; Datini's daughter by his slave: ibid., 345; the anxiety of Florentine fathers: ibid., 344; the orphanage and its clientele: ibid., 347.

A study of the archives of Genoa in the fifteenth century shows a pattern of slave ownership similar to that in Florence. Slaves owned by members of the liberal professions were as follows:

Owners	Female Slaves	Male Slaves
Notaries	70	9
Physicians	8	1
Doctors of law	4	3
Chancellors	4	–
Grammarians	3	–

Domenico Gioffré, *Il Mercato degli Schiavi A Genoa Nel Secolo XV* (Genoa: Fratelli Bozzi, 1971), 83. Including the slaves owned by artisans such as shoemakers, there were 242 women and 39 men held as slaves. Ibid., 88. A separate register in the city lists by name, age, seller, and buyer the sales of Tartar slaves, 1429–1439:

Margherita, age 10
Caterina, age 13
Melica, age 13
Maria, age 22
Maddalena, age 26
Lucia, age 22
Marta, age 27
Lisa, age 18
Marta, age 19
Lucia, age 12
Maria, age 27
Julian, age 29
Giorgio, age 18

That all on the register had baptismal Christian names was no obstacle to their enslavement. Over a dozen other nationalities or ethnicities were noted among the slaves, among them Bosnians, Bulgars, Canary Islanders, Circassians, Greeks, Hungarians, Jews, and Turks.

NINE.   Moral Masters

"This is the memorial of the slaves and slave girls who have been emancipated": Francesco Gatta and Giuseppe Plessi, eds., *Liber Paradisus* (Bologna, 1956), p. 5; prices: p. 6; precedents in Assisi, etc.: "Note Illustrative" by the editors, p. 129. In the background was political tension between the city and the rural magnates, the principal owners of slaves. See Rolando Dondarini, *Bologna Medievale Nella Storia Città* (Bologna, 2000); Guiseppe Coccolini, "La religione nella storia del popolo bolognese e la consequente 'bolognesita'," *Strena storica Bolognese* 53 (2003), 139.

the "transformation" occurred "very slowly": Marc Bloch, "Comment et pourquoi finit l'esclavage antique," *Annales* 2 (1947), 30–44, 161–171; "hard to explain": Marcel Bloch in *The Cambridge Economic History of Europe*. Volume I, *The Agrarian Life of the Middle Ages*, ed. M. M. Postan (Cambridge: at the University Press, 1961), 247; "one of the most notable facts": idem.

"The Church refused resolutely": Bloch, *The Agrarian Life*, 248.

"you incur a great sin": John VIII to the princes of Sardinia, December 14–16, 872: Denzinger, 1965, n.668; "robbery or booty": Council of Narbonne, canon 21, Mansi, 16, 831–832;"the wicked trade": Council of London, chap. 27, summarized in Mansi, 20, col. 1152; "contrary to the custom of the Latins": Guibert de Nogent, *Gesta Dei per Francos*, *PL* 156, 688.

Slaves in thirteenth-century Sicily: Verlinden, II, 138–154; in Sardinia: ibid., II, 343–344; in the kingdom of Naples: ibid., II, 284–287.

Danish slaves: Ruling on January 13, 1206, on a question presented to him by Andreas Sunesen, archbishop of Lund, Innocent III decreed that, guilty of attacking a priest, "the slaves ought to come to be absolved by the slave of the slaves" and so should be sent to Rome, unless, perchance, the slaves had "done this in fraud in order to withdraw from service to their masters." In that case, the interests of the masters were respected, and the slaves need not be sent to Rome. *Diplomaticum danicam*, ed. Niels Skyum Nielsen (Copenhagen: Ejnar Monkgaard Forlag, 1958), 6, 213. On the ownership of slaves in Scandinavia by churchmen and church institutions, see Ruth Mazo Karras, *Slavery and Society in Medieval Scandinavia* (New Haven: Yale University Press, 1988), 141.

Enslaving ends when opponents not different religiously: Charles Verlinden, "Slavery, Slave Trade," *Dictionary of the Middle Ages*, ed. Joseph R. Strayer (New York: Charles Scribner's Sons, 1983–1998), 11, 140.

"according to the mores of modern times": Bartolus de Saxoferrato, *Commentaria: cum additionibus Thomae Diplovatatii aliorumque excellentissimorum doctorum, una cum amplis-*

simo repertorio noviter elucubrato per dictum clarissimum doctorem dominum Thomam Diplo-vatatium, ed. G. Polari (Venice, 1526; facsimile Rome, 1996), at 49.15.24.1. The modern custom is not acknowledged by Johannes Teutonicus, the author in 1215–1216 of what became accepted as the ordinary gloss on Gratian. He writes: "If a war is just, he who is captured becomes the slave of his captor." The captive, he adds, sins if he attempts to escape: *Decretum gratiani . . . una cum glossis* (Lyons, 1584), at D.1, *Ius gentium.* Antoninus on custom of not enslaving: infra, this chapter.

on the effect of permitting slaves to marry: see Georges Duby, *The Early Growth of the European Economy,* trans. Howard B. Clarke (London: Weidenfeld & Nicholson, 1974), 34–35, 181.

Slavery as part of the *ius gentium:* Gratian, *Concordia discordantium canonum,* 1, 1; drunkenness and slavery: ibid., 1, 35; the marriage of slaves: ibid., 2, 29, 1–7, *CIC* I, 1002–1005; the kinds of mistake that prevent consent: ibid. The first version of the *Concordia* was published no earlier than 1139. Andreas Winroth, *The Making of Gratian's Decretum* (Cambridge: Cambridge University Press, 2000), 140.

At Paris, Peter Lombard agreed, adding only that as to slaves who married each other with their masters in ignorance of what they did, "to others it seems there can be marriage between them." Peter Lombard, *Sententiae In IV Libros Dictatae* (Grottaferrata: College of S. Bonaventure, 1981), Book IV, D.36. Another step away from Roman law.

"the masters opposing and unwilling": *Decretales* 4, 9, 1, *Dignum, CIC* II, 691–692; nullity if slave condition unknown: ibid., 4, 9, 2.

Slaves in Bologna: a resident of Bologna is found buying slaves in 1425, Verlinden, II, 647; in 1368, a Venetian license to export two slaves to Bologna is issued to a notary, ibid., 665; and in 1459, Venetian legislation regulates export of "souls" to Bologna, Florence and Siena, ibid., 685.

Natural law objections to slavery: Thomas Aquinas, *In libros sententiarim Petri Lombardi,* Book IV, D.36, art. 1; slavery inherited from a slave mother: ibid., art. 4; *"vernaculus."* *Summa theologiae,* 2–2, 76, 10; the term was used in the Vulgate translation of Jeremiah 1:14; the equivalent in the Septuagint was *oikogenes,* "house-born."

exceptions to the rule on offspring of a slave: as a ruling of Urban III inserted in the *Decretales* of Gregory IX made clear, in Rimini the male offspring of a free man and a slave girl was free. *Decretales* 4, 9, 3, *CIC* II, 692.

slavery instituted "by human reason for the utility of human life": Thomas Aquinas, *Summa theologiae,* Leonine edition, 1–2, Q.94, art. 5, *ad* 3; "for this one to be ruled by one wiser": ibid., 2–2, Q.57, art. 3, *ad* 2; "immutable" first principles: ibid., 1–2, Q.94, art. 5, *corpus;* applied to slave: *In libros Sent. IV,* D.36, art. 2; primacy of the conjugal debt, ibid., Reply, obj.3; selling of slave to distant place; ibid., Reply, obj. 4; slave's religious calling: ibid., Reply, obj. 5; "a slave is the tool [*instrumentum*], of the master," quoting Aristotle, *Politics*, 1.2, 1253–1254; in things "pertaining to the nature of the body" man is bound to obey God alone, *Summa theologiae*, 2–2, 107.

Stephen F. Brett, *Slavery and the Catholic Tradition: Rights in the Balance* (New York: Peter Lang, 1996), argues that Thomas believed that any dominion exercised by a slave-owner "must be analogous to the dominion which God exercises over creation" (193), that is, that unless such benevolent rule was maintained by the owner, the ownership of a slave was sinful. The idea is present in Thomas; the application is not; and only a modern writer could read Thomas as teaching that slavery was sinful.

The thought on slavery of John Duns Scotus has been preserved in two forms: the Oxford report of his commentary on the *Sentences* of Peter Lombard and the Parisian report. According to the Oxford report, slavery is just in only two cases: (1) a man sells himself as a slave and (2) the ruler of the community punishes with slavery those so vicious that liberty is harmful to them and to the public. War is not a justification for enslaving one defeated in a just war if the defeated will not rebel against his conqueror. Title to possessions such as gold can be acquired by prescription, but slaves by the law of nature are different from possessions like gold. Scotus, *In libros sententiarum* 4.36, *Opera omnia* (Lyons, 1639), vol. 9, 753–754.

In the later, Paris report, Scotus holds that slavery may be a proper penalty for crime, and it is also a proper penalty for one who, defeated in war and not killed, rebels unjustly against his conqueror. These two justifications, Scotus observes, "are really one." He then leaves open another justification, "prescription to the extent it is available to masters." As to its availability, he offers no judgment, adding only that "slavery, therefore, is from positive law." Scotus, *In libros sententiarum* 4.36, *Opera omnia*, ed. G. Lauriola. Markedly more reserved than Thomas in accepting slavery, Scotus did not leave an analysis developed to the point that it could have offset the teaching of Thomas.

Charity, by which God is within the person, and the person loves God for his goodness and loves all who are loved by God: Thomas Aquinas, *Summa theologiae*, 2–2, Q.23, art. 1; as one loves a friend's children or slaves: *ad* 2; "the double life" of body and mind: *ad* 1.

the multiple kinds of slavery: Antoninus, *Summa theologica* (Verona, 1740), pt. 3, title 3, chap. 6; "de facto," Christians don't enslave Christians defeated in war: ibid., 3.3.6, col. 197; variant rule on offspring in "parts of Italy": ibid., 3.1.3, col. 26; obedience as exalted virtue: ibid. 4.5.40, citing Thomas Aquinas, *Summa theologiae*, 2–2, Q.104; the duties, incapacities, treatment, and rights of slaves: 3.3.6 at col. 200; Christians "cannot be sold": ibid., at col. 199; baptism does not take away condition: ibid., col. 197; slaves baptized in Florence: Origo, "The Domestic Enemy," 334; duties of notaries: Antoninus, 3.6.6, cols. 275–276; of tradesmen: ibid., 3.8.3, cols. 303–307; on trumping of civil law, as to, e.g., divorce: ibid., 1.18.1, col. 834; on avarice: ibid., 2.1; on bankers: (*campsores*): ibid., 3.8.3; "To free slaves": 2.1.24, *De inhumanitate*, col. 333.

TEN. How the Portuguese Got the Guinea Trade

Nicholas V to Afonso V, June 18, 1452, quoted in relevant part: *European Treaties bearing on the History of the United States and its Dependencies to 1648,* ed. Frances Gardiner Davenport (Washington, D.C.: Carnegie Institution of Washington, 1917), 17, n.27.

Romanus pontifex: ibid., 13–20 (Latin), 20–26 (English); Boniface VIII, *Unam sanctam,* November 18, 1302, *CIC, Extra:* I, 8, I. The Portuguese were old hands at obtaining papal bulls to confirm their conquests of lands of the infidels and to exclude other nations. In the fifteenth century, beginning with Martin V at the Council of Constance in 1418, they obtained eleven bulls supporting their capture of Ceuta in Morocco from the Moslems. See Charles Martial de Witte, "Les Bulles Pontificales et L'Expansion Portugaise au XV siècle," *Revue d'histoire ecclésiastique* 48 (1953), 683, 686–690. In 1434, Prince Henrique, later known as the Navigator, landed on one of the Canary Islands. He reported baptizing four hundred natives, although a great number escaped and fled inland; the methods used for conversion may be imagined. He retreated to two small islands populated by Christians, where his men engaged in pillage. Ibid., 702. In response to the protests of the Christian Canary Islanders, Eugene IV in *Creator omnium* forbade the enslavement of Christian natives. Ibid., 711; but in the bull *Romanus pontifex* of 1436 the pope granted to Portugal the exclusive right of conquest over such of the Canaries as were populated by infidels so that the Portuguese could work "for the propagation of the Christian name." Ibid., 703. In response to the jealous complaint of Castille, the pope sought to provide against prejudice to the Castillians, ibid., 705; but the Canaries were substantially turned over to Portuguese domination. In 1437, Portugal obtained another crusade bull for the African continent, this time for the siege of Tangiers. Ibid., 709. By the time of the mid-century bulls the Portuguese knew well the ways of the Roman Curia.

Portuguese explorations under the infante Henrique: Bailey W. Diffie and George D. Winius, *Foundations of the Portuguese Empire 1415–1580* (Minneapolis: University of Minnesota Press, 1977), vol. I, 64–70, 74–92. Henrique's captain's comment and instructions: ibid., 77; Henrique another Alexander: ibid., 80; the breakup of slaves' families: ibid., 81.

The marriage of Donna Eleonora and Emperor Frederick III: Ludwig Pastor, *The History of the Popes from the Close of the Middle Ages,* ed. Frederick Ignatius Antrobus (London: Routledge & Kegan Paul, 1949), vol. 2, 154. The papal reaction to the fall of Constantinople and the reaction of the nations to the pope: ibid., 2, 274–286.

The style of *Romanus pontifex:* although the bull announces that it was issued *motu proprio,* unsolicited by Portugal, such declarations simply exempted Afonso from the payment of the ordinary fees set by the curia. See *European Treaties,* 17, n.28.

The islands disposed of in this bull were believed by the pope to belong to St. Peter's Patrimony by virtue of an expanded reading of the spurious Donation of Constantine.

Luis Weckmann-Muñoz, "The Alexandrine Bulls of 1493: Pseudo-Asiatic Documents," in Fredi Chiappelli, ed., *First Images of America* (Berkeley: University of California Press, 1976), 1, 204–205. This papal belief had been exhibited in Adrian IV's bull *Laudabiliter* in 1155 granting to Henry II the island of Ireland, which "belongs to the Holy Roman Church." The same theory was applied in the bulls that follow here of Calixtus III, Sixtus IV, and Leo X. Idem. But the popes did not demand homage from the kings of Portugal and Spain as though the papal donation was an act of infeudation. "Rather, Alexander VI [and his fifteenth-century predecessors] relied on the medieval theocratic doctrine developed by canonists attached to the Roman Curia and reinforced by the formula *papa vicarius Christi*." Miguel Batllori, S.J., "The Papal Division of the World and Its Consequences," in Chiappelli, op cit., 1, 215.

Calixtus III, *Inter Caetera: European Treaties,* 28–30 (Latin), 30–32 (English); Sixtus IV, *Aeterni Regis:* ibid., 50–52 (Latin), 53–55 (English); Leo X, *Praecelsae:* ibid., 113–115 (Latin), 115–117 (English).

"Lord of the conquest": Manuel I, quoted in Charles R. Boxer, *Race Relations in the Portuguese Colonial Empire 1415–1825* (Westport, Conn.: Greenwood Press, 1962), 2.

Alexander VI, *Inter caetera: European Treaties,* 58–61 (Latin), 61–63 (English); on the sense and importance of "vicar of Jesus Christ" in the curia of Alexander VI and in *Inter caetera:* Maccarone, 268–273.

"by the Holy Apostolic See": Testament of Queen Isabella quoted by Bartolomé de Las Casas to the Council of the Indies, January 20, 1531, in *Obras Completas,* vol. 13, p. 74.

"the most merciful, the most unconquerable": Juan Lopez de Palacios Rubios, *De las Islas del mar Océano,* trans. Augustín Millares Carlo (Mexico City: Fondo De Cultura Económica, 1954).

"any lands whatsoever": John Major, *In libros sententiarum Petri Lombardi* (1510), Book II, D.44, p. 13, Conclusion 2; "live bestially": ibid., Conclusion 3.

ELEVEN.   If John Major Were an Indian

"remains a slave in accordance with the custom of the heathen": Martin Luther, *Lectures on Philemon,* trans. Jaroslav Pelikan, *Luther's Works,* ed. Pelikan (St. Louis: Concordia Publishing House, 1968), vol. 29, 100; "we learn that the political order": John Calvin, *Commentarius in epistolam Ad Philemonem, Opera,* ed. W. Baum, E. Cunitz, and E. Reuss (Brunswick, 1895), vol. 52, 448; "because it was a bending": Calvin to William Cecil, March 1559 (explaining why he, Calvin, was not responsible for Knox's *The First*

Blast of the Trumpet Against the Monstrous Regiment and Empire of Women), Calvin, *Opera*, vol. 15, 490. In an incidental reference, Erasmus reads the letter to Philemon as a plea for "a fugitive slave": Erasmus, *Ecclesiastes*, ed. Jacques Clomarat, *Opera* V-4, 64.

Slaves in Utopia: Thomas More, *Utopia*, Book 2, ed. George M. Logan, Richard M. Adams, and Clarence H. Miller (Cambridge: Cambridge University Press, 1974); *"De servis,"* 184–193; *"De commercii materia,"* 138–150.

Alfonso de la Vera Cruz: see John T. Noonan, Jr., "Marriage in Michoacán," in Chiappelli, ed., *First Images of the Americas*, 1, 351–362.

Las Casas' ownership of slaves: Lewis Hanke, *All Mankind Is One: A Study of the Disputation Between Bartolomé de Las Casas and Juan Gines de Sepúlveda in 1550 on the Intellectual and Religious Capacity of the American Indians* (De Kalb: Northern Illinois University Press, 1974), 7.

"opening hell to the Spanish": Bartolomé de las Casas, *Historia de las Indias, Obras completas* III, chap. 107, vol. 5, 2220. The annotations of Las Casas on Palacios Rubios: Silvio Zavada, "Introduccion" to the 1954 edition of *De las Islas del mar Océano*, p. xviii; "Absurd": 108 (chap. 8, sec. 8); "false": idem; "Heretical": 112.

"And do you doubt that your king is in hell?": Las Casas, *Historia*, Book III, chap. 38, vol. 5, 1914–1915, quoting Cajetan to Peñafiel; "Against them no King": Cajetan, *Commentaria in summan theologiae S. Thomae Aquinatis* (Rome: Leonine ed.), 2–2, 66, 8. "On a human being, violence": idem.

Non-reference to the New World at Lateran V: John W. O'Malley, S.J., "The Discovery of America and Reform Thought at the Papal Court in the Early Cinquecento," in Chiappelli, *First Images*, 1, 187.

"to fulfill their natural purposes": Las Casas, *De unico vocationis modo, Obras completas*, vol. 2, Prologue. Quotation of Cajetan: idem. An English translation is given in Bartolomé de Las Casas, *The Only Way*, ed. Helen Rand Parish, trans. Francis Patrick Sullivan, S.J. (New York: Paulist Press, 1992).

On the religious friendly or hostile to the Indians, see Helen Rand Parish, *Las Casas En México* (Mexico City: Fondo De Cultura Económica, 1992), 25–26; "the Magna Carta of the Indians": ibid., 17; "the Indians are truly men": Paul III, *Sublimis Deus*, June 2, 1537, reprinted in ibid., 310–311.

"the lawful titles by which": Francisco de Vitoria, *Relección Primera De Los Indios Recientemente Descubiertos*, in Vitoria, *Relecciones Teológicas*, ed. Luis G. Alonso Getina (Madrid,

1934), vol. 2, 354–376; parallel drawn as to acts "in favor of the faith": ibid., 379. In "The Children of God: Natural Slavery in the Thought of Aquinas and Vitoria," *Theological Studies,* 63 (2002), 31, Joseph E. Capizzi notes Vitoria's hesitant acceptance of the mental incapacity of the Indians and observes at note 74: "By stressing the past Vitoria shows that he believes the subjugation no longer justified." But if the subjugation *had been* justified, then, according to all the theologians, the continued enslavement of those justly subjugated would have been justified as well as the enslavement of their descendants.

The reading of Las Casas' treatise: see *In Defense of the Indians: The Defense of the Most Reverend Lord, Don Fray Bartolomé de Las Casas, of the Order of Preachers, Late Bishop of Chiapas, Against the Persecutors and Slanderers of the Peoples of the New World Discovered Across the Seas,* trans. Stafford Poole, C.M. (De Kalb: Northern Illinois University Press, 1974), p. 9. This book is the translation of a Latin manuscript, written 1552–1553, translating the Spanish text of Las Casas' defense. No Spanish or Latin text has been published. The Latin manuscript is in the Bibliothéque Nationale, Nouveaux Fonds Latins, no. 12926. ibid. xiv–xv. "Mindful that I am a Christian": Las Casas to Philip, ibid., 21; Alexander VI's bull as major obstacle: *In Defense . . .,* chap. 1, p. 26; "for how could he permit": chap. 59, p. 348; "should be interpreted as 'to dispose'": chap. 60, p. 353; citation of *Sublimis Deus,* chap. 62, p. 360; cf. chap. 12, pp. 100–101; ignorance of John Major: chap. 53, p. 326; "ridiculous that this theologian": chap. 53, p. 329; "Away with John Major": idem; "famous and learned father" Vitoria: chap. 56, p. 340; "a little more careless": chap. 56, p. 341; "even if its literal meaning": chap. 62; p. 360; the "completely absurd" argument from Old Testament slaughter: chap. 13, pp. 106–107; "shins were showing": chap. 14, p. 113; denial of jurisdiction over unbelievers: chaps. 7–28, pp. 65–190; jurisdiction over heretics: chap. 6, p. 55.

"If he were an Indian": ibid., chap. 53. The significance of the shift in perspective to that of the Indian is captured by Gustavo Gutiérrez, *Las Casas: In Search of the Poor of Jesus Christ,* trans. Robert R. Barr (Maryknoll, N.Y.: Orbis Books, 1993), 87. Major appears in the history of contraception as a sensible defender of the pleasure of conjugal coupling, with sensitivity to the experience of married folk. See my *Contraception: A History of Its Treatment by the Catholic Theologians and Canonists* (Cambridge: Harvard University Press, 1967), 310–312. John Knox called him an "oracle of religions": idem.

Carlos de Aragón, a pupil of John Major in Paris, and now "a most solemn preacher," came to the Indies. When he mentioned Major in the pulpit, he would remove his cowl, saying with great reverence, "so says the great doctor Johannes Major." Las Casas found him insufferable. *Historia,* III, 35, vol. 5, 1904. Carlos de Aragón, according to Las Casas, annulled a marriage between a Spaniard and an Indian woman on the ground that she lacked reason. Later, Carlos returned to Spain and "was permitted by the just judgment of God to fall into many errors." He was imprisoned for life by the Inquisition. Las Casas, *In Defense,* chap. 56, p. 340.

"black and white slaves": Las Casas, "Memoral De Remedios Para Las Indias," *Obras Completas,* vol. 13, p. 36; "two black slaves and two black slave girls": ibid., 52. The editors suggest in the index that "the white slaves" were Moors: ibid., 430. The 1531 memorial: ibid., 80; the 1541 memorial: ibid., 116.

Las Casas' account of his recommendation of the importation of slaves from Africa and his judgment on himself: *Historia,* III, 129, vol. 5, 2322–2325. On June 30, 1560, Alonso de Montufar, archbishop of Mexico City, wrote Philip II, observing that the king had provided for the freedom of the Indians, but what happened to the Blacks here was "very contrary to such a just and Catholic provision." He went on: "We do not know what reason there is that the Blacks should be more captive than the Indians, since, as they say, they receive the Holy Gospel with good will and do not make war on the Christians." *Epistolario De Nueva España 1560–1563,* compiled by Francisco Del Paso y Troncoso (Mexico City, 1940), vol. 9, pp. 53–55.

In 1563, Las Casas extended his excoriation of Spanish injustice by attacking the invasion of Peru and the enslavement of the Incas, and teaching the religious duty of making restitution in a response to doubts posed by Bartolomé Vega, O.P. See Las Casas, *Doce Dudas,* ed. J. B. Lassegue, O.P., Las Casas, *Obras Completas,* 11.2. Las Casas' response was presented to Philip II and to the Council of the Indies in December 1565. Ibid., p. xx. Las Casas observed that in the last fifty years no Spaniard in the Indies had "in good faith" waged war on the Indians, enslaved them, or bought them. *Doce Dudas,* chap. xxii, ibid., p. 110.

"It is in accordance with nature for the strong": Juan Ginés de Sepúlveda, *Democrates Alter sive de iustis belli causis apud Indos,* trans. in John H. Parry and Robert G. Keith, eds., *New Iberian World* (New York: New York Times Books, 1984), vol. I, p. 324; war justified, ibid., 326.

TWELVE.   **Conventions, Cries and Murmurs, Repressions**

Documented sales of slaves in Italy: Verlinden 2, 1030–1046; Pius V's slaves received after Lepanto: ibid., 1031. At least as late as 1590, notarial acts from Venice show the sale of slaves in the Venetian market, where they were objects of luxury for the nobility and rich merchants. See Alberto Tenenti, "Gli Schiavi Di Venezia Alla Fine Del Cinquecento," *Rivista Storica Italiana* 681 (1955), 54.

"from a multitude of slaves, inheritances are augmented": Paul III, *motu proprio, Statutorum almae urbis Romae libri quinque* (Rome, 1567), *Liber bullarum* 19 v. This document, conservatively, specifies both *servi* and *sclavi* as alternatives as though one might escape by being one and not the other.

The position of Paul III on slavery became the subject of lively debate when an anticlerical Italian, speaking at the first anti-slavery congress in Italy in 1902, cited a ruling dated January 12, 1549, of the Roman municipal government notifying the inhabitants of

Rome of this *motu proprio* of Paul III. Salvatore M. Brandi, S.J., *Il Papato E La Schia-vitù: Studio Storico-Giuridico* (Rome: Civiltà Cattolica, 1903), 21–22. The charge that the popes had promoted slavery was responded to with asperity in the Jesuit journal, *Civiltà Catholica*, and the articles were collected to make up the small book just cited. Brandi supplied archival documents putting Paul III's *motu proprio* in context. In 1535, the pope had said that slavery was extinct in Rome but that fugitive slaves were fleeing to the Capitol to claim their liberty. Confirming this custom, Paul III authorized the Roman munic-ipality to treat such slaves as free men and Roman citizens. Ibid., 24. On November 27, 1544, the Roman Senate determined that the custom was a problem for the city and sent a delegation to the pope to ask him to moderate it. Nothing happened. On April 25, 1548, the Conservators of Rome stated that slavery was permitted in Rome on condition of freedom after ten years, but they now petitioned the pope to permit perpetual slavery in the city "as in other places where they are held." Paul III's *motu proprio* of November 8, 1548, was the response. Ibid., 26–27. A keen polemicist, Brandi mentioned the response but did not mention its celebration of the benefits of slavery. He argued that the slavery permitted was "mild" domestic slavery and was justified by the number of prisoners of war taken from the Turks. He offered no evidence for his claim of mildness and no com-ment on the Conservators' claim that slavery "in other places" was perpetual. Brandi cited Paul III's bull against enslavement of the Indians and other papal declarations of this sort directed at the enslavement of innocent free persons; he ignored the limited force of these documents, and he ignored the papal bulls authorizing enslavement in connection with the conquest of the New World. In 1571, Pius V restored the privilege of emancipation at the Capitol: Verlinden, 2, 1031. Estimates on the number of slaves in Rome from the sixteenth to the beginning of the nineteenth century are provided by Wipertus Rudt de Collenberg, "Slavery," *The Papacy: An Encyclopedia*, ed. Phillippe Levillain (New York: Routledge, 1994), 3, 1439–1443. The slaves include men, women, and children, with only male slaves employed in the papal galleys.

"if a free man" *Catechismus ex decretis Concilii Tridentini* (Rome: Vatican Polyglot Press, 1902), 399; "to be understood of captives": ibid., 427.

the supremacy of conscience: Giovanni Botero, *The Reason of State*, trans. P. J. and D. P. Waley (New Haven: Yale University Press, 1956), xiv; "nothing to which the ruler should pay more attention": ibid., Book 1, sec. 15; public works to be performed by slaves: Book 8, sec. 15; the Portuguese trade: idem.

"many or almost all" titles were unjust: Tomás Mercado, O.P., *Summa de Tratos y Con-tractos* (Seville, 1571), cxx. A strong sixteenth-century Portuguese critic of the slave trade, Fernando Oliveira, attacked its foundations in *A Arte Da Guerra No Mar* (Lisbon: Min-istero da Marinha, 1969): "We have been the inventors of an evil traffic never practised or heard of among men before now." It is "manifest tyranny" to take the lands or the per-sons of unbelievers who were never Christians, such as the Moors, the Jews, and the pagans. We compound the evil by enslaving their children, who are Christians. A man who buys what is wrongfully sold is guilty of sin, too. The judgment of God will overtake us (pp. 23–25). Oliveira cited no theologians, but did invoke Jesus Christ, St. Paul, Isaiah, and the Apocalypse. His book was originally printed in Coimbra in 1555 by a printer to the king.

"The general consent of almost all people": Jean Bodin, *Six Books of the Republic* (English and Latin trans. of the edition of 1606), 3, 7; the pro and con argument and the case of the German merchant: 1, 5. Bodin's biography and attitude toward authority: George Goyau, "Bodin, Jean," *The Catholic Encyclopedia* (New York: Robert Appleton, 1907), 2, 609.

"What judgment shall I dread" William Shakespeare, *The Merchant of Venice*, 4, 1, 89–100, *The Complete Plays and Poems of William Shakespeare*, ed. William Allan Neilson and Charles Jarvis Hill (Cambridge: Houghton Mifflin Company, 1942), 138.

"*strenuissimus*": Paul V quoted in *Epistola Dedicatoria* to Tomás Sanchez, *Consilia seu opuscula* in the first German edition, Cologne, 1640; other references are to the Lyons edition of 1635. The good, bad, and mixed titles to ownership, and the duty of a purchaser: Book 1, chap. 1, doubt 4; flight of slave captured in war: doubt 6; flight by abused slave girl: doubt 9; undesirability of emancipation: doubt 10.

Slaves generally from "a hostile commonwealth": Juan de Lugo, *Disputationes de iustitia et iure* (Lyons, 1652); Dist. VI, sec. 2; "They are part of the hostile commonwealth [*republica*]": idem; "not against the prohibition of nature": idem; the rights of slaves: ibid., sec. 3; "in these matters not considered a slave": D. III, sec. 2.

"sure sign of falsity": Jacques Bossuet, *Histoire des variations des églises protestantes*, preface, *Oeuvres complètes de Bossuet*, ed. E. N. Guillaume (Lyons: Librairie ecclésiastique de Briday, 1877), 3, 150; Jurieu on contracts and Bossuet's response on slavery: Bossuet, *Avertissement aux Protestants sur les lettres du ministre Jurieu contre l'Histoire des variations*, ibid., 3, 541–542; "In his sermons": Ferdinand Brunetière, "Bossuet, Literary and Theological Appreciation of," *The Catholic Encyclopedia* (New York: Robert Appleton Company, 1907), 2, 702.

A Spanish Capuchin, Epifano de Moirans, preached in Havana in 1681 in favor of the immediate emancipation of the Blacks and wrote a Latin treatise teaching that by natural and divine law they had a duty to escape. This position could scarcely be countenanced by the bishop. Moirons departed for Spain. It does not appear that he attracted support there. Phillipe Delisle, "Clergé et esclavage aux Antilles et en Guyane français. De l'Ancien Régime à 1848," *Mémoire Spiritaine*, 9, 162 (1999).

"May slaves captured in a just war": Ligouri, *Theologia moralis*, Book III, n.350. "I myself dare": ibid., Book III, n.520, q.1. The slave population of Naples: Théodule Rey-Mermet,

C.SS.T., *Le Saint Du Siècle des Lumières, Alfonso de Ligouri* (1696–1787), (Paris: Nouvelle Cité, 2d ed., 1987), 44; a "good number" in the Ligouri household: idem.; Alfonso's personal slave: ibid., 110–111.

In the same century, Germain Fromageau of the faculty of theology at the Sorbonne took a position not far from that of Sanchez: "One cannot with a sure conscience buy or sell Blacks, because there is injustice in the trade. If, nonetheless, when everything has been examined, the Blacks being bought are slaves by a just title, and on the side of the buyers there is neither injustice, nor deceit, then according to the principles established, one may buy and sell them under the conditions indicated." De Lamet and Fromageau, *Dictionnaire des cas de conscience*, 1, 1437–1444 (Paris, 1733), quoted by Michel Legrain, "Éthique Chretienne et Esclavgisme," *Mémoire Spiritaine*, 9, 60 (1999). Failing to condemn the traffic absolutely, Fromageau left it to the individual conscience.

THIRTEEN. Advice to the Missions

"Black ivory": Charles R. Boxer, *Portuguese Society in the Tropics* (Madison: University of Wisconsin Press, 1965), 132; the complaint of the nuns at Goa: ibid., 37–38; the beneficiaries of the trade in Angola: ibid., 131–132. In 1592, the Jesuits in Angola reported receiving 300 slaves each year from a tribe conquered by the Portuguese. The Jesuits kept 100 for work, sold 150 for food and clothes, and freed 50. It was decided to change this routine and send to Brazil all the slaves annually received and get construction material in return. Louis Jadin, "L'oeuvre missionarie en Afrique noir," in *Sacrae Congregationis De Propaganda Fidei Memoria Rerum,* ed. J. Metzler (Rome: Herder, 1972), vol. 1:2, 441–443. For Jesuit slaveholdings in Peru, see note "Mission St. Francis Borgia," infra.

The will of María Barros: Angel Valtierra, S.J., *St. Peter Claver: Saint of the Slaves,* trans. Janet H. Perry and J. Woodward (Westminster, Md.: The Newman Press, 1960), 87–88. This work is a translation of *El santo que liberto una raza: San Pedro Claver, S.J.* (Bogotá, 1954), and draws largely on testimony offered during the process of Claver's canonization. Three hundred thousand baptisms: the testimony of Brother Nicolás González, Claver's companion and biographer, testifying in the process as to what Claver estimated: ibid., 103–104; the necessity of interpreters, Claver's purchase of them, and those he acquired: ibid., 116–119; "ever the slave of the Africans": ibid., 71; "the great mercy of the Lord": Sandoval, quoted in ibid., 112–113. Valtierra estimates the slave population of Cadiz, Spain, in 1650 as 1,500: ibid., 77. Slaves were part of the dowry of girls entering the Dominican nuns in Kentucky. Frances Jerome Woods, C.D.P., "Congregations of Religious Women in the Old South," in *Catholics in the Old South,* ed. Randall M. Miller and Jon L. Wakelyn, 114.

"It is lawful to capture," "It is not lawful.": Holy Office, March 20, 1686: *Collectanea,* vol. I, n.230. The story of Lourenço: Richard Gray, "The Papacy and the Atlantic Slave

Trade," *Past and Present,* vol. 115, pp. 52–59 (1987); the subsequent 1686 decision and the "Instructions for Monsignor Cibo": ibid. pp. 60–68. Evidence of watering-down: Richard Gray, *Black Christians and White Missionaries* (New Haven: Yale University Press, 1990), 30.

"May Cambodian Christians buy Laotians": Holy Office, September 12, 1776, for Indochina: *Collectanea,* vol. I, n.515.

"May a Christian sell a slave who is of bad character": Holy Office, April 29, 1840, for Korea: ibid. I, n.900.

"May a Christian lend money and get his debtor's labor as a slave": Holy Office, November 29, 1854 for Cambodia: ibid., I, n.1107.

"Mission St. Francis Borgia": Report of William Hunter, S.J., to the provincial, in Thomas Hughes, S.J., *History of the Society of Jesus in North America: Colonial and Federal Documents* (London: Longmans, Green & Co., 1910), vol. I, pt. I, p. 336. For comparable plantations operated by slaves in South America, see Nicholas P. Cushner, S.J., "Slave Mortality and Reproduction on Jesuit Haciendas in Colonial Peru," *The Hispanic American Historical Review* 55:177–198 (1975). The haciendas were owned by eleven Jesuit colleges in Peru during the period studied, 1714–1767. At the date of the expulsion of the Jesuits in 1767, these haciendas employed 5,234 slaves, making the Jesuit colleges among the largest slaveholders in South America. The account books recorded their number, and it was triennially reported to Jesuit headquarters in Rome. The slaves planted sugarcane and ground cane at the mill, the mill shifts working past midnight. Other slaves shod mules or worked at carpentry, repairs, and construction. Minor infractions were punished by twenty-five lashes, theft or flight by fifty lashes. The slaves were run by overseers, often recruited from ex-army officers. Fertility was low, and almost half the recorded deaths were of slave children fifteen and under. Increase came by purchase.

In the French Caribbean, the Dominicans on Martinique in 1700 owned ninety slaves, and the Jesuits owned two hundred; on Guadaloupe, the Jesuits held more land and over three hundred slaves. Philippe Delisle, "Clergé et esclavage aux Antilles et en Guyane français: De'l Ancien Régime à 1848," *Mémoire Spiritaine* 9, 162 (1999).

Sales by Maréchal and dispute over proceeds: "M. Maréchal's notes of buying and selling," Hughes, *History,* vol. I, pt. II, 749–750; objection to Maréchal's right to proceeds: Proceedings of the Corporation, August 21, 1795, ibid., 750.

"stumbling blocks": John Ryan, O.P,. to John Carroll, circa 1814, quoted in Robert Emmett Curran, S.J., "Rome, the American Church and Slavery," in *Building the Church in America: Studies in Honor of Monsignor Robert E. Trisco on the Occasion of His Seventieth Birthday* (Washington: The Catholic University of America Press, 1999), 36. Carroll had actually removed a priest, John Thayer, from Kentucky because, among other things, he had stirred up the people by his opposition to slavery. Ibid., 35. The Dominicans' recourse to Propaganda and its nonresponse: ibid., 37.

Maréchal to Somaglia, January 15, 1826: Hughes, History vol. I, pt. I, 533–559; number and value, 544; Kohlmann's rebuttal, 545, n.29.

"a great and crying national sin": see John T. Noonan, Jr., *The Lustre of Our Country* (Berkeley: University of California Press, 1998), 126.

"the blacks . . . are our sons": Francis Dzierozynski, S.J. to Roothaan, quoted in Robert Emmett Curran, S.J., "'Splendid Poverty': Jesuit Slaveholding in Maryland, 1805–1838" in *Catholics in the Old South*, ed. Randall M. Miller and Jon L. Wakelyn (Macon: Mercer University Press, 1983), 140; aversion to Deep South, 131; roundup and escapes: 142–143. According to the diary of Joseph Moberley, S.J., the slaves could marry only with the permission of the Jesuits. When in 1837 all the slaves were sold, the only ones at St. Inigoes who escaped were Aunt Louisa and her mother, who hid in the woods. Joseph Agonite, "St. Inigoes Manor: A Nineteenth Century Jesuit Plantation," *Maryland Historical Magazine* 72 (1972), 95 and 98.

Familiarity with the institution bred acceptance, however regretful: Another illustration is provided by the correspondence of Mother Mary Hyacinth (1817–1897), a member of the Daughters of the Cross, who came to Louisiana from France in 1854. Dorothea O. McCants, *They Came to Louisiana: Letters of a Catholic Mission 1854–1882*, (Baton Rouge: Louisiana State University Press, 1970). On November 17, 1855, Mother Mary Hyacinth wrote her brother Yves-Marie in France: "The first time I saw a rational human being exposed 'For Sale' in New Orleans I was seized with horror. The bishop proposed that we buy one slave. I showed my repugnance, and he did not insist!" (p. 160). On January 12, 1856, she wrote Bishop Martin that their chaplain was thinking of buying a Negro at a sale on the twentieth. She asked, "If he is not too expensive, may we buy him?" (p. 161). On March 24, 1856, she wrote her brother: "The day I signed the bill of sale for our slave, I wanted to cry all day." (p. 161).

Rules governing sales: Edward Warfield Beitzell, *The Jesuit Missions of St. Mary's County, Maryland* (Abell, Md.: Beitzell, 2nd ed., 1974), 211; purchasers: ibid.; distribution: idem.; information on Johnson: *The Louisiana Governors*, ed. Joseph G. Dawson III (Baton Rouge: Louisiana State University Press, 1964), 98–102; the sale price and uses of it: Thomas V. Spalding, *The Premier See: A History of the Archdiocese of Baltimore, 1789–1989* (Baltimore: The John Hopkins University Press, 1989), 113; the mortgages and the delayed payments: Thomas Murphy, S.J., *Jesuit Slaveholding in Maryland, 1717–1838* (New York: Routledge, 2001), 203–204. In 1848, a Jesuit visited the slaves sold to the Louisiana buyers and found their opportunities to attend mass or to catechize their children to be severely limited. Ibid., 205.

FOURTEEN.   Only if Christianity Is a Lye

To buy "Souls and Bodies": George Keith, "An Exhortation & Caution To Friends Concerning Buying Or Keeping Of Negroes," reprinted from George Moore, ed., "The First Printed Protest Against Slavery in America," *The Pennsylvania Magazine of History and Biography* (Philadelphia, 1880), available 5/23/03 on the Quaker Writings Home Page. On George Keith, see Davis, 1966, 309–310.

Locke was of the opinion that captives taken in a just war are "by the Right of Nature subjected to the Absolute Dominion and Arbitrary Power of their Masters," *Two Treaties of Government*, II, sec. 84. As secretary of the Lord Proprietors of Carolina, he helped draft the Fundamental Constitution of Carolina, which provided: "Every freeman of Carolina shall have absolute power and authority over his negro slaves, of what opinion or religion soever." Locke, *The Works of John Locke* (1825). It is argued that, although in Locke's hand, this draft does not reflect Locke's own ideas. See John W. Yolton, *A Locke Dictionary* (Oxford: Blackwell, 1993), 258.

Jefferson as drafter of Virginia slave law: John T. Noonan, Jr., *Persons and Masks of the Law: Cardozo, Holmes, Jefferson and Wythe as Makers of the Masks* (New York: Farrar, Strauss and Giroux, 1976), 50–54; Madison's attitude toward: ibid., 51, see also John T. Noonan, Jr., *The Lustre of Our Country: The American Experience of Religious Freedom* (Berkeley: University of California Press, 1998), 70–71.

Nantes as the Liverpool of France: Philip D. Curtin, *The Atlantic Slave Trade: A Census* (Madison: University of Wisconsin Press, 1969), 163; the importance of the colonial commerce to France: Richard W. Sanders, "French Declaration of the Rights of Man and of Citizen," *The Historical Encyclopedia of World Slavery*, ed. Junius P. Rodriguez (Santa Barbara: ABC-Clio, 1997), 1, 284.

"It is impossible that we should suppose those people to be men": Charles de Secondat, Baron de Montesquieu, *L'Esprit des lois*, 15.5, *Oeuvres complètes* (1843), 309.

"It's the custom": Voltaire, *Candide ou L'Optimisme*, ed. Christopher Thacker (Geneva: Droz, 1968), chap. 19; sale of Cunegonde: chap. 7; sales of the old woman: chap. 12. Voltaire on slavery: *A Philosophical Dictionary*, translated in *Slavery*, ed. Stanley Engerman, Seymour Drescher, and Robert Paquette (New York: Oxford University Press, 2001), 24–25.

cruelties of slavery: Guillaume Raynal, *Histoire philosophique et politique des établissements et du commerce des Européens dans les deux Indes* (Geneva: J. L. Pellet, 1781).

"repugnant to our religion": "Slavery," by Jarecourt in Denis Diderot, ed., *Encyclopédie*, trans. in *Slavery*, 28.

Brissot: see Robert Darnton, *George Washington's False Teeth: An Unconventional Guide to the Eighteenth Century* (New York: W.W. Norton & Co., 2003), 135 (founding of the "Friends of the Blacks"); 171 (Brissot probably a police spy).

"set up for a Guiney Trader": Daniel Defoe, *The Life and Strange Surprising Adventures of Robinson Crusoe, of York, Mariner,* ed. J. Donald Crowley (London: Oxford University Press, 1972), 18; "a Negro Slave": p. 37; Friday enslaves self: 206; Friday catechized: 216–221; "one of the anonymous productions of the race": Woolf, quoted, p. vii.

"the emergence of a widespread conviction that New World slavery was deeply evil": Davis, 2001, p. 131. After a careful examination of conflicting motives, Davis has warned "against the simplistic impression that 'industrialists' promoted abolitionist doctrine as a means of distracting attention from their own forms of exploitation." Ibid., 223.

"abhors and will not endure": William Blackstone, *Commentaries on the Laws of England* (1765), Book I, chap. 14, pp. 411–412. Somerset's release: *Sommerset v. Stewart* (1772), Lofft, *English Reports,* 98, 499; on the case and its influence: William M. Wiecek, "Somerset: Lord Mansfield and the Legitimacy of Slavery in the Anglo-American World," *University of Chicago Law Review* (1974), 42, 84–146. On Blackstone's hedging and Mansfield's qualifications, Davis (1975), 485–486, 496, 500.

"How is it that we hear": James Boswell, *Life of Johnson* (London: Oxford University Press, 1953), 876 (Sept. 23, 1777); "to contribute": ibid., 783 (July 6, 1776); "that a negro cannot be taken": idem.; "never was examined": 877 (Sept. 23, 1777); "Here's to the next insurrection": 876; "perhaps, he was in the right": 878; "African savages": idem.

"the business of his life": Ellen Wilson, *Thomas Clarkson* (New York: St. Martin's Press, 1990), 17; "Am I Not a Man and a Brother": ibid., 29–46.

Methodists against slavery: Seymour Drescher, *Capitalism and Antislavery: British Mobilization in Comparative Perspective* (New York: Oxford University Press, 1978), 120–22.

"Unless the divine power": John Wesley to William Wilberforce, February 24, 1791, *Letters of the Rev. John Wesley,* ed. John Telford (London: Epworth Press, 1931), VIII, 265.

Abolition "the lengthened shadow" of Clarkson: Ralph Waldo Emerson, "Self-Reliance," *Essays: First Series, The Collected Works of Ralph Waldo Emerson,* ed. Joseph Slater (Cambridge: Belknap Press, 1979), II, 35.

"Clarkson! it was an obstinate hill": William Wordsworth, "To Thomas Clarkson," *The Poetical Works of Wordsworth,* ed. Paul D. Sheats (Boston: Houghton Mifflin Company, 1982), 356–357.

"any property whatever in the *human species*": Clarkson quoted in Wilson, *Thomas Clarkson*, 15. "Never was any cause": Clarkson, quoted ibid., 17.

FIFTEEN.   The Pope Is Prompted

Slaves in the Papal States: Claude Prudhomme, "La papauté face à l'esclavage: quelle condemnation?" *Mémoire Spiritaine*, 9 (1999), 156; Alberto Guglielmotti, O.P., *Storia della marina pontificia* (Rome: Vatican Press, 1886), I, 175.

Defense of the trade: Jose Joaquiem de Cunha de Azervedo Coutinho, bishop of Elvas and inquisitor general, *Obras econômicas: Analise Solve A Justicia Do Coércio Do Resgate Dos Escravos Da Costa Africa*, ed. Sérgio Buarque de Holanda (São Paulo, 1966), 233–256.

public opinion "was sharply divided": Lorenz A. Eitner, *Géricault: His Life and Work* (London: Orbis Publishing Co., 1983), 275; the Academy and the Société de la Morale Chrétienne: idem; Géricault's *African Slave Trade:* idem; *La Jeune Eugénie* in Boston: John T. Noonan, Jr., *The Antelope* (Berkeley: University of California Press, 1977), 69–74. Alexis de Tocqueville headed a commission in 1839 that recommended abolition. The colonists resisted. In Martinique, Guadeloupe, and Reunion, there were a total of over 370,000 slaves and no more than 139,000 free persons. Immediately after the revolution of 1848, a decree of March 4, 1848, enacted by the provisional government of the French Republic, abolished slavery in all the colonies. Napoleon III did not restore it. See Augustin Cochin, *The Results of Slavery*, trans. Mary L. Booth (Boston, 1863), 62 and 243.

"the lands inhabited by the Negro": Immanuel Kant, *Perpetual Peace*, ed. Lewis White Beck (New York: Liberal Arts Press, 1957), sec. II, pp. 21–23; "inborn rights which are inalienable": ibid., p. 11, n.2.

"the foundation of all morality": Johann M. Sailer, *Handbuch der christlichen Moral* (Munich, 1917), II, 275–276.

O'Connell on abolition: Fergus O'Farrall, *Daniel O'Connell* (Dublin: Gill & Macmillan, 1981), 109–110.

Freetown: Granville Sharp, the lawyer who had engineered Somerset's case, persuaded Parliament to permit the Province of Freedom to be founded in Sierra Leone by freed slaves. In 1787, the first shipment arrived—former slaves in America, more recently in Nova Scotia. With difficulties and mishaps, this experiment in a haven for the emancipated continued. Eventually, Freetown, Sierra Leone, became a port where the British navy would bring persons rescued from captivity on slavers. See Christopher Fyfe, *Sierra Leone Inheritance* (London: Oxford University Press, 1964), 5–8.

Castlereagh's request to Consalvi and the response: François Renault, "Aux origines de la lettre apostolique de Grégoire XVI, In Supremo (1839)," *Mémoire Spiritaine,* 2 (1995), 145; the 1822 request of Castlereagh and response: ibid., 146–147. The British objection to Tuscan transportation of slaves from Tunis: Report of Thomas Reade, consul general at Tunis, forwarded to Henry Edward Fox in Florence, June 11, 1839. Public Record Office: Foreign Office 84.292, p. 129. The subsequent references to papers of the Foreign Office (the F.O.), are to this file.

"loves me like a son": Capaccini to L. Armellini, February 18, 1831, quoted in Lajos Pásztor, *La Segreteria Di Stato E Il Suo Archivo 1814–1833,* I, 165–166 (vol. 23:1 of *Päpste Und Papstum.* Stuttgart: Anton Hiersemann, 1984). "Pupo" and Consalvi: ibid., 137; Capaccini's career as *sustituto* or Undersecretary: ibid., 165–171.

"the pope would accede to our wishes": Aubin to W. F. Strangeways, May 23, 1839, F.O. file, p. 165: "suppression of the African Slave Trade": draft note for Aubin to present to the papal government, sent to Fox, June 28, 1839, F.O. file, p. 134; Aubin's reasons for translating the note and his interview with Lambruschini: Aubin to Fox, July 15, 1839, F.O. file, p. 171; Aubin to press for answer: P. to Fox, October 18, 1839, F.O. file, p. 151; Buxton given introduction to Aubin: F.O. file, p. 153; Aubin's title: *British Diplomatic Representatives, 1789–1852,* ed., S. T. Bindoff et al., (London: Royal Historical Society, 1934), 108. A modern biographer believes the position taken on slavery by Palmerston, a notoriously cool cat, did not show greater sensitivity on the subject than that of his cabinet colleagues. Kenneth Bourne, *Palmerston: The Early Years 1784–1841* (New York: Macmillan, 1982), 624. "If there was any passion in his policy, it was probably more against Frenchmen and, still more, Portuguese, than for the slaves." But his instructions for approaching the pope appear to reflect what he declared in 1848: "I hold that the real policy of England—apart from questions which involve her own particular interests, political or commercial—is to be the champion of justice and right, pursuing this course with moderation and prudence, not becoming the Quixote of the world, but giving the weight of her moral sanction and support wherever she thinks that justice is and wherever she thinks that wrong has been done." Ibid., 622. Bourne does not deal with Palmerston's prompting of the pope.

"If the truth I must tell": Thomas Foxwell Buxton, *Memoirs,* ed. Charles Buxton (London: J. M. Dent, 1985), 204; "a capital bull": idem. Buxton himself in 1839 wrote *The African Slave Trade and Its Remedy* (London: J. Murray), a book that noted that Britain was once an exporter of slaves: "what we find the African, the Romans found us" (p. 13). Based on various estimates, he concluded that between 200,000 and 250,000 slaves were annually exported from Africa to the West in the 1830s (p. 58), and that 50,000 were annually exported by Moslems to Egypt and Arabia (p. 69). Among other things, he remarked on Spanish evasion of the treaty with England outlawing the trade, so the treaty was "an impudent fraud" (p. 218), while the United States had made international slaving the crime of piracy in 1820 with death as the penalty but had failed to execute a single slaver since the law was passed (p. 219). Buxton wrote, he said, confident of what was required by "humanity, justice, and the duties of Christian men" (p. 529). "My desire has been to lay it upon the national conscience of Great Britain" (p. 531).

"the most competent among the authors": *Ponenza*, quoted by François Renault, "Aux origines de la lettre apostolique de Grégoire XVI, In Supremo (1839)," *Mémoire Spiritaine*, 2, 147 (1995); the considerations of the pope: idem and Claude Prudhomme, "La Papauté face à l'esclavage: Quelle condemnation?" *Mémoire Spiritaine*, 9, 141–144 (1999); "ambiguities and silences": Prudhomme at 144.

"circumstances he could not prevent": Aubin to Fox, F.O. file, p. 179.

De Nigritarum Commercio non exercendo: title page of the bull printed by the Camera Apostolica.

"from the inhuman trade": *In supremo Apostolatus, Acta Gregorii Papae XVI*, ed. A. M. Bernasconi (Rome, 1901–1904), Vol. II, 387; references to popes: 387–388; posting: 388.

"My dear Aubin": W. F. Strangeways to Aubin, December 23, 1839, F.O. file, p. 157; "a strong and salutary effect": idem; "too openly shown": Note to Palmerston, December 20, 1839, F.O. file, p. 186.

cheers at Faneuil Hall: McGreevy, 50; "have not engaged in the negro traffic": Gregory XVI, quoted in John England to John Forsyth, October 7, 1840, in *The Works of the Right Reverend John England* (New York: Arno Press reprint, 1978), 111, 117; "not incompatible": ibid., 119. On John England's see and reputation: Peter Guilday, *The Life and Times of John England* (Arno Press reprint, 1969), vol. I, p. vii.

Joel S. Panzer, a priest of the diocese of Lincoln, Nebraska, has authored a short book, *The Popes and Slavery* (New York: Alba House, 1996), in which at pp. 67–68 he contended that *In supremo* condemned slavery as it existed in the United States and that Bishop England and all the bishops of the United States at the First Council of Baltimore in 1840 had misinterpreted the pope. Panzer did not mention England's report of what Gregory XVI had said to him. Strenuously maintaining that the Church had always condemned "racial slavery," Panzer stated that "we can look to the practice of noncompliance with the teachings of the Papal Magisterium as a key reason why slavery was not directly opposed by the Church in the United States" (p. 70). Panzer reads the papal documents condemning the enslavement of innocent Canary Islanders and of blameless Indians as a condemnation of the institution of slavery. *Sublimis Deus* of Paul III is a prime exhibit (pp. 16–22). Panzer does not refer to the moral theologians who continued to defend slavery. He is under the impression that what he calls "just title servitude" can be distinguished from the slavery practiced in the New World (pp. 4–5). His declared purpose is to clear "the Papal Magisterium" from what he terms "a great shadow" (p. 6). The great shadow is its failure to condemn a sin which Panzer seems to suppose to have been evident to everyone, even while popes, bishops, and religious orders owned, acquired, and disposed of slaves.

Panzer's thesis has been relied upon by an American sociologist of religion, Rodney Stark, in *For the Glory of God: How Monotheism Led to Reformations, Science, Witch-Hunts and the End of Slavery* (Princeton: Princeton University Press, 2003). Declaring that he is not a Catholic and that he does not write as an apologist (p. 13), Stark finds "militant anti-Catholicism" in the histories he has read. Alert to the dangers of political correctness and to the bias against recognition of the Christian part in the abolition of slavery, he goes further. In a chapter entitled "God's Justice of Slavery," he states: "When Europeans subsequently instituted slavery in the New World, they did so over strenuous papal opposition, a fact that was conveniently 'lost' from history until recently" (p. 291). He goes on to state without qualification: "in the thirteenth century, St. Thomas Aquinas deduced that slavery was a sin, and a series of popes upheld his position, beginning in 1435 and culminating in three major pronouncements against slavery by Pope Paul III in 1537" (p. 329). His footnote for this statement references Panzer and the thesis of Stephen Brett that is discussed here in a footnote to Chapter 9, "Moral Masters." Stark treats with undeserved scorn a pioneering work, John Francis Maxwell's *Slavery and the Catholic Church: The History of Catholic Teaching Concerning the Moral Legitimacy of the Institution of Slavery* (Chichester and London: Rose for the Anti-Slavery Society for the Protection of Human Rights, 1975).

prescription cures the defect in title: Kenrick, *Theologia moralis* (Philadelphia, 1843), III, 333; "evidence that the Gospel is not directed to disturb the actual order of society": Kenrick, *The Acts of the Apostles, the Epistles of St. Paul, the Catholic Epistles, and the Apocalypse* (New York: Edward Dunigan and Brother, 1851), 497; "may be an intimation": ibid., 500, n.9. McGreevy, pp. 48–90, provides a thorough and balanced account of the voices raised for and against slavery by Catholics in the United States. Orestes Brownson, a convert to Catholicism from New England Transcendentalism, moved cautiously toward an antislavery position (p. 49). In October 1862, John B. Purcell, archbishop of Cincinnati, endorsed immediate emancipation (p. 84). The majority of those who wrote, whether clerical or lay, were hostile to emancipation (pp. 84–88).

The American response was not unusual. Compare seminary teaching in France: The equivalent in France to John England's defense of slavery was the *Institutions théologiques* (1834), of Jean-Baptiste Bouvier, bishop of Mans. This book was adopted by sixty French seminaries, including those preparing priests for the colonies, and, from 1834 to 1880, underwent fifteen editions. Claude Prudhomme, "L'Église catholique et l'esclavage: une aussi longue attente," in Guy Bedouelle, O.P., et al., *L'Église et L'abolition de l'esclavage* (Paris: le centre d'études du Saulchoir, 1999), 11. Bouvier maintained that slavery was not prohibited by natural law, divine law, positive civil, or ecclesiastical law, but rather approved by them. He did not change his text after Gregory XVI's encyclical. Benoit Truffet, the vicar-apostolic at Dakar, wrote him, September 2, 1847, to inform him that in the conditions he saw in Africa the masters were debased by slavery and the slaves disgusted by a religion that allowed it. This letter, too, had no effect: ibid., 15.

Ending of the Brazilian trade: Leslie Bethell, *The Abolition of the Brazilian Slave Trade* (Cambridge: Cambridge University Press, 1970), 359.

Emphasis on the effective intervention of Britain in the trade should not be taken as a denial of the growth of antislavery sentiment in Brazil or of the later action of Brazilians to end the sordid trade within the country. Three examples, brought to my attention by Hilgard Sternberg: (1) the numerous manumissions in the cattle country of Ceará State in the northeast, topped in 1880 by the founding by Masons of the Cearenese Liberator Society, dedicated to liberation, cited in Raimundo Girão, *Pequena História de Ceará* (Fortaleza: Impresa Universitário, 1962), chap. 23; (2) the *jangadeiros*, a type of raftman, in 1881 refusing to transport slaves in Ceará aboard ship for the southern provinces, ibid., 224; and (3) the province of Ceará freeing all slaves within the province on March 25, 1883, idem.

SIXTEEN. Emancipators' Éclat

"This country is not likely to gain or lose": Julian Pauncefort to George Granville, Minute, November 14, 1884, F.O. 84/1814, quoted in Suzanne Miers, *Britain and the Ending of the Slave Trade* (New York: Africana Publishing Co., 1975), 171; declaration against the trade: Berlin Act, Article IV in idem., 172–173.

"Master more may gaze": *The Poems of Gerard Manley Hopkins*, ed. Robert Bridges (Oxford University Press, 1930).

Lavigerie's memorandum to Rome and the "great crusade of faith and humanity": François Renault, *Lavigerie: L'esclavage Africain et L'Europe 1868–1892* (Paris: E. De Brocard, 1971), vol. I, pp. 165–166.

The encyclical of Leo XIII: *In plurimis, ASS*, vol. 20, pp. 545–559 (1888); "the Apostle of the Moors": *Leonis XIII Acta* (Rome, 1889), vol. 8, 12–14. Claver was canonized along with two other Jesuits and the seven founders of the order of the Slaves of Mary.

After Claver had been beatified by Pius IX on July 16, 1850, a pro-slavery writer in the Catholic press in the United States explicitly contrasted his life of heroic service to the slaves with the noisy efforts of abolitionists on behalf of emancipation. See McGreevy, 52.

In plurimis interpreted to reject slavery in principle: Prudhomme, "L'Église catholique" at 18. The comment of a modern historian is acidulous and accurate: "Pope Leo XIII's self-congratulatory letter to the bishops of Brazil on the (very belated) abolition of slavery there in 1888 is riddled with historical inaccuracies and totally unjustified claims of earlier papal opposition to Negro slavery." Charles Ralph Boxer, *The Church Militant and Iberian Expansion 1440–1770* (Baltimore: The Johns Hopkins University Press, 1978), 126, n.45.

Lavigerie's advice to Leo XIII and the pope's response: François Renault, *Le Cardinal Lavigerie* (Paris: Fayard, 1992), 556–557.

"safeguarding . . . the dignity of the human person": Leo XIII to Lavigerie, October 27, 1888, *ASS*, vol. 21, 195.

Lavigerie and Leo and other antislavery societies: Renault, *Le Cardinal Lavigerie,* 574.

Leo's second encyclical: *Catholicae Ecclesiae, ASS*, 23, 257 (1890); "to rescue workers":, Leo XIII to a meeting of Catholic workers, August 6, 1893, *ASS*, 26 (1893–1894), 74–75.

The collection of rulings: *Collectanea*, I, "Praefatio".

Question 1: What is the status of a fugitive slave?: Holy Office, June 20, 1866: *Collectanea*, I, n.1293, sec. V (fugitive slave); sec. VI (killing slave); sec. VII (concubinage).

The case of Titius and Lola: Holy Office, November 22, 1871, for Siam, ibid., II, n.1377. A similar case was dealt with by the Holy Office in its ruling of July 4, 1855, for Siam: I, n.1114.

The case of the man who had sold his wife: Holy Office, July 8, 1891, for Nyasa, ibid., II, n.1760.

"You ask, How slavery": Arthur Vermeersch, *Quaestiones de iustitia* (Bruges, 2d ed., 1904), n.1151. Later in the century, Benoit Merkelbach, a Dominican moralist at the Angelicum in Rome, published the second edition of his *Summa theologiae moralis* with the imprimatur of M. S. Gillet, the master general of his order. Merkelbach taught that slavery in perpetuity was not per se opposed to natural law if there was not "an excess of oppression and tyranny." He added that it was "less fitting (*minus conveniens*) for human dignity." In a footnote he noted it was not unlawful by Scripture and that there were four titles to ownership of a slave—purchase; war; birth; and criminal penalty. In a footnote to the footnote, he said apropos of birth that "it could seem less just (*minus aequa*) if the slavery was perpetual." See his *Summa theologiae moralis* (Paris: Desclée De Brouwer, 1936), vol. 2, "De virtutibus moralibus," 168.3.

Mistake as to slavery: *CIC* (1917), canon 1083, sec. 3; slavery a bar to orders: canon 987, sec. 4.

"a state of perpetual subjection": Tommaso Angelo Iorio, *Theologia moralis* (Naples: M. D'Auria, 5th ed., 1960), vol. 2, p. 329.

Condemnations of usury: Denzinger 1955: n.365, 394, 403, 448, 479, 716, 739, 1081, 1475, 1609.

The 1965 edition of Denzinger, issued during the council, showed a new awareness of slavery as a moral issue. A systematic index to the work had the entry "Personal Liberty" and under it on p. 917: "Liberty from slavery. The purchase and sale of human beings are forbidden as contrary to the laws of justice and humanity. 668, 1495, 2745a." The first number referred to the letter of John VIII to the Sardinians, cited supra, chap. 9; the second number, to Paul III's brief accompanying *Sublimis Deus;* the third number, to Gregory XVI's *In supremo.* The first and third quotations were reproduced under the misleading rubric "The Slavery of Human Beings Should Be Removed." Strikingly, Leo XIII was not quoted. No text condemning slavery had been found.

"chattel slavery": John C. Ford and Gerald Kelly, *Contemporary Moral Theology* (Westminster, Md.: Newman Press, 1963), II, 67. American Catholics in the twentieth century had a hard time recognizing that slavery as an institution had always been accepted by the Church. See, e.g., James J. Fox, "Slavery, Ethical Aspects of," *The Catholic Encyclopedia* (New York: Robert Appleton Co., 1912), vol. 14, p. 46: Slavery was accepted "as not in itself incompatible with the Christian laws" until towards the end of the eighteenth century. Later moralists, unnamed by Fox, "hold that it is hardly compatible with the dignity of personality and is to be condemned as immoral on account of the evil consequences it almost inevitably leads to." Bishop John England, whose defense of slavery had come out in 1840, would have been surprised to see the difference made by the Civil War and a Northern perspective.

SEVENTEEN.   **The Sin Perceived, Categorized, Condemned**

probra: Second Vatican Council, *Constitutio Pastoralis De Ecclesia In Mundo Huius Temporis.* "Reverence Toward the Human Person": I.2.27, *Vat. II,* IV, pt. VII, 750; compare the draft of its "The Human Community," I. 2. 27, ibid., 251–253; the addition of slavery is noted by the drafting commission at 414. As an addition, slavery was italicized in the text at 254. Final vote and promulgation: 860.

"is *the* underlying issue": John Courtney Murray, "This Matter of Religious Freedom," *America* 112 (January 9, 1965), 43.

preparation of *Catechism of the Catholic Church:* John Paul II, *Fidei depositum*, October 11, 1992; English translation: *CCC*, 3–4; "a sure norm": ibid., 5; "The seventh commandment": ibid., 580.

"It is fitting that there be confessed": John Paul II, Allocution, February 2, 1992, *La Documentation catholique*, April 5, 1992, p. 326.

"a complete and full exposition": John Paul II, *Veritatis splendor* 5.3, *AAS*, vol. 85, p. 1137 (1993); the council's list: sec. 80.1.

The present position of the Church that slavery is intrinsically evil may be contrasted with that of an influential modern philosopher, John Rawls. In his *A Theory of Justice* (Cambridge: Harvard University Press, 1971), p. 248, Rawls states: "There may be transition cases where enslavement is better than current practice." He supposes warring states that kill their captives, but then agree by treaty only to enslave them. "The arrangement seems defensible as an advance on established institutions, if slaves are not treated too severely. In time it will presumably be abandoned altogether, since the exchange of prisoners of war is a still more desirable arrangement, the return of the captured members of the community being preferable to the services of slaves." The "transition cases," it seems, could last a long time. Who would judge whether the slaves were treated "too severely"?

"the distinguished defender of the rights of conscience": *Veritatis splendor*, sec. 34.1, *AAS*, vol. 85, p. 1161; "Fortified by the Holy Spirit": ibid., 4.1, p. 1136.

The "average Catholic" as "an improbable stereotype": I cite three examples culled from my discussing the topic of this book. A scientist, a woman brought up in Italy, now teaching in the United States, told me "Italy never had any slaves." She, of course, did not mean Roman Italy, but she did mean medieval and renaissance Italy. An Argentinian woman, in her sixties: "They thought they had no souls." She did not identify the second "they," but meant slaves generally. "That's how they were able to do it." A Brazilian woman, now an American citizen, in her eighties: "As a girl, I knew a woman who had been a slave of my grandmother. She told me how mean my grandmother had been to her." Three representative attitudes: Italian Catholics never had slaves. Spanish Catholics had slaves but thought them soulless. Brazilian Catholics had slaves and did not treat them well.

EIGHTEEN.   Unnatural Reproduction

The Jesuit commission of 1573: John T. Noonan, Jr., "The Amendment of Papal Teaching by Theologians," *Contraception: Authority and Dissent*, ed. Charles E. Curran (New York, 1969), 60–61; the commission of 1581: ibid., 64.

Money-changers are not bankers: see David Daube, "Civil Disobedience in Antiquity," *Biblical Law and Literature*, ed. Calum Carmichael (Berkeley: The Robbins Collection, 2002), 646, n.111; the Temple's exchange policy: *Jerome Bible Commentary*, 429.

"mutuum date": Luke 6:35, *Biblia sacra juxta vulgatam versionem*, ed. Robert Weber (Stuttgart: 2nd ed., 1975). It is sometimes incorrectly assumed that there was only one Vulgate, that produced by Jerome. But errors in transcriptions of Jerome's work multiplied over the centuries. The Council of Trent in 1546 declared "the Vulgate" to be free from any error in faith and morals and so could be quoted with complete authority in disputations, lectures, and preaching. Council of Trent, *Insuper*, April 8, 1546, Mansi, vol. 33, p. 23. Nonetheless, the version of the Vulgate commonly in use translated Luke 6:35 *"mutuum date, nihil inde sperantes,"* and from 1189 on this translation played a critical role in morals. The most authoritative modern translation of the Vulgate follows the Greek and translates *"mutuum date, nihil desperantes."* *Nova Vulgata Bibliorum Sacrorum editio* (Vatican City: Libreria Editrice Vaticana, 1979).

"I have seen a piteous sight": Basil, *Homilia* II, 4, *PG* 29, 277; Ambrose, *De Tobia* 29, *PL* 14, 769. Other Fathers on usury: Jerome: "They do not understand that whatever excess there is is called usury." *In Ezechiel* 6:18, *PL* 25, 176. The Law prohibited usury from one's brothers; the Prophets prohibited it from all; the Gospel, where virtue is increased, tells you to lend "to those from whom you do not hope to receive." "Some, who think themselves just, say, 'I gave a measure, which you sowed and made 10 measures. Is it not just that I take half a measure for mine, when from my generosity you have had 9½?'" It is still usury, and God will not be mocked. Ibid., at 176. Augustine: Usury is when you "give your money in a loan from which you expect to receive more than you have given." "How detestable, how odious, how execrable I think the usurers themselves know." Sermon 3.6, on Psalm 36, *PL* 36, 386. Usurers dare to say in defense of their usury, "'I don't have else from which to live'. A thief would say this to me. . . . A pimp would say this to me, buying girls for prostitution." Augustine, *Enchiridion in Psalm* 128, *PL* 37, 1692. A leading Greek Father satirized as beset by anxiety the usurer who made maritime loans and mocked the usurer who tried to make money out of a poor man: Gregory of Nyssa to Letoius, bishop of Militene, *PG* 45, 234. How, he asked, could the usurer pray the Lord's prayer as reported in Matthew 18:28 and ask God's forgiveness "as we forgive our debtors." *Against the Usurers*, *PG* 46, 443–444. Gregory of Nazianzen: money cannot produce offspring. *Oratio XVI*, 18, *PG* 35, 957. See generally the very helpful article of Robert P. Maloney, "The Teaching of the Fathers on Usury: An Historical Study on the Development of Christian Thinking," *Vigiliae Christianae* 27 (1973), 241–265.

No judge would order restitution: Augustine to Macedonia, Epistle 153, n.25, *CSEL* 44.426.

Development under Charlemagne: John T. Noonan, Jr., *The Scholastic Analysis of Usury* (Cambridge: Harvard University Press, 1957), 15.

NINETEEN. In Your City You Say It Often Happens

"Behold, it is evident": Gratian, *Concordia*, II, C.14, Q.3, dictum after C.4, *CIC*, vol. I.

Usury reprobated by both Testaments: Second Lateran Council, canon 13, Mansi, 21, 530.

Fruits of the land to be counted toward principal: Eugene III, *Epistola, PL* 180, 1567.

"In your city you say": *In tua civitate, Decretales*, 5.19.6, *CIC*, vol. II; "since Sacred Scripture prohibits lying": ibid., "Super eo", 5.19.4; "with many giving up other businesses": *Quia in omnibus*, 5, 19, 3, and in Mansi, 22, 232.

The "intention of profit": *Consuluit, Decretales*, 5.19.10.

the universal teaching on the sin of seeking profit from a loan: Noonan, *The Scholastic Analysis*, 193, 357; the teaching on partnership: ibid., 134–153; on annuities: ibid., 154–170, 230–248.

Sharia law on usury: see Frank E. Vogel and Samuel L. Hayes, III, *Islamic Law and Finance, Religion, Risk and Return* (Cambridge: Kluwer Law International, 1998), and Yusuf DeLorenzo, "The Religious Foundation of Islamic Finance," *The Jurist* 60 (2000), 146–154.

the sweep of usury law in Bernardino's Siena: see Noonan, *Scholastic Analysis*, 73–75.

"dry exchange": Noonan, *Scholastic Analysis*, 184–189.

"Go back a little": Dante Alighieri, *Inferno*, XI, 94–96, *La Divina Comedia*, ed. Charles S. Singleton (Princeton: Princeton University Press, 1970), 114.

charity could replace usury: Noonan, *Scholastic Analysis*, 73; the *montes pietatis:* ibid., 295–312.

TWENTY. The Custom of the Country

The new analyses: Noonan, *Scholastic Analysis*, 199–201; "Do not disturb them": ibid., 378–382.

"full of usury": quoted in Noonan, "The Amendment," 48; the objections of Peter Canisius: ibid., 49; the commission of 1581: ibid., 64–65; the general's order: *ibid.*, 67.

Cum onus: ibid., 52.

Detestabilis avaritia: ibid., 55–56; its treatment by the theologians: ibid., 70–72.

Damnum emergens: Noonan, *Scholastic Analysis,* 115–116, 303–304; *lucrum cessans:* ibid., 262–267; risk of default: ibid., 389–393.

The responses on usury from Rome, 1822–1836: see ibid., 378–382.

Luke 6:35 a counsel: ibid., 365, 390; Marie-Joseph Lagrange, O.P., *L'Évangile selon S. Luc* (Paris; Gabalda, 1921), 196, n.4.

Criticism of usury by *The Catholic Worker:* ibid., 399.

Keynes's charge of "usury": Robert Skidelsky, *John Maynard Keynes* (New York: Viking, 2000), vol. 3, p. 377, quoting Keynes to Cornelius Gregg, Chairman of the Board of Trade, April 9, 1945.

"the reduction, if not the entire forgiveness": John Paul II, *Tertio adveniente millenio,* sec. 51, November 10, 1994, *AAS* 87, 36.

The aged Maritain on the usury rule: Jacques Maritain, *De l'Église du Christ: La personne de l'Église et son personnel* (Paris: Desclée De Brouwer, 1970), 58; great Thomist though he was, it may be doubted that Maritain had studied Cajetan on exchange bankers.

TWENTY-ONE.   **The Future Is Put Off**

"the first daily newspaper": *Mémoire* presented to Gregory XVI by the editors of *L'Avenir,* February 3, 1832, reproduced in *La Condamnation de Lamennais, dossier présenté* by M. J. Le Guillou and Louis Le Guillou (Paris: Beauchesne, 1982), 573–574.

The ideas advocated by *L'Avenir: Mémoire* in ibid., 542–592.

"May God rise up": Leo XII, *Ubi primum,* May 5, 1824, *Bullarii romani continuatio* (Rome, 1854), 16, 47.

On Cappellari's choice of name: Owen Chadwick, *A History of the Popes 1830–1914* (Oxford: Clarendon Press, 1998), 2.

"very respectfully kissing your most holy feet": Cardinal Bartolomeo to Gregory XVI, February 28, 1832, reproduced in *La Condamnation,* pp. 130–131.

"The sovereign pontiff will judge": *Mémoire* in ibid., 592.

The audience with the pope: excerpt from the diary of Montalembert in *La Condamnation*, pp. 141–142.

"François" Lamennais: Frezza, Report to the Congregation for Extraordinary Ecclesiastical Affairs for its session of February 28, 1832, reproduced in ibid., p. 291; "no stranger to the revolutions": ibid., p. 294; "a criminal act": Frezza, *votum*, submitted to Gregory XVI, July 1832, in ibid., p. 192; "an absurd and shameful system." ibid., 198; citation of Leo XII's encyclical: ibid., 201. Frezza, rather than Secretary of State Tommaso Bernetti, was relied on in ecclesiastical-political affairs by Gregory XVI. See Lajos Pásztor, *La Segreteria Di Stato E Il Suo Archivo, 1814–1833,* I, 155 (*Päpste Und Papstum,* vol. 23.1, Stuttgart: Anton Hiersemann 1984).

Metternich's influence: see Chadwick, *A History*, 19; Austrian interception of Lamennais letters: Lambruschini to Gregory XVI, March 13, 1832, reproduced in *La Condamnation*, pp. 143–144.

"You want to live?": Félicité de Lamennais, *Affaires de Rome* (Brussels: J-P. Melise, 1837), 121.

"patron and saviour" (*sospita*, applying to Mary what pagan Romans had applied to Juno): *Mirari vos: Acta Gregorii Papae XVI,* ed. A. M. Bernasconi (Rome: Propaganda Fide, 1901–04), vol. I, 169; "unrestrained wickedness": ibid., 170; "Academies and schools": 170; "keep the deposit": 170; "taught by the Holy Spirit": 171; "*indifferentism*": 171; *deliramentum:* 172; "What worse death," quoting Augustine, Epistle 166, and *"pit of the abyss,"* quoting Apocalypse 9:2; freedom of publishing: 170; burning of books: 171.

TWENTY-TWO. **With Words for Infidels, with Fire for the Faltering Baptized**

like "bad slaves": Augustine to Boniface, Governor of Africa, *Epistola* 185, "The Correction of the Donatists," *PL* 33, 803; the Lord's force on Saul: ibid. The blinding of Saul as precedent for persecution: if the Acts of the Apostles were used as precedent, reneging on a gift to the Church would have been subject to the death penalty on the basis of how Ananias and his wife Sapphira were struck down after they held back from the apostles part of the sales price of their property and lied about it (Acts 5:1–10).

Thomas Aquinas, *Summa theologiae*, 2–2, 11, 3 (death penalty; comparison to forgery); 11, 4 *ad* 1 (Church does not forgive).

Lucius III, *Ad abolendam, Decretales,* 5, 7, 9, *CIC II,* col. 780–782.

"To burn heretics is contrary to the will of the Spirit": a proposition condemned by Leo X, *Exsurge Domine,* June 16, 1520, *MBR* I, 611; orders and penalties: ibid., 615.

Erasmus' deliberate play on More's name: Desiderius Erasmus to Thomas More, printed as foreword to Erasmus, *Moriae Encomium Id Est Stultitiae Laus*, ed. Clarence H. Miller, in Erasmus, *Opera omnia* (Amsterdam: North Holland Publishing Co., 1979), IV-3, p. 67; place of composition: Miller, "Introduction," p. 14; "a sour old fellow": Erasmus, *Moriae Encomium*, p. 186; "impotently shout, 'Heresy! Heresy!'": Erasmus, *De sarcienda Ecclesiae concordia*, ed. R. Stupperich, *Opera omnia*, V-3, p. 302.

"great minds": John Paul II, *Tertio millenio adveniente*, November 10, 1994, sec. 35, *AAS* 87, 27.

TWENTY-THREE.   The Requirements of the Human Person

The new doctrine on religious freedom: Vatican II, *Dignitatis humanae personae*, sec. 2, *Vat. II* 4:7. For the old doctrine, see John A. Ryan and Francis Boland, *Catholic Principles of Politics* (New York: Macmillan, 1940), 317–321. The same teaching appears in John A. Ryan and Moorhouse F. X. Millar, S.J., *The State and the Church* (New York: Macmillan, 1922), 35–39.

Maritain's position: Maritain, *The Person and the Common Good*, trans. John J. Fitzgerald (New York: Scribner's, 1947), 81–83; Maritain, *Man & the State*, ed. Richard O'Sullivan (London: Hollis and Carter, 1954), 136–137. The attacks on Maritain: see Jean-Dominique Durand, "La grand attaque de 1956," *Cahiers Jacques Maritain* 30 (June, 1995), 2–31. *De Lamennais à Maritain* by Abbé Jules Meinville was published in Buenos Aires and found favor both in Peronist Argentina and Franco Spain: ibid., 3–4. A senior editor of *Civiltà Catholica* and Cardinals Siri and Pizzardo, as well as Ottaviani, were among Maritain's chief critics: ibid., 8–15.

The silencing of Murray: Donald E. Pelotte, S.S.S., *John Courtney Murray: Theologian in Conflict* (New York: Paulist Press, 1976), 53; Murray's appearance at the council: ibid., 82.

"the very recent Catholic liberalism": Alfredo Ottaviani, *Institutiones iuris publici ecclesiastici*, 4th ed. (Vatican City: Vatican Polyglot Press, 1960), II, 55; quotation of Mussolini: ibid., 69, n.193.

quotation of Gregory XVI and Pius IX: Ernesto Ruffini, *Oratio*, Sept. 23, 1964, *Vat. II* 3:3, 355; "a new law": Lefebvre, Intervention, Sept. 20, 1965, *Vat. II* 4:1, 409; "The reporter": Lefebvre, *Oratio*, Sept. 16, 1965, ibid., 409–410. In the printed version, Lefebvre added "It seems to me" at the start of the second paragraph quoted here. The editors moved "Voltaire" from the text to a footnote. Lefebvre does not seem to have checked the dates for Hobbes or Locke, and he elides Lamennais with those condemned by Pius IX.

Final vote on *Dignitatis: Vat. II* 4:7, 807.

The development of the ideal of religious freedom in the seventeenth and eighteenth centuries: see John T. Noonan, *The Lustre of Our Country: The American Experience of Religious Freedom* (Berkeley: University of California Press, 1998), 53–57; "a contradiction to the Christian Religion itself": James Madison, "Memorial and Remonstrance," *The Papers of James Madison,* ed. Robert A. Rutland and William M. E. Rachal (Chicago: University of Chicago Press, 1973), 8, 298–304.

Development of doctrine the underlying issue of the council: John Courtney Murray, "This Matter of Religious Freedom," *America* 112 (Jan. 9, 1965), 43.

"the vicissitudes of history": *Dignitatis humanae personae,* n.11, *Vat. II* 4:7.

"If what is being taught is true": Lefebvre, Commentary, Sept. 20, 1965, *Vat. II* 4:1, 792; "married the [French] Revolution": Lefebvre, homily at Lille, Aug. 29, 1976, quoted in Jean-Anne Chalet, *Monseigneur Lefebvre* (Paris: Pygmalion, 1976), 209–210. The 1965 edition of Denzinger, the authoritative collection of teachings of the magisterium, continued to reproduce Pius IX's Syllabus of Errors. Denzinger, 1965, n.2901–2980. Vatican II had not yet spoken, but John XXIII had already taught in *Pacem in terris,* April 11, 1963, that the rights of the human being arose from human nature and are "inviolable" and that "the dignity of the human person was taught by revelation." This teaching was excerpted in Denzinger, 1965, n.3957, without any attempt to reconcile it with the repressive teachings of the past popes who were still solemnly quoted.

TWENTY-FOUR.   If the Unbeliever Separates

Djakarta, August 19, 1959: "Dissolution of the Natural Bond Between Two Infidels Without Any Conversion," *CLD,* V (1963), 543–546.

"the most difficult of all": Erasmus, *Annotationes in Primam Epistolam ad Corinthios* in *Erasmus' Annotations on the New Testament,* ed. Anne Reeve and M. A. Screech (London: E. J. Brill, 1971), at 1 Corinthians 7. David Daube has argued that the basis of Paul's teaching is this: according to rabbinic thought, a convert is literally a new person; hence his or her old marriage no longer exists. Daube, "Biblical Landmarks in the Struggle for Women's Rights," *New Testament Judaism,* ed. Calum Carmichael (Berkeley: The Robbins Collection, 2000), 236–237. Much as I have benefitted from Daube's insights, this novel explanation is unconvincing to me. If Paul thought converts were new persons, why would he have not given the same freedom to marry as each chose to husband and wife if they both converted and parted? Paul tells his converts that each "must continue in the station which the Lord has appointed for him and in which he was when God's call came to him" (1 Cor 7:17). That is a strange prescription if Paul believed them literally reborn. That theory was a favorite of Daube's. See *New Testament Judaism*, 476–477; 530–531 (arguing that Paul believes Useful has been freed by baptism; it is superfluous to ask Philemon to free him); 537–538; 545–547 ("the traditional construction of the [Pauline] Privilege will have to be revised"); 554 (again, Useful as a new, free man).

Could Paul be speaking of his own case? A devout Jew, he very likely was married. His wife would not have had his experience on the road to Damascus and would have found his sudden conversion intolerable; he would be now without a wife (1 Cor 7:7). If this conjecture were correct, he would be free because no longer bound to an unbeliever.

The changing rate of divorce in England: Lawrence Stone, *Road to Divorce* (New York: Oxford University Press, 1990), 2; "History is messier than that": ibid., 27.

"If the unbeliever separates": Ambrosiaster (= Isaac), *Commentarius in Epistulas Paulinas*, ed. H. S. Vogels (Vienna, 1968), at 1 Cor 7:15, p. 76.

Augustine's silence on the convert's right to remarry: Augustine: *De sermone Domini in monte* 1.16: 44–45, *CC* 35, 49–52. Augustine's own argument against divorce by a couple that was sterile was that "from the first coupling of two human beings, marriage bears a certain sacramental sign (*sacramentum*)." It would seem that this argument prevented his acceptance of Isaac's position. See Augustine, *De bono coniugali* 15, 17, *CSEL* 41, 209–210. But Augustine also wrote of the case of a convert in the marriage of two unbaptized persons: "It is not on account of the conjugal bond to be preserved with such spouses, but he [Paul] forbids withdrawal from the unbelieving spouse that the spouse may be gained in Christ." Augustine, *De adulterinis coniugiis*, chap. 13, *CC* 41, 363. In the background was the history of his own parents: the pious Monica married to the pagan Patrick, who did not leave her entirely at peace, yet was won over by her gentleness.

A teaching that comes close to Isaac's is the roughly contemporary commentary of John Chrysostom, patriarch of Constantinople, on the same text in Paul. He interprets it as applying if the pagan spouse orders you to perform sacrifices or be a companion in impiety; then, "it is better that the marriage be torn apart than your piety." John Chrysostom, *Homily 19 on the First Letter to the Corinthians*, *PG* 61, 155. The implication is that the convert is free to remarry. The implication remains unstated.

Canon 9 of Basil, after quoting 1 Corinthians 7:16 on the convert not knowing whether she will save her husband, adds, "Therefore, she who leaves is an adulterer if she goes to another man. But he who is left is worthy of pardon, and she who lives with him is not condemned." Basil to Amphiliochius, Canon 9, *PG* 32, 677. This brief comment appears to be an unenthusiastic acceptance of the right of remarriage, by its choice of pronouns restricting it to a male convert. Basil had declared that "custom" treated a woman more severely than a man and under no circumstances should a wife dismiss even her adulterous husband.

ratum: As an adjective meaning "valid", *ratus* was regularly used in Roman law, for example in the Digest XXIV, 1, 65, of a gift and, again, in 67: "If a wife buys a slave with money given to her by her husband or by one who is in his power, and then, after the slave has been made hers, she delivers him to her husband as a gift, the delivery will be valid (*rata*). . . ."

Isaac's history: Erasmus was the first to state that the author of the commentary on Paul's letters was not one of the Fathers. Erasmus assigned him the down-putting name "Ambrosiaster," adding to "Ambrosius" the pejorative suffix "*aster.*" Erasmus didn't know who the author was. The identification continues to be a matter of debate. Alessandra Pollastri, "Ambrosiaster," *Encyclopedia of the Early Church*, ed. Angelo Di Berardino, trans. Adrian Walford (Oxford University Press, 1992), I, 30. In *Power to Dissolve* (1972), p. 454, n.3, after a review of the evidence, I thought Isaac was the author. Nothing in the last thirty years has changed my view. This identification is accepted as "not *invraisemblable*" by the *DHGE*, XXVI, 82 (1997). The principal reasons for my conclusion are:

1. The commentator had "a profound knowledge of the institutions of the Jews." Pollastri at 30. Therefore he was a convert from Judaism.

2. Although the commentary on Paul was the first Latin commentary and one of great importance in its insights, the name of the author disappeared. The complete suppression of his name can most plausibly be accounted for by the author's opponents, victorious in a conflict, following the old Roman custom of eliminating the loser's name, the so-called *damnatio memoriae*. See Charles W. Hendrick Jr., *History and Silence: Purge and Rehabilitation of Memory in Antiquity* (Austin: University of Texas Press, 2000), 43. Isaac was such a loser. He was an ally of Ursinus, a deacon of the Roman Church who in 366 was elected bishop of Rome at Santa Maria in Trastevere. Ursinus was driven from this church by Damasus, a priest of the Roman Church, and his followers. Reportedly, there was heavy loss of life. See the anonymous anti-Damasus account in *Avellana Quae Dicitur Collectio*, ed. Otto Guenther, *CSEL* 35, 2–3. Damasus was then elected by his followers, meeting at the Lateran Basilica. Ursinus and his supporters, including some bishops, continued the opposition for years and eventually established themselves in Milan, the capital of the Western Empire. Isaac took the lead in accusing Damasus of a capital crime, probably adultery; and Damasus was brought to trial before an imperial court, according to the *Liber pontificalis*. See A. Van Roey, "Damase," *DHGE XIV*, 50 (1960). Damasus was acquitted and the accusation pronounced "a most foul calumny." Idem.

In 378, a group of bishops favorable to Damasus gathered in Rome and asked the emperor's help in restraining Ursinus and his followers, accused, inter alia, of the heresy of rebaptizing. Mansi, III, 626. Isaac "a suborned Jew," was accused of "having returned to the synagogue and profaned the heavenly mysteries" and of being led by Ursinus "so that the head of our holy brother Damasus was sought, the blood of the innocent was shed, and frauds were accomplished." But Isaac "could not prove what he argued." The emperor issued orders banishing Isaac to Spain. Ibid., 628. Damasus was, postmortem, given status as a saint.

The fierceness of the fight and Isaac's actual prosecution of Damasus would have qualified Isaac as a mortal enemy, deserving of having his name blotted out by the victors, who, most probably, would have had control of the manuscripts after Isaac's banishment. We need not accept at face value the Roman charge against Isaac of apostasy. Vituperation of one's opponents came easily.

3. The author of the commentary is unmentioned by Jerome in his *De viris illustribus*. Jerome, the foremost biblical scholar of the age, overlooks the most important Latin writer on Paul. Why? Jerome was the secretary of Pope Damasus. He had a very strong motive for eliminating Isaac from his list of the illustrious.

4. The commentator was a lawyer. The succinct interpretation of 1 Corinthians 7:13 demonstrates his skill. Isaac, the prosecutor of Damasus, was a lawyer.

5. The elimination of Isaac's name was accomplished efficiently and early. Augustine, writing in 420 against Pelagius, attributed a quotation from the commentator's work on Romans to St. Hilary. *Contra duas epistulas Pelagii*, 4.7, *CSEL* 60:528. Who was in a better position to so effectively remove Isaac's name than Damasus and his followers?

The first writer to suggest that Isaac could be the author was a Benedictine, Germain Morin, "L'Ambrosiaster et le juif converti Isaac," *Revue d'histoire et de littér. religeux* 4 (1899), 197–211. Four years later, Morin denied that he had decided on Isaac and now thought the author was Hilary, proconsul of Africa in 377, one of the Christian aristocrats of Rome. Morin, "Hilarius l'Ambrosiaster," *Revue bénédictine* 20 (1903), 121. After World War I, Morin published "Qui Est L'Ambrosiaster? Solution Nouvelle," *Revue bénédictine* 31 (1914–1919), 1–34. Here, after rejecting another Hilary, he said his "definitive candidate" was Evagrius, bishop of Antioch, who had "lived and written in Rome and openly taken the part of Pope Damasus" (p. 3). Then in 1928, after thirty years of thinking about the author, Morin confessed defeat in "La Critique dans une impasse: à propos du cas de l'Ambrosiaster," *Revue bénédictine* 40 (1928), 251–255. Morin now rejected Isaac because "there is in Ambrosiaster some phrases that a Jew by birth could never write." (p. 252).

I don't know how one can say what a zealous convert "could never write." It is, no doubt, rash to disregard Morin's explorations, but it seems to me that he gave very little weight to the elimination of the name of the author from Jerome's account of famous men and from the author's own manuscripts. If, as Morin admits at ibid., 252, the author wrote works "of an exceptional value and originality" and was "*un haut personnage*, in more or less direct contact with the principal ecclesiastical milieus of the fourth century," how on earth could his name and identity disappear except by the design of enemies to obliterate his memory?

"That marriage is not confirmed": Gratian, dictum post c.17, Part II, C.28, q.1, *CIC* I, 1089; "it is not necessary to follow": ibid., dictum post c.2, C.28, q.2, *CIC* I, 1090; Peter Lombard, *Libri Quattuor Sententiarim*, IV, D.39 (Quaracchi, 1916) (same result without using the canonical term *ratum* or quoting the text of Isaac).

Quanto te: Decretales, 4, 19, 7, *CIC* II, 722; the overruled decretal of Celestine III is now printed in the Friedberg edition at 3, 33, 1, *CIC* II, 588. Of the nine canons composing *De divortiis,* only *Quanto te* permitted dissolution of a marriage.

Procedure for divorce by convert: Hostiensis, *In quinque libros decretalium commentaria* (Venice, 1582), 4, 19, 7; dissolution by contempt: Guillaume of Auxeere, *Summa aurea in quattuor libros sententiarum* (Paris, 1500), f.291 r; on Richard of Middleton, see George Hayward Joyce, S.J., *Christian Marriage* (London: Sheed and Ward, 1933), 427. Petrus Cantor, a theologian teaching at Paris at the end of the twelfth century, asked how many times an infidel spouse had to engage in blasphemy before the marriage bond with the convert was broken. His answer: the convert should get the judgment of ecclesiastical authority. But what if the blasphemies were secret and the convert could not prove them? Then the convert has the authority to withdraw and to marry someone else "in a remote place." Pierre Le Chantre, *Summa de sacramentis et animae consiliis,* ed. Jean-Albert Dugauquier (Louvain: Éditions Nauwelaerts, 1967), pt. III, chap. 13, p. 443. The willingness to let divorce occur on one's own authority is noteworthy.

"the more firm": Thomas Aquinas, *In libros sententiarum,* Book IV, D.39, 1.5; "in punishment": ibid. *ad* 3. This harsh penalty for the unconverted partner of the first marriage was current in the eighteenth century when Benedict XIV applied it to a Jewish woman whose husband had become a Christian. According to some, their marriage had been dissolved by his conversion; according to "the more common opinion," their marriage was dissolved by his remarriage. But she could remarry only on his death! Benedict XIV, *Nuper quaestio,* September 16, 1747, *Colección de Bulas, Breves, y otros Documentos Relativos A La Iglesia De America y Filipinas,* ed. Francisco Javier Hernaez, S.J. (Brussels, 1879), I, 85–88.

TWENTY-FIVE.   If Necessity Urges

The problem of the polygamous chiefs: see John T. Noonan, Jr., *Power to Dissolve: Lawyers and Marriages in the Courts of the Roman Curia* (Cambridge: Harvard University Press, 1970), 347–352.

Altitudo: printed as an appendix to *CIC* (1917); *Romani pontificis:* ibid.; *Populis et nationibus:* ibid. "Urgent necessity" as a reason justifying the pope to dissolve the marriage of a bishop to his diocese was advanced by Innocent III in *Inter corporalia, Decretales,* 1, 7, 2, although the phrase was eliminated in the decretal collection and only restored in the nineteenth century by Friedburg, *CIC* II, 98.

"by virtue of the privilege of Christ": Tomás Sanchez, *De sancto matrimonii sacramento* (Venice, 1737), 7.74.10. The practice of the curia before recent times was to describe the

Pauline privilege as "privilege in favor of the faith promulgated by the Apostle": e.g., a ruling of Propaganda to the Vicar Apostolic of Setchuen, January 16, 1797, *Collectanea*, n.634, I, 390.

The treatment of the decrees in the following centuries: Noonan, *Power to Dissolve*, 357–367. A case before the Sacred Congregation of the Council in 1726 raised the question whether the papal power could be exercised in regard to the marriage of two Jews in Florence. The ambiguous evidence suggests that the power was used to dissolve their marriage, unconsummated after they had each independently converted. See ibid., 362–364.

"Full Divorce": Pietro Gasparri, *Tractatus canonicus de matrimonio* (Paris: Delhomme et Briguet, 1893), secs. 1084, 1109.

"extended to other regions": *CIC* (1917), Canon 1925. *Populis et nationibus* of Gregory XIII had been extended to the East Indies and to China and adjoining regions including Siam. Instruction of the Holy Office, January 13, 1757, for the East Indies, *Collectanea*, n.400, I, 256; instruction of the Holy Office, July 4, 1855, for Siam, ibid., n.1114, I, 593; "successive polygamists": T. Lincoln Bouscaren, S.J., and Adam C. Ellis, S.J., *Canon Law: A Text and Commentary* (Milwaukee: Bruce Publishing Co., 1946), 559.

TWENTY-SIX. Out of Deeds Comes Law

Helena, 1924: reported, "Dispensation from Natural Marriage 'In Favorem Fidei'—An Important Decision," *The Ecclesiastical Review* 72 (1925), 188. LaHood is a common name in Lebanon, so presumably Lulu LaHood was of Lebanese descent. For how the case proceeded abstractly without reference to the real parties, and how it was misinterpreted as a Pauline privilege case by the chancellor of the Helena diocese, see Noonan, *Power to Dissolve*, 371.

Prior to the Code of 1917, a marriage between a baptized person and an unbaptized person was recognized by the Church as valid only if the Church granted a dispensation for it. This rule was applied to Protestants as well as Catholics. As no Protestant would ask for a dispensation, the marriage of a Protestant to an unbaptized person would be treated by the Church as null. The Marsh-Groom marriage would have been no barrier to the Marsh-LaHood marriage. Canon 1070 of the 1917 Code, with more sensitivity to the scope of the Church's law, removed the Church's impediment to the marriage of the unbaptized with non-Catholic Christians. The result was that the Marsh-Groom marriage was viewed as valid but dissoluble. The Church's asserted power over marrying was moved as to its object, not denied as to its reach. The dissolution of the Marsh-Groom marriage was interpreted as effected by the papal rescript. Bouscaren and Ellis, *Canon Law*, 565.

papal grace not to be granted if scandal caused: "Norms for the Dissolution of Marriage in Favor of the Faith by the Supreme Authority of the Sovereign Pontiff" (copy furnished the author by Peter Shannon, then of the chancery of the archdiocese of Chicago).

Monterey-Fresno, 7/18/47, reported: *CLD*, IV, 349–350. The contrary had been standard teaching: e.g., Instruction of the Holy Office for Siam, July 4, 1855, *Collectanea*, n.1114, I, 594.

"an exaggerated indissolubility": Franz Hürth, S.J., "Notae quaedam ad Privilegium Petrinum," *Periodica* 45 (1956), 379.

Intrinsic dissolubility was defined as dissolubility at the will of the parties to the marriage: Benoît H. Merkelbach, O.P,. *Summa theologiae moralis ad mentem D. Thomae et ad normam iuris novi* (Bruges: Desclée De Brouwer, 5th ed., 1947), n.816. Extrinsic dissolubility meant dissoluble by authority. By natural law, Merkelbach maintained, marriage was intrinsically and extrinsically indissoluble. By divine law, however, marriage was dissolved by a new marriage in accordance with the Pauline privilege: ibid., n.819. Merkelbach at n.821 mentioned the sixteenth-century papal rulings, did not take a position on their basis, and did not mention the modern papal cases beginning in 1924.

In an influential encyclopedia of theology published in the wake of Vatican II, Waldemar Molinski spoke of dissolution "extrinsically" as the equivalent of dissolution "by human authority" and referred to the Pauline and Petrine privileges. Molinski, "Marriage," *Sacramentum Mundi* V, 397–398. He notes that only in the second millennium did the Church "recognize more clearly its competence and duties with respect to marriage." He adds with remarkable caution: "It is not quite clear how far non-Christian religious bodies and civil society have jurisdiction over non-sacramental marriages." Ibid., 398.

Thousands of cases: Lawrence G. Wrenn, "Some Notes on the Petrine Privilege," *The Jurist* 43 (1983), 399; cost: ibid., 396, n.9; suspension of the privilege: ibid., 399. A survey of 119 dioceses in the United States by the Canon Law Society of America reported these figures on privilege of the faith cases in the year 1963–1964:

Submitted to diocese:	7,137
Forwarded to Rome:	4,061
Granted:	2,634

Paul E. Demuth, "The Nature and Origin of the Privilege of the Faith," *Resonance* 4 (1967), 71.

The privilege denied during the suspension: e.g., *Joliet, June 4, 1973, CLD*, 8, 840–841.

Proposed canons 1104 and 1659–1662: Pontifical Commission for the Revision of the Code of Canon Law, *Schema Codicis Iuris Canonici* (Vatican City: Libreria Editrice Vaticana, 1980), pp. 250, 365–366.

Promulgation of the new code: John Paul II, "*Sacrae disciplinae leges,*" January 25, 1983, *CIC* (1983), p. xviii.

"derogate from the laws of nature": Umberto Betti, "In margine al nuovo Codice di Diritto Canonico," *Antonianum* 58 (January–March, 1983), 633; "disappeared without a trace": ibid.

Canons 1148 and 1149 of the *CIC* (1983): important commentaries on these canons do not develop the theology, see, e.g., *Code of Canon Law Annotated* with commentary prepared by the Instituto Martín de Azpilcueta (Montreal: Wilson & Lafleur, 1993), 722–723, and James A. Coriden, Thomas J. Green, and Donald E. Heintschel, *The Code of Canon Law: A Text and Commentary* (New York: Paulist Press, 1985), 817–818. This commentary notes as to canon 1149: "The law presumes that a reconciliation between the original spouses is either impossible or not desired by them."

In exercising even the Pauline privilege, canons 1144 and 1145 of the current Code of Canon Law set out content and timing for interpellations or interrogatories to be addressed to the nonbaptized party. He or she is asked, "Do you wish to receive baptism?" and "Do you wish to cohabit peacefully with the baptized party without offense to the Creator?" If these questions are answered negatively, the conditions exist for exercise of the Pauline privilege. If they are answered affirmatively but "it is de facto impossible to restore conjugal cohabitation because of distance, confinement, or some other circumstances," the unbeliever is considered to have separated and the privilege may be exercised. John P. Beal, James A. Coriden, and Thomas J. Green, eds., *New Commentary on the Code of Canon Law* (New York: Paulist Press, 2000), 1367.

Privilege of the faith cases for 1979: "Tribunal Statistical Report," Canon Law Society of America, *Proceedings of the Forty-Second Annual Convention* (1980), 222–230; for 1989: "Tribunal Statistics 1989," Canon Law Society of America, *Proceedings of the Fifty-Second Annual Convention* (1990), 277–292; for 1999: "Tribunal Statistics 1999," Canon Law Society of America, *Proceedings of the Sixty-Second Annual Convention* (2000), 458–466. That the statistics show some kind of failure is implied by William H. Woestman, O.M.I., "Respecting the Petitioner's Rights to Dissolution Procedures," *The Jurist* 50:343–344.

The new norms: Janusz Kowal, S.J., "Nuove Norme Per Lo Scioglimento Del Matrimonio *In Favorem Fidei,*" *Periodica* 91 (2002), 500.

anomalous concealment: That the norms governing the grant of the privilege of the faith were not made public until 2001 raises the question of whether such concealment violated what has been called "the inner morality of law" by Lon L. Fuller, *The Morality of Law* (New Haven: Yale University Press, rev. ed., 1964), 96, or "the morality that makes law possible," 49–51. Undisclosed laws may exist. Handbooks on the administrative process in an agency may be retained by an agency for its own use without sharing them with the public, as Fuller acknowledges, p. 50. Acts appropriating funds for classified projects and activities do not cease to be law because they are secret (p. 92). Article V of the Constitution of the United States explicitly provides that the two houses of Congress may refrain from publishing such parts of their proceedings "as may in their judgment require secrecy." Nonetheless, laws that affect the rights of those subject to them should normally be published so that they may be invoked if necessary and interpreted and criticized by professionals (pp. 50–51). Keeping the norms secret enhances the power of those dispensing the favor (p. 213). The secrecy surrounding the Norms of 1934 was not total but did deter discussion. The norms published in 2001 are anomalous in a different way; they set out a procedure for a privilege unprovided for in the Code of 1983.

2002 privilege of the faith cases: *L'Attività delle Sante Sede nel 2002* (Vatican City: Libreria Editrice Vaticana, 2003), 691; "to facilitate": idem. No statistics are furnished on the number of dissolutions granted. Statistics are reported for judgments of the Roman Rota, which, in 2002, upheld 73 marriages and found 62 to be null: ibid., 859. The Apostolic Signatura, the appeals court, handled 7 marriage cases, whose results are not reported: ibid., 845–846.

Form of rescript; same form was used under Pius XII: see the rescript of February 23, 1957, granting the favor in regard to the marriage of two Moslems, El Keir and Sessya: René Leguerrier, O.F.M. Cap., "Recent Practice of the Holy See in Regard to the Dissolution of Marriage Between Non-Baptized Persons Without Conversion," *The Jurist* 25 (1965), 456.

The two-step process: Pietro Gasparri, *De matrimonio* (Rome, 1932 ed.), II, 239; the prevailing view that the pope dissolves: Heinrich Molitor, "Die Auflösung von Naturehen durch päpstlichen Gnademakt," in Karl Siepen, Joseph Weitzel, and Paul Wirth, ed., *Ecclesia Et Jus* (Munich: Ferdinand Schöningh, 1968), 528–530.

On the prevailing view, odd cases could occur—for example, the case of the would-be bachelor: A Catholic married to an unbaptized wife sought the dissolution of the marriage with no particular second wife in mind, but in order, "if the circumstances are favorable and a good and suitable woman is found, that he may be able to enter another marriage." On May 18, 1975, Paul VI granted the dissolution. *CLD* IX, 675–677. And the case of the tentative vocation: On June 23, 1982, H.L., a Catholic woman in the diocese of Rockville Center, was granted a dissolution of her marriage to an unbaptized man in order that she might enter religious life. Two conditions were attached: (1) that, before making her final profession as a religious, she again apply to the Holy See, and (2) if she should leave religious life before her final profession, she again apply to the Holy See. *CLD* X (1986), 184–185.

What Newman would call "a difficulty": e.g., "Ten thousand difficulties do not make one doubt." John Henry Newman, *Apologia pro vita sua,* ed. Martin J. Svaglic (Oxford, 1967), 214.

TWENTY-SEVEN.   Out of Difficulties Comes Development

"a grave offense against the natural law": *CCC,* sec. 2384, p. 573.

"The greater a friendship is, the firmer": Thomas Aquinas, *Liber de veritate catholicae fidei contra errores infidelium seu Summa contra Gentiles,* ed. Celsas Pera, Peter Mars, and Pietro Caravello (Turin: Marietti, 1961), 3, 123.

"Love is not love": William Shakespeare, Sonnet 116, lines 2–3, *Shakespeare's Sonnets,* ed. Stephen Booth (New Haven: Yale University Press, 1977), 100. Booth sees an echo in the sonnet of Paul to the Ephesians: ibid., 385.

"their indissoluble unity": *Gaudium et spes,* n.48, *Vat. II,* IV, 7, 767–768; "the sacrament of something": John Paul II to the Roman Rota, February 2001, *AAS* 93 (2001), 360–361; "essential property": John Paul II to the Roman Rota, January 28, 2002, *AAS* 94 (2002), 342; reference to papal dissolution: ibid., 344; "an end contrary to justice": ibid., 346.

natural marriages extrinsically dissoluble: For a creative modern writer on marriage, the Pauline privilege and the privilege of the faith have been difficult to explain or to accommodate to his new theory. In *The Way of the Lord Jesus* (Quincy, Ill.: The Franciscan Press, 1992), III, 557, Germain Grisez rejects St. Augustine's approach to marriage because it makes marriage "an instrumental good." For Grisez, marriage is "intrinsically good," sought for its own sake (ibid., 555). It becomes a question how such a good may be subordinated to the faith of one not a party to the marriage (584–595).

Grisez's proposed solution is this: Some marriages of the unbaptized are valid but "imperfect" because they lack a commitment to exclusivity and indissolubility due "to fallen mankind's hardness of heart" (594). It is these marriages that are dissolved by the Pauline privilege and the privilege of the faith.

The difficulties attendant on this explanation are evident. First, Grisez has created a category of marriage unknown to traditional theology: the imperfect marriage. Theology must have scope to be creative. This difficulty is not fatal, although the coherence of the new category with the tradition needs to be explored and demonstrated. Grisez himself states that parenthood is "the specific, intrinsic perfection of marriage" (570). He moves to a different meaning of perfect when he speaks of imperfect marriages. Second, if these marriages have the characteristics ascribed to them by Grisez, they are invalid and do not need to be dissolved by a privilege. Again, this difficulty is not fatal, although it makes the exercise of the privilege a kind of shortcut to a declaration of nullity. It would be surprising if most canonists would agree that, because of their cultural context, most marriages are invalid. Third, the two privileges are put into effect by the Church without the slightest consideration of whether the marriage in question was imperfect in the sense used by Grisez. Does he mean to maintain that without knowing what they are doing the popes dissolve imperfect marriages and the Church accepts the Pauline privilege?

"Sacred Scripture has taught us": Innocent III to Bernardo Balbi of Faenza, August 8, 1198, *Die Register Innocenz' III*, ed. Othmar Hageneder and Anton Haidacher (Graz-Cologne: Hermann Böhlaus Nachf. 1964), I, 472–474; "not by human but rather by divine authority": *Quanto personam, Decretales*, 1, 7, 3, *CIC* II, 98–99; "Between bodily matters and spiritual matters": *Inter corporalia, Decretales*, 1, 7, 2, *CIC* II, 97.

Boniface VIII, *Unam sanctam: Extravagantes* I, 8, 1, *CIC* II, 1245.

Innocent accepts England as a fief: Innocent III to King John, *PL* 216, 881–882. On the day of his coronation as bishop of Rome, Innocent declared the pope to be "set in the middle between God and man, less than God but bigger than man." Innocent III, *Sermo II in consecrationem Pontificis Maximi, PL* 217, 657–658.

"The vicarial power is exercised": Alfredo Ottaviani, *Institutiones iuris publici ecclesiastici*, n.348 (Vatican City: Vatican Polyglot Press, 4th ed., 1960), II, 215; the power "touches the rights and the duties of the unbaptized" party: idem.

"the pope in using vicarious authority": William H. Woestman, O.M.I., *Special Marriage Cases* (Ottawa: St. Paul University, 1992), 9. A standard reference work lists not only the three sixteenth-century rulings, but *Unam sanctam* of Boniface VIII, Nicholas V's ruling in favor of Portugal, and Alexander VI's *Inter caetera*. Pietro Palazzini, "Privilegium Fidei," in Palazzini, *Dictionarium Morale et Canonicum* (Rome: Catholic Book Agency, 1966), 801–802.

"The opposite affirmation would imply": John Paul II to the Judges and Officers of the Roman Rota, January 21, 2000, *AAS* 92 (2000), 353; see also Janusz Kowal, S.J., "L'Indissolubità Del Matrimonio Rato E Consummato: Status quaestionis," *Periodica* 90 (2002), 272, 295, following John Paul II's teaching and explicitly stating that the consummated marriage of two baptized persons has "extrinsic indissolubility."

"stuck" in unhappy marriages: Erasmus, *Annotationes* 471; God destroys what "he did": 475. Erasmus' views were attacked by several contemporaries, among them Johannes Dietenberger, O.P., a professor at Mainz. In 1532, Erasmus answered him: *Responsio Ad Disputationem Cuiusdam Phimostom; De Divortio*, ed. Edwin Rabbie, Erasmus, *Opera omnin* IX–4, 375–398, (The Hague: Elsevier Science, 2003).

Erasmus' emphasis on his English experience makes one ask if he discussed divorce with his friend Thomas More, who in his *Utopia* permitted divorce for adultery and other "intolerable offenses to morals," and also divorce by mutual consent with the approval of the senate and the wives of the senators. See Thomas More, *Utopia*, ed. George M. Logan, Robert M. Adams, and Clarence H. McMillen (Cambridge: Cambridge University Press, 1995), 190. More carefully preserves the whimsy of his work so that it is hard to be sure what reforms he seriously endorses. It seems fair to infer that he did not believe that divorce was against nature.

The present position on the noneffectiveness of a civil divorce: see John J. Coughlin, O.F.M., "Divorce and the Catholic Lawyer," *The Jurist* 61 (2001), 304, simply citing *CIC* (1983), canon 1141 ("no human power can dissolve").

The state as God's agent in execution: Avery Dulles, S.J., "Catholicism and Capital Punishment," *First Things* (April 2001), 32, citing Rom 13:4, 1 Pet 2:13, and even Jn 19:11.

Papal dissolution of valid, sacramental, but unconsummated marriages: the practice was codified in canon 1119 of the 1917 *CIC* and is now codified in canon 1142 of the 1983 *CIC*. *The Code of Canon Law: A Text and Commentary,* ed. James A. Coriden, Thomas J. Green, and Donald E. Heintschel (New York: Paulist Press, 1985), 813, takes the position that dissolution is by the pope's "vicarious power which cannot be delegated." In the fifteenth century, however, Oddo Colonna, Pope Martin V, delegated dissolution of this kind to a bishop in one case, to a deacon in another, and to an apostolic notary in a third. See Noonan, *Power to Dissolve,* 130–131.

"refused to cooperate", "It is understood": "Communication of Grant of Dissolution to Respondent Is at Discretion of Ordinary," *CLD* V, 548. In a private instruction issued in 1986 by the Congregation for the Doctrine of the Faith, bishops were told: "According to the Norms, the Respondent has a right to be heard. While the person in question may sometimes not wish to be involved, every honest effort should be made to present both sides of the case." *CLD* 12, 712 (2002).

the power of the Church as a complete society: Kowal, "Nuove Norme," 483, following Urbano Navarrete, S.J., "Potestas vicaria Ecclesiae: Evolutio historica conceptus atque observationes attenta doctrina concilii Vaticani II," *Periodica* 60 (1971), 421–459. Navarette had observed at 272 that Vatican II's *Lumen gentium,* n.27, treated all the bishops as "vicars of Christ."

"Let each spouse be heard": *Normae De Conficiendo Processu De Solutione Vinculi Matrimonialis In Favorem Fidei,* art. 10 in Kowal, "Nuove Norme," 501; requirement of civil decree: ibid., art. 19. In the case of marriage dissolved pursuant to canons 1148 and 1149, it is not even clear that the Norms of 2001 apply or that any notice to the unbaptized spouse has to be supplied. See the ambiguous reference to these canons. ibid., 500.

An annulment "suffers from the defect of irremediable nullity where one party not heard." *CIC* (1983), canon 1619. The European Court of Human Rights held Italy in violation of the Convention of Human Rights when an Italian civil court enforced the judgment of nullity of marriage given by a tribunal of the Vicariate of Rome, appeal from which had been dismissed by the Roman Rota. The European Court held that the complainant had not been notified of the reasons her husband was alleging that their marriage was null, nor had she been informed of her right to counsel. The European Court noted that each party should have the opportunity to know and to argue each piece of evidence presented. The complainant had not had this opportunity, and, without counsel, she should have been presumed not to know the law. The European Court would not determine the loss the complainant had suffered, but held she had suffered "a certain moral prejudice" and awarded her 10 million lira to be paid by Italy, plus 18,253,946 lira for attorneys' fees and other expenses. *Affaire Pellegrini c. Italie,* Strasburg, July 20, 2001, reported *Revue de droit canonique* 51 (2001), 127–140. This case does not involve papal dissolution. It is not clear that such a dissolution could be civilly enforced in Italy by a civil *exequatur*. It is clear that the right of defense of a marriage is an accepted principle of jurisprudence. The concordat with Italy, executed February 11, 1929, and signed by Mussolini for Italy and by Pietro Gasparri for the Holy See, specified in Article 23: "The norms of international law will apply to the execution in the Kingdom of the judgments emanating from the tribunals of Vatican City." *Raccolta,* II, 90. Was a papal dissolution of marriage in favor of faith a judgment emanating from a tribunal of Vatican City? Arguably, it was if the pope was issuing a judgment of divorce. A procedure for securing the civil effects of a declaration of nullity by a church tribunal has been published, *CLD* 12, 896–897 (2002), but not a similar procedure following a papal ruling on the privilege of the faith.

Exercise of the privilege turned not only upon a power not believed in by at least one party affected; it also turned upon a fact whose relevance would not have struck many persons as significant: the absence of baptism. Not many people today, it is possible to surmise, know that, if they have not been baptized, their marriage may be dissolved by the Catholic Church. "What's lack of baptism got to do with it?" they might ask. To a couple in love, wanting to get married, the investigation, the paperwork, the $200 fee, the year's delay—all small obstacles from an olympian perspective—could seem intolerable; and if all it takes to clear their way is the nod of the pope, the impediment to be removed may strike them as not worth the trouble. How often such polite scepticism occurs is hard to say; that it does occur is known from my observation of people in this situation.

The routine administration of the privilege was exercised by the Congregation for the Doctrine of the Faith. On December 8, 1965, the congregation turned down, without giving a reason, a request from the bishops of the Antilles that they be delegated the power to dissolve in favor of the faith. *CLD* 7, 765.

On October 19, 1977, the congregation rejected a request from the bishops of Zambia to abrogate Article 5 of the Norms, which denied the privilege on behalf of a person who wanted to enter a second marriage with an unbeliever. Informed by the bishops that their flocks did not understand the rule, the congregation briskly told the bishops it was their job to make them understand. *CLD* 9, 995–996.

The number of Catholic Christians, other Christians, and the world population: *The World Almanac and Book of Facts* (New York: World Almanac Books, 2003), 638 and 857.

The pope's power debated: Umberto Betti, "Appunto sulla mia partecipazione alla revisione ultima del nuovo Codice di Diritto Canonico," in D. J. Andrés, ed., *Il processo di designazione dei vescovi. Storia, legislazione, prassi. Atti del X Symposium Canonistico-romanistico, April 24–28, 1995. In onore del Rev.mo P. Umberto Betti, O.F.M.* (Vatican City: PUL, 1996), 37; "such a grave question": ibid., 38; devoid of theological foundation: ibid., 37. As Betti records, this meeting took place between 12:50 and 3:40, September 17, 1982. It was one of twelve three-hour meetings of the pope with a small group of experts systematically going over the proposed code. Betti's memoir was published in the Festschrift in his honor, preceded by a letter to Betti from the pope thanking him for his work; it may be inferred that Betti believed his recollections of the meetings on the code to have accurately captured the papal response.

"he had reached the same certainty": Kowal, "Nuove Norme," 483; "an always more unitary explanation": ibid., 478.

"Petrine privilege" never used officially: Urbano Navarrete, S.J., "De termine 'privilegium petrinum' non adhibendo," *Periodica* 53 (1964), 369; Navarrete thought the term misleading.

The response of the Church in the nineteenth century to civil divorce: see, e.g., Instruction of the Holy Office, June 6, 1817, for Martinique and Guadeloupe: lawyers and judges sin mortally by legislating divorce or carrying out divorce laws. *Collectanea*, n.725, I, 425–427.

TWENTY-EIGHT.   How Development Can Be Dated, Cannot Be Denied,
and Should Neither Be Exaggerated Nor Ignored

"that we may hold to be believed": Vincent of Lérins, *Commentorium*, chap. 2, *PL* 50, 640. "But perhaps someone asks": ibid., chap. 23, *PL* 50, 667.

TWENTY-NINE.   How We Are Innocent Despite the
Development of Our Descendants

Empathy with the bigot: In my own experience I have encountered one man who gave me a glimpse into the way of thinking of a Christian bigot. I omit his name, his nationality, his religious order, but not the context: our encounter occurred during the discussions of the commission set up to advise the pope on contraception. This theologian was of small stature and of a thinness suggestive of ascetic consumption of food. His mind was sharp, his learning very bookish. Not a canonist, he carried on his person the 1917 *Code of Canon Law,* to which he referred when I said that the rule on usury had changed. (In the black letter of the code, read abstracting from modern life, it had not). I was convinced after an hour of one-on-one debate with him that he would cheerfully have lit the fire if I were at the stake, at the same time assuring me with complete sincerity that he was acting for my good and that by an act of contrition I could still save my immortal soul, although not my mortal skin.

Harm done by drivers: see U.S. Department of Transportation, Bureau of Transportation Statistics, *National Transportation Statistics 2000,* p. 129 (accidents and casualties); pp. 294–299 (pollution). The toll is even greater on a world basis; over 1 million persons killed, over 50 million injured annually on the road. "Road traffic deaths," *The Economist,* April 17, 2004, referring to a joint report by the World Health Organization and the World Bank.

Animal rights: see Laurence H. Tribe, "Ten Lessons Our Constitutional Experience Can Teach Us about the Puzzle of Human Rights: The Work of Steven M. Wise," 7 *Animal Law,* 1–6 (2001); Peter Singer, *Animal Liberation* (2nd edition, 1990); David Bank, "Is a Chimp a Person with a Legal Right to a Lawyer in Court?" *Wall Street Journal,* April 25, 2002, p. 1; "that animal welfare is not just a moral problem": Matthew Scully, *Dominion: The Power of Man, the Suffering of Animals, and the Call to Mercy* (New York: St. Martin: Griffin, 2002), 398.

On prison reform: see Charles Colson, *Justice That Restores* (Tyndale House Publications, 2000); official punishment of family: Brian McKnight, *Law and Order in Sung China* (Cambridge: Cambridge University Press, 1992), 327 (official sign of crime hung on family gate); "joint adjudication," i.e., spouses jointly held responsible for crime of one: ibid., 53 and 403.

Jefferson as legislator of slavery in Virginia: John T. Noonan, Jr., *Persons and Masks of the Law: Cardozo, Holmes, Jefferson, and Wythe as Makers of the Masks* (New York: Farrar, Straus and Giroux, 1976), 50–54; James Madison as slaveowner: John T. Noonan, Jr., *The Lustre of Our Country: The American Experience of Religious Freedom* (Berkeley: University of California Press, 1998), 70–71.

　　Brandeis, Holmes, Hughes held racially segregated schools to be no denial of equal protection—"it is the same question which has been many times decided": *Gong Lum v. Rice,* 275 U.S. 78 (1927), (a unanimous court, opinion by Taft, C.J.).

"efforts to coerce rational minds themselves": *Gaudium et spes,* chap. 22, cited in John Paul II, *Veritatis splendor,* sec. 80, *AAS* 85, 1198.

The forged donation of Constantine: see Walter Ullmann, *The Growth of Papal Government in the Middle Ages* (London: Methuen, 1962), 74–86; for the expansion to include the islands of the world: see note to chapter 10, "How the Portuguese Got the Guinea Trade," supra; Pius IX's teaching: Denzinger, 1955, n.1776. A note added a reference to six other allocutions of Pius IX between 1849 and 1862 on the civil power of the pope, "teaching that all Catholics ought to retain most firmly."

"holy and always in need of purification": *Lumen gentium*, n.8, *Vat. II*, III:8.

"all those times in history departed": John Paul II, *Adveniente millenio tertio*, November 10, 1994, n.33, *AAS* 87, 35; "errors": ibid., at 36. "Although many acted here in good faith": John Paul II, Catechesis in the series "God The Father," September 1, 1999, *The Pope Speaks*, vol. 43, p. 50.

"many doctrines which were once universally held have proved to be problematic or erroneous": Karl Rahner, S.J., "Magisterium," *Sacramentum Mundi*, 5, 334.

THIRTY.   How Precedent Deters but Does Not Defeat Development

Reception of the law: see Ladislas Orsy, S.J., "The Reception of Laws by the People of God: A Theological and Canonical Inquiry in the Light of Vatican Council II," *The Jurist* 55 (1995), 516–522.

Häring's experience: see Bernard Häring, C.SS.R., *Embattled Witness: Memories of a Time of War* (New York: The Seabury Press 1976).

"They watch each other like hawks," Ivo Thomas, O.P., oral observation to me in 1963. "It was all I could say in Rome at the time," Bernard Häring responded to me when, driving him in the 1960s from Notre Dame to Chicago, I remarked how curious it was that Catholic colleges and Catholic high schools in the United States regularly sponsored dances for their mixed student bodies, while he wrote that dancing was "not always mortally sinful." See Häring, *Das Gesetz Christi* (Munich: Erich Wewel, 1967), 3, 312.

"explicitly set out to be definitively held": Karl Rahner, S.J., "Magisterium," *Sacramentum Mundi*, 5, 351.

The "ordinary magisterium" as a technical term appeared in the reaction of Pius IX to a theological congress in Munich in 1863 organized by Johann Döllinger, the learned Church historian. Writing the archbishop of Munich, the pope scolded the rationalist spirit of the congress and declared that "the act of divine faith . . . should be extended to those things that the ordinary magisterium of the whole Church, as the Church is ranged across the world, hands on as divinely revealed and therefore by universal and steady agreement are held by Catholic theologians to belong to the faith." Pius IX, *Tuas libenter*, December 21, 1863. Denzinger (1955), n.1683. If the authority of the ordinary magisterium is restricted to what it proposes as divinely revealed, the scope of the authority is restricted at the same time that its binding force is heightened.

"mere de facto universality . . . is not enough": Rahner, "Magisterium," *Sacramentum Mundi*, 3, 356.

"The faithful ought to concur": *Lumen gentium*, n.25, *Vat. II*, III:8, p. 805;

"Investigation of the truth": Congregation for the Doctrine of the Faith, *De ecclesiali theologi vocatione*, 82 *AAS* (May 24, 1990), n.1, p. 1550; "arguments to the contrary appear to prevail": n.31, p. 1502.

THIRTY-ONE.   **That Form and Formula Fail to Foil Development**

"Just as the ordering of right reason": Thomas Aquinas, *Summa theologiae* 2–2, 154, 12 *ad* 1; for a fuller treatment of theologians on sins against nature, see John T. Noonan, Jr., *Contraception: A History of Its Treatment by the Catholic Theologians and Canonists* (Cambridge: Belknap Press of the Harvard University Press, enlarged ed., 1986), 238–246.

THIRTY-TWO.   **That Development Cannot Exceed Capacity**

"All that is received": Thomas Aquinas, *Summa theologiae* I, Q. 75, art. 5. See the over one hundred uses or variants of this maxim in the *Index Thomisticus*, ed. Roberto Busa, S.J. (Stuttgart, Frommann-Holzboog 1975), sec. II, vol. 19, 118-123.

THIRTY-THREE.   **That Development Runs by No Rule Except the Rule of Faith**

"The love is from God": e.g., John S. Dunne, C.S.C., *The Road of the Heart's Desire: An Essay on the Cycles of Story and Song* (Notre Dame, Ind.: University of Notre Dame Press, 2002), 110.

the rule of faith (*praescriptio fidei*): Augustine, *De doctrina christiana* I, XXXVI, 40, *CC* 32, 29.

JOHN T. NOONAN, JR., is a judge of the United States Court of Appeals for the Ninth Circut in San Francisco, California. He is a historian of ideas, distinguished lecturer, and author of thirteen books.